May 5:86

Dear Colleen,
with all best
wishes for a
marvelously successful
future —
Gabe Weisberg

The European
Realist
Tradition

EDITED BY

Gabriel P. Weisberg

INDIANA UNIVERSITY PRESS
Bloomington

The European
Realist
Tradition

This book was brought to publication with the assistance of grants from
the Samuel H. Kress Foundation and Mrs. Muriel S. Butkin.

Manufactured in the United States of America

Library of Congress Cataloging in Publication Data
Main entry under title:

The European realist tradition.

Includes index.
1. Realism in art—Europe—Themes, motives.
2. Painting, European—Themes, motives.   3. Painting,
Modern—19th century—Europe—Themes, motives.
I. Weisberg, Gabriel P.
N6757.E93   759.94   81-48399
ISBN 0-253-32084-4   AACR2
1 2 3 4 5 86 85 84 83 82

Contents

Plates for chapters 1–4 following page 52
Plates for chapters 5–7 following page 148
Plates for chapters 8–10 following page 244

Preface

In an international symposium held at the Cleveland Museum of Art in November 1980, a group of scholars met to discuss French realism in conjunction with an exhibition of the art that had resulted from it, entitled "The Realist Tradition: French Painting and Drawing, 1830–1900." The art historians, historians, and museum curators who gathered in Cleveland all realized that only a small sample of the many questions realism poses could be broached at a single symposium, but they made it a goal of the group at least to determine what aspects of realism had still to be studied. Some of these neglected areas are included in this volume.

Several of the authors seek reasons for the enduring appeal of realism as a cultural and artistic force throughout Europe; whether in Germany (Françoise Foster-Hahn), Switzerland (Hans Lüthy), England (Kenneth McConkey), or Russia (Alison Hilton), the common denominator was the requirement that art reach a broad, general public by using images that could be easily understood. As a result, wherever realism emerged, its stylistic traits were similar: it was always an art form that examined the commonplaces of everyday life and meticulously rendered their details in order to record the world as each artist saw it.

These similarities in Europe's realist styles have up to now been ignored, though the questions why realism became popular simultaneously in a number of countries and why it was so ubiquitous in the nineteenth century have often enough been asked. One answer has been that the middle class required an intelligible art form, and realism met that criterion of intelligibility. Wealthy industrialists and landowners and the regional art societies they fostered to nurture culture readily shifted their allegiance from romanticism to realism. French nationalism, too, required a democratic art with broad popular appeal to solidify the aspirations, customs, and traditions of the nation.

How the realist painters reacted to the social problems of the time is most commonly exemplified in the literature by the paintings of Gustave Courbet, who is equally commonly regarded as the only realist painter worthy of serious attention. The preoccupation with Courbet has tended to disguise the fact that, while realism could be put to the service of social reform, it was equally frequently put to the service of preserving the status quo, justifying and even glorifying the ruling class and the central authority. In his essay on the cultural politics of

vii

the Second Empire, Albert Boime shows how Napoleon III used the realists to help him subvert radicalism and glorify his own position and demonstrates clearly how the realist style could be used as an aid to state control. Alison Hilton describes much the same phenomenon in Russia. In our own time Hitler's Third Reich can be adduced as an instance of realism used to support an authoritarian regime.

In the hands of an artistic innovator like Courbet, realism did, however, undeniably challenge its audience, though, as Robert Bezucha writes, the social criticism expressed in realist works was not always recognized. To the viewer, as Alison Hilton points out, narrative painting can simply be seen as accurate, and its critical implications can easily be lost, whatever the intentions of the painter might have been.

Why realism appeared when it did remains a complex problem, and accounting for the various guises it assumed presents an equally formidable challenge. Petra Chu finds that realism relied on the artist's memory to assure a truthful, honest, almost naïve recording of the natural world both in intimate drawings and in paintings; H. W. Janson explains it as a way of re-creating the reality of appearance and actuality through trickery and illusion. Occasionally, it was used to overwhelm its audience with huge, panoramic canvases reminiscent of the cinematic extravaganzas of our own times. When exhibited at a public salon, these large canvases compelled attention and forced the onlooker to test the accuracy of the transcription of type, place, and personality, writes Geneviève Lacambre. The realism that resulted when science and perception forced a new interpretation of the world was given the name "naturalism."

Many of these points were raised at the Cleveland symposium, but the question of realism's importance remained unresolved. Critics have tended to shrink from the task of assigning significance to it, because confronting the problem involved dealing with other than the recognized master painters who contributed to the evolution of modernism. Realist painters who worked in a style that made them important in their own time are now largely forgotten by critics and collectors. Esthetic criteria change; we stress innovation in art and find the realists lacking in imagination. In the process we have failed to notice that several styles flourished at the same time. Art historians intent only on tracing the development of modernism are blind to the artistic interchange that went on between members of a whole range of artistic camps, if only through their viewing one another's work at public exhibitions. Even today, the defenders of modernism seem to regard the existence of any other way of painting as a threat. The nineteenth century was artistically as complex a period as any other; to limit consideration to artists of "modernist individuality" is to misrepresent it.

With realism once again in vogue, and its forerunners once more of esthetic interest, those who have relegated realist art to their scholarly attics should reconsider whether it is necessarily either "tedious," "sentimental," or "banal." A new generation is trying to understand the origins of the realist tradition and to evaluate its work. Realist art was meant to inform, to educate, to instruct, to propagandize, and to elevate through its content. To attack it simply because it succeeded in appealing to the middle class through its use of mundane themes is not to prove that it was of poor quality. Much of it was worthy of the name of art. If the avant-garde appealed to an elite who often stressed the autonomy of the image, the realist continually tried to reach a larger audience. Realist painting is now ready for rediscovery by those tired of abstraction and willing to recognize pluralism in artistic taste.

The spectrum of creativity that realism encompasses is also expanding. No longer can one artist be identified with a single style, as Gustave Courbet once was. As the numerous adherents of the realist tradition are rediscovered, their work promises to provide discoveries and food for discussion for years to come.

My personal thanks go to the Department of Fine Arts at the University of Pittsburgh for their initiative, encouragement, and support during my year there. And all the contributors to this volume join me in expressing deep gratitude to the Samuel H. Kress Foundation and Mrs. Muriel S. Butkin. Without their generous support, this book would never have appeared.

Gabriel P. Weisberg

The European
Realist
Tradition

Being Realistic about Realism

Art and the Social History of Nineteenth-Century France

Robert Bezucha 1

REALISM SEEMED TO BURST UPON THE art world in the Salon of 1850/1851. It took some time to sort out what was happening. In 1855—the year a Universal Exposition was held in Paris to celebrate international recognition that the restoration of an empire did, as Napoleon III had promised, mean peace—the critic Champfleury published an open letter to George Sand: "The term [realism] horrifies me with its pedantic terminology; I fear schools like cholera. . . . I won't define realism for you, Madame; I don't know where it comes from, where it goes, what it is. Homer would be a realist since he observed with exactitude the customs of his time."[1]

Fear of cholera was real—it had driven Millet to Barbizon in 1849—and Champfleury's metaphor was well chosen. I also think he meant it. 1855 was also the year of Courbet's ill-fated independent exhibition, and his so-termed realist "manifesto" (which Champfleury probably edited) begins on a curiously defensive note: "The title 'realist' has been imposed on me in the same way as the title 'romantic' was imposed on the men of 1830. Titles have never given the right idea of things; if they did, works would be unnecessary."[2] Not only had the political and social climate changed with the coup d'état that ended the Second Republic, but also what Linda Nochlin calls the realists' battlecry—"*Il faut être de son temps*"—had proven sufficiently complicated that Champfleury felt he had to back off from his earlier enthusiasm.[3] There was no realist school.

The purpose of the present exhibition is, however, to demonstrate that there is a realist tradition. Gabriel Weisberg has suggested in the catalogue that realist artists can be divided into three groups: those

1

whose work was regarded as dangerous (Courbet and, in some cases, Millet), those who painted social themes but who were never considered a threat to the social order (his example is Jules Breton), and those (such as Pils and Antigna) who painted "official propaganda and, in the process, formulated an official realism palatable to the bourgeoisie and the government." "Realist art," he states, "did not necessarily imply radical politics, but it did imply social consciousness."[4] These distinctions are helpful (although I think the second and third groups can often be conflated), and I will use them to pursue the meaning of Weisberg's problematic phrase, "social consciousness." Because the style itself so closely approximates the way we see things with our own eyes or in a photograph, we must resist looking at a realist painting as though it were an open window on life in nineteenth-century France. Being realistic about realism means that we acknowledge that the problems of representation found in the interpretation of any painting are not reduced, and, in some cases, may actually be *increased*.[5] I propose to illustrate my argument by discussing one such case, where the artist's "social consciousness" diverts our attention in important ways from the social reality he appears to be depicting.

The Realist Tradition has brought a number of lesser-known painters to our attention, none more so than Jules Breton, whose work is represented eighteen times in the exhibition. Breton's painting *The Gleaners* (fig. 1.1) won him critical approval and his first Salon prize, a third-class medal at the age of twenty-eight, in 1855—again that important date. This was the initial triumph of a long and distinguished career, which included the awarding of the *Légion d'honneur* in 1861 (seven years before Millet, who was thirteen years older) and membership in the *Institut de France* in 1886, the first realist painter to be so honored. Breton, like Millet, was known as a *peintre paysan,* and it has been suggested that his *Gleaners* was one inspiration for the latter's famous painting with the same title, which was exhibited in the Salon of 1857 (where Breton won a second-class medal for *The Blessing of the Grain*).[6] In the Salon of 1859, Breton's *The Recall of the Gleaners* was displayed in the prestigious *Salon carré*, won a first-class medal, and was purchased by the emperor and hung in the St. Cloud palace. (Millet's *Woman Tending Her Cow* was attacked by critics in the same Salon.) From acclaim in his own day, Breton's reputation dropped to the status of footnotes in ours. His current revival offers us an intriguing example of the social history of taste: a realist painter whose "social consciousness" was acceptable to many of the same persons who rejected Courbet's and Millet's.

Direct comparison of Breton's *Gleaners* and *Recall of the Gleaners*

with Millet's *Gleaners* (fig. 1.2) reveals some obvious reasons for
Breton's initial popularity. Above all else, his paintings are pleasant
to look at, whereas Millet's is not. Breton's women are pretty, and, in
the case of the central figure of *Recall of the Gleaners*, even alluring.
Millet, whose women have weathered faces and hardened hands, commented that "Breton always paints the village girls who will not remain there."[7] Breton depicts gleaning as a social occasion, but Millet
sees it as hard and painful. Breton includes children, who turn work
into play alongside their mothers and older sisters, while Millet's
"three Fates of pauperism," as Paul de Saint-Victor described them,[8]
labor in isolation, even (we feel) from one another. Both artists
portray a rich harvest: for Breton there is much wheat left to be
gathered; for Millet there remains only stubble. Small wonder that
Breton's *Recall of the Gleaners* was purchased by a banker and captain
of industry, Isaac Pereire, while Millet's *Gleaners* went unsold for
seven years. There is, after all, *some* accounting for taste.

Breton's style epitomizes the contemporaneity associated with
realism. He wants us to feel we are looking at real people in an actual
place, and, indeed, the young woman seen in profile in his *Gleaners*
is a portrait of the artist's future bride, Elodie.[9] Millet's *Gleaners*, on
the other hand, has a timeless, even classic quality; Paul de Saint-
Victor criticized the figures as "conceited" in their debt to Michelangelo
and Poussin.[10] Nevertheless, the effect of Millet's painting disturbed
many critics, while Breton's made them feel reassured. Why was this so?

Breton presents a picture of an integrated, well-ordered society. On
the right side of his *Gleaners* we see the village steeple in the background, as the women and children go about their work under the gaze
of the male figure of civil authority, the *garde champêtre*. Family,
church, and state form an eternal triangle, while in the background
the work of the harvest goes on. And in *The Recall of the Gleaners*,
the rules of gleaning are obeyed: the women and children leave the
fields at dusk without a word of protest. Millet's gleaners, by contrast,
seem marginal, even outside society. In the distance, the harvest boss
astride his horse oversees the collection of the earth's bounty from
which they are excluded. Millet omitted so much from his painting
that he caused the critic Jean Rousseau to see what wasn't there.
"Behind these three gleaners," he wrote, "outlined on the leaded horizon are the pikes of popular uprisings and the scaffolds of '93."[11]

Millet's gleaners are from the commune of Chailly, in the Brie region of the Paris basin. Breton's are from his native village of Courrières, in the Pas-de-Calais department, where he spent two years preparing the canvas. These paintings captured public attention because
their subject was both biblical (Breton and Millet each felt as much)

and timely: as Weisberg reminds us, the French Senate was engaged
in an extended debate over the introduction of a rural code in the
mid-1850s. He states:

> At a time when gleaning was coming under harsh criticism by
> the press and by politicians, Breton recorded the practice as a
> natural aspect of regional life. He remained somehow immune to
> the changes being advocated, although he must have been well
> aware of the articles and discussions in parliament because of the
> considerable amount of time he is known to have spent in Paris.
> Gleaning had always been practiced in Courrières, and Breton's
> attitude—reinforced by this canvas—suggests that there was no
> need for modification of the tradition in this small village.[12]

Here the social historian and the art historian part company. My
questions begin where Weisberg's answers end. To what extent did
Breton actually "record" the practice of gleaning in his region? By what
process was he able to remain "somehow immune" from the debate?
These, you may have gathered, are questions about the artist's "social
consciousness." In order to answer them we must accompany Breton
back to Courrières in search of more information.

Courrières lies on the Lens plain, thirty-three kilometers from the
industrializing city of Lille and fifteen kilometers from Arras, the
chef lieu of the Pas-de-Calais department, in the heart of what, in
the middle of the nineteenth century, was certainly the most *urbanized*
area of rural France.[13] There was, of course, no railroad station in
Courrières then, but a major canal passed near the village, one that
linked Paris with the English Channel. The Artois region was famous
for the abundance of its farm products and also for the problems of
overpopulation. Throughout the first half of the nineteenth century
one-eighth of the inhabitants of the Pas-de-Calais department were
indigent.[14] During the famine of 1846–47, there were at least five
incidents of grain barges on the canal being seized and pillaged by
villagers, although I do not know if any of them were residents of
Courrières.[15] In any case, poverty in the midst of plenty did not
disappear with the Revolution of 1848. Here is a report written by the
juge de paix of the commune of Croisilles, about thirty-five kilometers
from Courrières, describing the situation in June 1854, the exact
moment that Breton was painting his *Gleaners:*

> In the past two weeks I have become aware of an almost hostile
> movement among the farm workers of my canton toward the
> growers. The principal cause of this movement is the anxiety in-
> spired by the likelihood of a disastrous grain harvest. And the
> method used here for paying harvest workers explains this anxiety.
> The growers have, in effect, conserved and maintained relations of

a completely patriarchal nature with the families attached in service to the farms. An estate of one hundred hectares, for example, employs eight families for the work of harvesting and threshing. As their wage these families are entitled to the tenth sheaf of wheat and the sixth hectoliter threshed in the barn. This . . . would be too costly for the farmer, if he were not compensated by the daily rate for weeding and other [tasks], which varies from 60 centimes to one franc. This form of payment has existed from time immemorial in our countryside; it is so advantageous for the worker that our peasants seek a place as a harvester with as much ardor as a bourgeois [does] for a salaried position, [and] it should not be changed. But human memory does not recall having seen as terrible a winter for grain as we have just experienced. On certain estates . . . only a quarter of the crop survived, and it is very poor. It has been replaced by oats, oleaginous grains and sugar beets.

This unfortunate event has forcibly destroyed . . . our old system of wages. Also, the harvester, called upon to do all the work of cultivating sugar beets, flax . . . [etc.], demands to know under what conditions he will work and how he will survive.

This anxiety which, with reason, torments the worker and which places him in defiance toward his master, who cannot be generous, has not yet . . . resulted in reprehensible actions. Nevertheless, I believe that it is urgent to halt this separation which is making itself felt between masters and workers. There is still an old tie of former times, of former customs between them. If it is broken nothing will remain of the good old days. I am going to visit each commune of my canton. I will do all I can to prevent a rupture prejudicial to the interests of each.[16]

A thousand words are sometimes worth more than a picture. The *juge de paix*'s report is a remarkable document because it articulates, at a precise moment, the inherent tension between two coexisting economic and social systems. On the one hand, we hear the persistence of what E. P. Thompson has called "the moral economy" of precapitalist social relations:[17] patriarchal ties between growers and workers, the hiring of entire families, the customary payment in kind. On the other hand, there is talk of the introduction of market-oriented polyculture, the emergence of wage-based day labor, and the implication of capitalist social relations (the comment that the masters "cannot be generous"). The disastrous grain harvest of 1854 caused the price of bread to double and worsened the lot of the poor throughout France,[18] but we should not lose sight of the fact that the shift to flax and sugar beets was part of a long-term trend toward agricultural diversification in the Artois region.[19] The wheat fields were shrinking, and the *juge de paix* foresaw the end of the "good old days" in the accompanying "movement of separation" between field-workers and landowners.

Many of the growers, of course, embraced such change and called it progress. In 1868, the Agricultural Society of Béthune (about twenty kilometers from Courrières) held a banquet to honor Guislain Decrombecque, whose farm had won the *grand prix d'agriculture* at the Universal Exposition the previous year. Known locally as "the veteran of the Lens plain," Decrombecque was seventy-one years old and had seen it all. "Agriculture," he told his audience, "is an industry" that requires "intelligent activity and capital." And, he continued: "Great is the error . . . of those who still accredit ignorant and uncapitalized agriculture, the deplorable legacy of an unfortunate past, which the men of our day cannot accept without abdicating their task and compromising the hope of the country."[20]

The Artois, in short, was a region ripe for agricultural capitalism. It was exactly the sort of place where landowners might resent gleaning not only as a violation of their private property but also as a reminder of "the deplorable legacy of an unfortunate past." The small village of Courrières, it seems, was surrounded by big changes.

How could Jules Breton have missed all this? Or did he see it and fail to "record" it in his paintings? One way to begin to answer is by posing yet another question: since Courrières was a place where, as Weisberg puts it, "everyone knew one another,"[21] who did the villagers think the artist was as he sketched them at their work?

For those who remembered Jules Breton as a boy, he was both the son and the nephew of men whom the prefect of the Pas-de-Calais department had appointed as mayor of Courrières during the July Monarchy. At various times his father was also a rent collector for the estate of the duc de Duras, a tax collector, a *juge de paix*, manager of the family brewery, and, finally, an investor in forest property. Although the family experienced financial trouble around the time of his father's death in the spring of 1848 (the temporary collapse of credit drove many small enterprises into bankruptcy), the Bretons were respected members of the rural bourgeoisie: they could afford to send young Jules away to a church-run school in 1837 and later supported him while he studied painting in Belgium. They were the sort of people who might exchange greetings with "the veteran of the Lens plain," Guislain Decrombecque. And in the summer of 1854, all of the villagers must have known that Jules's uncle had recently built an atelier for him behind the brewery. Breton's painting of *The Garden of the Brewery at Courrières* suggests that it was a substantial commercial enterprise.

Jules Breton had returned to Courrières to find inspiration for his art. There can be no doubt that he was as deeply attached to his native region as Courbet and Millet were to theirs. It is equally clear that the Revolution of 1848 made a strong impression on him. As he wrote in *La Vie d'un artiste:*

> The causes and consequences of that revolution . . . had a keen influence on my spirits, on those of all artists, on the general move-ment of arts and literature. There was an ardent upsurge of new efforts.
>
> We studied what Gambetta would later call the new social strata and the natural setting which surrounded it. We studied the streets and the fields more deeply; we associated ourselves with the passions and feelings of the humble, and art was to do for them the honor formerly reserved exclusively for the gods and the mighty.[22]

At first reading this passage sounds as though it could be Courbet talking about his *Stonebreakers* or Millet about his *Sower*. The refer-ence to Gambetta is a clue to an important difference, however. Léon Gambetta was a founding father of the Third Republic and, at the time of his premature death in 1882, Prime Minister of France. He is still remembered in textbooks as the man who coined the term "new social strata" (*nouvelles couches sociales*) to describe those whom democracy (universal male suffrage was established in France in 1848) and economic progress would eventually and inevitably bring to power. Gambetta saw French society as composed of "individuals in the process of rising" and, therefore, denied the existence of class conflict. A champion of the "spirit of enterprise," he was the political hero of small proprietors, small industrialists, and shopkeepers.[23] One can well imagine Gambetta's photograph hanging in the office of the brewery in Courrières.

Jules Breton looked at the world and the future with an optimistic eye. Although he painted many of the same themes as Courbet and Millet, his sensibility—his "social consciousness"—was different. Where they saw the poor, he saw "the humble." This was a persistent quality in their art, moreover. Courbet painted sensuous nudes and hunting scenes in the 1860s, but he also produced *The Poor Woman of the Village, Ornans* (1867), and *The Charity of a Beggar at Ornans: The Beggar's Alms* (1867–68). And Millet's *The Vine-Tender* (1869–70) is a powerful contrast to Breton's *The Grape Harvest at Chateau-Lagrange* (1864).[24] What makes this observation interesting, rather than banal, is the fact that the three artists—particularly Courbet and Breton—came from similar backgrounds.

Millet was the son of a comfortable peasant-farmer from the Nor-man village of Gruchy on the English Channel. There is scholarly dis-agreement about the exact status of the Millet family, but I believe there is justification for T. J. Clark to ask "whether Millet's art was a compensatory myth—whether he tried to redefine a peasant status he had lost, or never had."[25] Courbet came from the highlands of the Franche-Comté, and, although Clark has directed our attention to "the family's ambivalent situation, their status between the peasantry and the rural bourgeoisie" in the artist's work,[26] his father was clearly a wealthy man. Régis Courbet owned enough scattered parcels of land to qualify as a voter under the July Monarchy (the requirement was a minimum annual payment of 200 francs in direct taxes), maintained two houses (one in the village of Flagy, the other in the town of Ornans), and provided his children with the accoutrements of bourgeois life: music lessons, new parasols and bonnets for the girls (cf. *Young Ladies of the Village Giving Alms to a Cowherd*), and talk of a law career for young Gustave.[27] Courbet, furthermore, was never so remote from the patronage of the aristocracy and the *grande bourgeoisie* as the socialist legend he spun around himself would imply: he sold his *Young Ladies of the Village* to the comte de Morny before the opening of the Salon of 1852, completed a commissioned canvas of the comte de Choiseul's greyhounds in 1866, and enjoyed a reputation as a society portrait-painter at the new resort of Trouville.[28] In short, he shared much in common with Jules Breton. How, then, are we to explain their discrepant visions of rural life?

In his book *Image of the People*, T. J. Clark discusses the emergence in the 1840s and the 1850s of what he calls "a distinct bourgeois myth of rural society—a myth which was central to the structure of bourgeois self-consciousness." Masking the reality of social and economic conflict in the countryside, the myth projected rural society to be "a unity, a one-class society in which peasant and master worked in harmony."[29] Courbet's imagery, Clark goes on to argue, was considered offensive or dangerous precisely because he pulled away the mask. (Robert Herbert's masterful catalogue of the Millet exhibition at the Grand Palais convinces me that Clark is mistaken not to include Millet as an unmasker.[30]) Jules Breton, in other words, was a realist purveyor of the bourgeois myth of rural society.

This is circular reasoning, however. Our discussion has returned to the point where it began: Breton's peasant scenes were acceptable to many of the same persons who rejected Courbet's and Millet's. What remains at issue is *why* Breton painted his *Gleaners* and *Recall of the Gleaners* the way he did. The journey back to Courrières has yielded enough information for me to attempt an answer. Before offering my interpretation, however, I want to make a few remarks about the relationship between art history and social history.

"Politics in a work of literature," wrote Stendhal a century and a half ago, "is like a pistol-shot in the middle of a concert, something loud and vulgar, and yet a thing to which it is not possible to refuse one's attention." Many have tried, however. If scientific inquiry is commonly symbolized by the classical figure of Prometheus, who stole fire from the gods, scholarship in the arts and humanities can often be represented by the myth of Hermes Trismegistus, who created a magic seal to keep vessels airtight. In a recent article Griselda Pollock has succinctly stated the current Marxist critique of art history, citing "the failure of that discipline which purports to provide a *history* of art, to engage with, or even acknowledge, any but the most simplistic, recognisable notion of history let alone of production, class, or ideology." In art history, she continues, the "fields of discourse" have created "an ideological 'pure' space for something called 'art', sealed off from and impenetrable to any attempt to locate art practice within a history of production and social relations."[31] Certainly not every one of the art historians I have cited here—Weisberg, Nochlin, Herbert and Clark—is explicitly Marxist in his or her approach, yet none of them appears reluctant to, as Pollock puts it, "reclaim art for history."[32] Others may be disturbed by the direction their work has taken and long for a return to connoisseurship, but it has been a pleasure for me to discover them as interdisciplinary colleagues. I might add that the reverse of Pollock's dictum—to reclaim history for art—strikes me as equally valid and important.

The hermetic seal has been struck from the paintings of Courbet and Millet, and they are now accessible to the host of historians actively engaged in reinterpreting the Revolution of 1848 and the Second French Republic.[33] *The Realist Tradition* exhibition is an important event for art history and social history because it provides the opportunity to extend the process of reclamation—in the dual sense I have just mentioned—to lesser-known painters of the Second Empire and the Third Republic. Clearly there are significant problems here that must be reserved for art historians. Social historians simply lack the skill—the ways of seeing—to address, for example, the relationship of realism and photography (Linda Nochlin has noted in passing the appearance of the wrinkle in mid-nineteenth century painting[34]), the impact of mechanical reproduction on art (Breton's *Recall of the Gleaners* was on the cover of *L'Illustration* in June 1859), or the problems of stylistic tradition and innovation. Social historians, on the other hand, are trained to think about such matters as means of production, class, and ideology. Although we vigorously disagree about their meaning for social relations—the range of interpretation extends from economic determinists such as Albert Soboul to self-proclaimed "*pointillistes*" like Richard Cobb and Theodore Zeldin—we, too, have special skills. As art historians and social historians seek new ways to pool their talents we may yet prove that the social history of art is not a chimera.

It would be chimeral, however, for me to think it possible to de-

termine completely why Jules Breton "recorded" gleaning in Courrières the way he did. Nevertheless, I agree with T. J. Clark that "the
search for determinacy, in the work, of that which determines it—is
the interesting one."[35] In this case because it draws our attention to the
problem of art-as-social-document.

"Painting" as Robert Herbert states, "is a form of high poetry. Its
meaning lies behind the images, just as the meaning of poetry lies
behind the words."[36] The meaning behind Breton's images appears to
be that life in Courrières was harmonious, that relations between
man and nature, between property owners and the property-less, flowed
smoothly. Weisberg accurately perceives the atmosphere of *The
Gleaners* as "free of anxiety or hardship."[37] Yet, as I have tried to indicate, there is every reason to believe that anxiety and hardship were
all around. This is more than bourgeois myth-making; it is self-decep-
tion. And, as if I weren't in enough trouble already, I want to suggest
that unconscious denial was a powerful source of these images.

The poor and indigent of the Artois were not pretty, and Jules
Breton knew it. As a child he saw them when they came to his grandmother's house to beg. Raised as a devout Catholic, he was told to
feel compassion, but the sight and sound of them made a different impression, which he recalled in his memoirs: "I felt an internal con-
tentment at overcoming the fear which the raggedness of the poor,
and especially the sight of physical deformity, caused in me; fear that
in special cases extended to horror. I often felt myself trembling as I
held out a sou which my grandmother had given me to give to certain
cripples. I shuddered at the mere sound of certain crutches on the
pavement."[38]

These dirty, ragged, diseased, and crippled people—research on
the medical condition of nineteenth-century army conscripts sub-
stantiates the fact[39]—depended on gleaning in fields and forests for
the margin of their survival. None of them, I suppose, looked like
Breton's future bride, herself a child of the bourgeoisie, whom he
portrayed in his *Gleaners*. Breton was not incapable of painting true
poverty. In Paris in 1849, he produced "Misery and Despair" and
"Starvation," melodramatic scenes from the life of the *urban* poor;
the exhibition of the latter canvas in the Salon of 1850/1851 furnished
his initial reputation as a realist artist.[40] It is all the more significant,
therefore, that he never painted the poor he knew best, the *rural*
poor, as they actually looked. His art served instead to deny the reality
of life in Courrières.

Denial is a common psychological defense against feelings of guilt
and anxiety, and there were plenty of signs of it among the bourgeoisie
during the nineteenth century. The factory owner who insisted that
his wage-hands did not mind their labor or living conditions, the

politician who proclaimed that all careers were open to talent and hard work, the professor who declared that "progress" had no victims, all believed in what Peter Gay has called "a largely imaginary class: the poor who did not suffer."[41] It would be wrong to see this as hypocrisy, for, to cite Gay again, the "invention of the happy poor was actually a distortion of vision, all the more cherished, no doubt, for being so profitable, but a defensive distortion nonetheless."[42]

Class attitudes are not a simple or uniform matter, moreover. They may originate in a shared social and historical setting, but they are played out in the personalities of individual human beings. Courbet was extremely ambivalent about his family's background, and he reacted with anger at the lot of the rural proletariat. So, too, Jules Breton was neither a hypocrite nor a puppet dangling from the strings of crude economic or psychological determinism. The reasons he denied the fact that the poor of Courrières suffered lie far deeper than his Belgian training or the Flemish tradition in painting; they are probably beyond recovery. Nevertheless, we can safely say that he was not "somehow immune" from the debate over a rural code, and that he "recorded" gleaning in his native village through a distorted vision.

All this need not stop us from speculating. As Breton himself said: "Ideas are born in the form of images in the mind of the child. Man is a seeing being before he is a thinking being."[43] We may guess about the effect of the small child's frightening encounters with the beggars at the door. We may wonder if the boy who played with "friends of an inferior position to my own" knew that as mayor his father kept the list of those who were entitled to glean in Courrières and hired the *garde champêtre* to watch the fields, and that as *juge de paix* he levied fines on those who broke the rules.[44] We may ask whether the teenager who accompanied his father to Paris for the printing of a "forest guide" (*guide forestier*), which the elder Breton had written, ever read what it said about the problem of gleaning in private woodlands. And we may imagine that when the family's fortune collapsed briefly in 1848, the young man learned the lesson that the bourgeoisie, too, could fall. Each of these elements from his personal history may have influenced the development of his "social consciousness." Being realistic about realism also means, however, that there are limits to what the art historian and the social historian can know.

NOTES

1. *L'Artiste*, 2 September 1855.

2. Alan Bowness, Marie Thérèse de Forges, Michel Laclotte, and Hélène Toussaint, eds., *Gustave Courbet, 1819–1877* (London: Arts Council of Great Britain, 1978), p. 77.

3. Linda Nochlin, *Realism* (New York: Penguin Books, 1971), p. 28. To add a contemporary scholarly complication, Hugh Honour has even suggested that "to be of one's time" originated as a romantic concept (*Romanticism* [New York: Harper & Row, 1979], p. 321).

4. Gabriel P. Weisberg, ed., *The Realist Tradition: French Painting and Drawing, 1830-1900* (Bloomington, Indiana: The Cleveland Museum of Art and Indiana University Press, 1980), pp. 13–14.

5. E. H. Gombrich reminds us in *Art and Illusion* (New York: Phaidon Press, 1960) that "style in art enables the world to be organized and apprehended in a certain way, granting the user a power he would not otherwise have, while at the same time setting limits on how he can see and represent reality."

6. Weisberg, *Realist Tradition*, p. 85.

7. Helen O. Borowitz, *The Realist Tradition: French Painting and Drawing, 1830–1900. Notes on the Exhibition* (Cleveland: The Cleveland Museum of Art, 1980), p. 28.

8. Robert L. Herbert, Roseline Bacou, and Michel Laclotte, eds., *Jean-François Millet* (Paris: Editions des Musées Nationaux, 1975), p. 101.

9. Weisberg, *Realist Tradition*, p. 85.

10. T. J. Clark, *The Absolute Bourgeois: Artists and Politics in France, 1848–1851* (London: Thames and Hudson, 1973), p. 73.

11. Herbert et al., *Millet*, p. 101.

12. Gabriel P. Weisberg, "Jules Breton's 'The Gleaners' of Courrières: A Traditional Aspect of Regional Life," *Arts Magazine* 55, no. 5 (January 1981): 106.

13. The term "urbanized" is taken from sociology. For an example of its application in social history, see Charles Tilly, *The Vendée: A Sociological Analysis of the Counterrevolution of 1793* (Cambridge, Mass.: Harvard University Press, 1964), chapter 2.

14. Louis Trenard, ed., *Histoire des Pays-Bas Français* (Toulouse: Privat, Éditeur, 1972), p. 404.

15. R. Gossez, "Carte des troubles en 1846–1847 (Cherté des grains)" in E. Labrousse, ed., *Aspects de la crise et de la dépression de l'économie française au milieu du XIXe siècle* (Paris: Bibliothèque de la Révolution de 1848, tome XIX, 1956), p. 1.

16. Louis Trenard, ed., *Histoire des Pays-Bas Français: Documents* (Toulouse: Privat, Éditeur, 1974), pp. 312–13.

17. E. P. Thompson, "The Moral Economy of the English Crowd in the Eighteenth Century," *Past & Present* 50 (February 1971): 76–136.

18. E. Labrousse, "The Evolution of Peasant Society in France from the Eighteenth Century to the Present," in Evelyn M. Acomb and Marvin L. Brown, Jr., eds., *French Society and Culture Since the Old Regime* (New York: Holt, Rinehart and Winston, 1966), p. 59.

19. Trenard, ed., *Histoire des Pays-Bas Français*, p. 427.

20. Trenard, ed., *Histoire des Pays-Bas Français: Documents*, pp. 310–12.

21. Weisberg, "Jules Breton's 'The Gleaners,' " p. 106.

22. Jules Breton, *La Vie d'un artiste* (Paris, 1890), p. 177.

23. Theodore Zeldin, *France, 1845-1945. Volume One: Ambition, Love and Politics* (Oxford: Clarendon Press, 1973), pp. 613–14.

24. Bowness et al., *Gustave Courbet*, pp. 175–76, 182; Herbert et al.,

Millet, pp. 225–26; Gabriel P. Weisberg with Annette Bourrut-Lacouture, "Jules Breton's 'The Grape Harvest at Chateau-Lagrange,'" *Arts Magazine* 55, no.5 (January 1981): 98–103.

25. Clark, *Absolute Bourgeois*, p. 98.

26. T. J. Clark, *Image of the People: Gustave Courbet and the Second French Republic, 1848–1851* (Greenwich, Conn.: New York Graphic Society, 1973), p. 114.

27. Bowness et al., *Gustave Courbet*, p. 27.

28. Ibid., pp. 29, 171, and 172.

29. Clark, *Image of the People*, pp. 150–51.

30. See, in particular, Herbert's analysis of "L'Angélus," in Herbert et al., *Millet*, pp. 103–106.

31. Griselda Pollock, "Artists, Mythologies and Media Genius, Madness and Art History," *Screen* 21, no. 3 (1980): 57.

32. Ibid., p. 58.

33. For a discussion of current controversies, see Eugen Weber, "The Second Republic, Politics, and the Peasant," *French Historical Studies* XI, no. 4 (Fall 1980): 521–50.

34. Nochlin's remark was made at the symposium held upon the occasion of the opening of The Realist Tradition exhibition at the Cleveland Museum of Art, November 1980.

35. T. J. Clark, "A Note in Reply to Peter Wollen," *Screen* 21, no. 3 (1980): 100.

36. Robert L. Herbert, *Barbizon Revisited* (Boston: Museum of Fine Arts, 1962), p. 66.

37. Weisberg, *Realist Tradition*, p. 84.

38. Breton, *La Vie d'un artiste*, p. 17.

39. E. Leroy Ladurie and Paul Dumont, "Quantitative and Catographical Exploitation of French Military Archives, 1819–1826," in Felix Gilbert and Stephen R. Graubard, eds., *Historical Studies Today* (New York: W. W. Norton and Co., 1972), pp. 62–106.

40. Breton, *La Vie d'un artiste*, pp. 197–99; Weisberg, *Realist Tradition*, p. 13.

41. Peter Gay, "On the Bourgeoisie: A Psychological Interpretation," in John M. Merriman, ed., *Consciousness and Class Experience in Nineteenth-Century Europe* (New York and London: Holmes & Meier Publishers, 1979), p. 198.

42. Ibid.

43. Breton, *La Vie d'un artiste*, p. 70.

44. Ibid., p. 17.

The New Maecenas

Regional and Private Patronage of Realism in France, 1830–70

Gabriel P. Weisberg **2**

THE EVOLUTION OF AN ART FOR THE people—imagery that could be easily understood and readily appreciated by the public—was stimulated by many factors, not the least of which was the revolutionary zeal of 1830 and 1848.[1] Encouraged by democratic ideals and a growing desire to unify the country under the banner of nationalism, artists tried to create a realist imagery that would reflect traditions and ideas from all sections of the country.[2] With numerous provincials moving to Paris to find work in an urban environment, the Salons (the one source of mass, free entertainment)—and the pictures created solely for the Salons—reflected, in turn, the need to record the life of the provinces as well as the city before customs and folklore disappeared forever. In effect, much of the art of the realist tradition reflected the life of the period, as paintings were often appreciated by Salon visitors for their content and as documentary records of a way of life that was fast disappearing.

Art works were exhibited not only in Paris, at the annual Salons, but also throughout the provinces in a well-established system of local shows. Artists living in Marseille or Nantes, for example, could exhibit first locally and later in Paris. If their works proved popular, they would often send canvases "on tour" to exhibitions held in cities and locales far removed from the capital, where their works might then be purchased by local art societies, municipal museums, or—in an increasing number of cases—by astute private collectors. The role and number of art societies and private benefactors increased throughout the century, although the origins of this tendency can be found in earlier periods.[3] It is important to evaluate art patronage and its impact on contemporary creativity from 1830 until the end of the Second Empire, for in this patronage lies the impetus behind much of the realist tradition in France.

Early Stages of Support

Interest in the arts received the continued support of the royal family until the July Revolution destroyed this traditional patronage system.[4] By September 1830 artists eager to gain full control of their own careers saw an opportunity to legislate for changes that would not only ensure their livelihood but also provide new avenues for their work. A key figure in this movement to provide freer jury selection at the Salons and to decentralize art patronage by establishing an active Ministry of Fine Arts was Philippe Auguste Jeanron, an artist and activist soon to become one of the major proponents of realism.[5] In his famous *Pétition nationale*, 1830, Jeanron advocated equality in the arts. Jeanron hated state-dominated control, and he advocated a turn away from art imagery that reflected esoteric court themes or mythological stories in favor of an art of the "here and now." His petition stands as one of the strongest attacks ever mounted against the dominance of the Institute in matters of art exhibitions and state support of painters. In advocating that artists elect their own members to the Salon jury, Jeanron was democratizing the system and trying to wrest control away from absolutist state dominance. Jeanron urged the dissolution of the stranglehold of royal authority that, more often than not, favored only those artists who were admired by the court or who were willing to compromise creativity to comply with the rigid proscriptions that controlled the choice of styles and themes.[6]

The ideals envisioned by Jeanron and his radical compatriots were all but forgotten, even though control of art patronage shifted from the king to the Ministry of Fine Arts at the time of the July Monarchy.[7] The time was just not right for a complete revamping of the state of the arts. Those who now assumed the position of preeminence in the absence of a royal family were essentially politicians and civil servants, deputies charged with the support of the arts and artists, the dispersal of funds, and the assignment of specific governmental commissions. Because of their own limited backgrounds, traditional themes became the natural choice for churches and public buildings then being sponsored. This type of support was inadequate for younger artists, especially those who were essentially landscapists or genre painters and whose images reflected the newer tendencies of the time.[8] The younger painters of this persuasion found the patronage they needed in the growing number of the increasingly affluent middle class, eager to obtain images that they could easily understand.

Much has been written on the role of the middle class in supporting art during the later half of the nineteenth century. The bourgeoisie has been severely chastised for failing to support the newer forms of art that emphasized formal change and tended toward abstraction.[9] While such a viewpoint is partially correct, it is also an oversimplification: the role of the middle class in patronage of the visual arts was dependent upon, and affected by, changes taking place within the Parisian government and the newly emerging awareness of all types of painting throughout the provinces.

The types of patronage available during the reign of Louis Philippe and Napoleon III, the ways in which painters attracted viewers and solicited attention for their canvases, the exhibitions that took place, and the coverage provided by critics and writers all influenced the diffusion of a realist vision in private and public collections.[10] Research and evaluation of these aspects may eventually lead to a long-awaited revelation: the identity of the elusive bourgeoisie—those individuals who actually provided the support for the mid-century renaissance of easel painting.[11]

The Role of Art Societies

Although art historians have traditionally devoted much attention to the Parisian Salon, at the expense of art exhibitions elsewhere, the influence of regional art societies in the propagation of art support was an important aspect of the rise of realism. The large Paris Salons, where paintings were often purchased by the government, were only one way in which art objects were acquired by the state and then assigned to provincial museums. A second means of enlarging the collections in regional museums was through increased provincial exhibitions in which local artists presented their works.

Often, these provincial art exhibitions were held at the urging of local art societies—groups of influential businessmen, industrialists, and the wealthy "establishment" of the community—organized for the specific purpose of promoting art for their cities. Some of these groups originated as early as the seventeenth century as a means of establishing the artist as an independent figure in his own right.[12] Art societies in the most important regional centers, such as Lyon, Bordeaux, Nancy, Rouen, Reims, Toulouse, and Marseille, often were also responsible for founding and sponsoring local art academies to assure traditional and formal instruction in the arts and to contribute to the growth of regional pride in the arts. The contribution of these societies was varied, although essentially they supported promising local painters, giving them an opportunity to earn a living comparable to that of other community professions. After the Revolution of 1789, when regional academies were transformed, art training was channeled through the central Academy (under the direction of the Institute des Beaux-Arts), which dictated traditional styles based upon classical references or themes from past history; this centralization of authority allowed little opportunity for independent response. Recognizing the need for regional creativity, however, the societies that had flourished prior to the Revolution were eventually restructured, regrouping after 1830 in order to decentralize control and to provide recognition for local painters. The activities of provincial art societies did much to prepare the atmosphere for free thought and new imagery that would contribute to both the later stages of romanticism and the realist cause.[13] The local art societies also did much to encourage the establishment and expansion of regional museums, often working together with members of the town council in the selection and purchase of works of art from provincial exhibitions. A number of realist paintings became part of regional depositories in this way.

Occasionally, the central government, in an attempt to promote contemporary art in the provinces, purchased art objects from the Salons and sent them to a regional municipal museum. An early realist work by Isidore Pils, *The Death of a Sister of Charity* (1850-51), was purchased by the government of the Second Empire for 4000 francs and allocated to the museum in Toulouse (fig. 2.1).

Pils's image of the dying mother superior had been well received by Salon reviewers, many of whom regarded it as a representative realist endeavor, since it reflected the poverty of the masses and the dedication of the church in trying to alleviate suffering among the poor. Why this particular painting was selected for Toulouse, however, has never been fully determined.[14] If the government had wanted simply to demonstrate its beneficence to a provincial museum, it could have done so by exhibiting the work for a time in the provinces, without permanently consigning it to a regional location. It is more likely that the gift of a work with a realist theme (albeit a realism tinged with romanticism and sentimentality) reflected another line of reasoning by the state: it demonstrated munificence to the masses while underscoring the state's decentralization policy and its intention to distribute major paintings among regional collections.[15]

Frequently the regional *Sociétés des amis des arts* were the sole voices in effecting the distribution of newer forms of art for their particular provinces, because they encountered little competition from a central government that, despite its profession of "active" policies, actually did little to promote the cultivation of regional art. The government sent few works to the provinces (even under the more liberalized decentralization policy of the Third Republic), and the money allotted to local societies by the state continued to be minimal at best. More often, if the goal of a regional art collection for the people was realized, it was because of the efforts of regional societies themselves to purchase works of art.

Regional Art Exhibits

There can be little doubt that regional art exhibits, held on an annual basis, did much to promote the collection and appreciation of contemporary nineteenth-century paintings. Canvases that were successful in Paris were often shown in the provinces, where an even larger audience—already alerted to the stir the work had caused in the capital—anxiously awaited the opportunity to see the work themselves firsthand.[16] Occasionally, a painting that had been well received in Paris would be scheduled to tour in several exhibitions, in the hope of attracting a patron who might thus assure a permanent home for the work.[17] It is even possible that, with governmental sanction of realism underway—as recorded in an official document of 1856— artists may have been encouraged to use contemporary images or regional themes that were then popular in order to promote their own careers.[18]

Gustave Brion's *Potato Harvest during the Flooding of the Rhine* is an important early realist work (fig. 2.2). It was exhibited at the 1853 Paris Salon but did not become part of a permanent collection until 1858, when it was purchased by the museum in Nantes.[19] Brion regarded this canvas as one of his few works to be completed in a purely realist vein, and Parisian critics found the painting both "sad and somber"—a designation especially significant for the evolution of a realist style. The painting also reflected the painter's interest in the tribulations of the poor, for his work conveyed a deep sense of sympathy for workers desperately trying to save their only source of food.

As a native Alsatian, Brion agreed to show the canvas at an exhibition in Strasbourg, perhaps in the hope of attracting interest from the local *Société des amis des arts* or of winning support from a private patron. *The Potato Harvest* also mirrored a contemporary event pertinent to the livelihood of the local people and an event that had become part of the history of the region. These are reasons that would have encouraged Brion to believe the work would attract sympathetic support in his homeland.

The painting did not inspire the response Brion thought it merited, although there is little known documentation of the reaction of local art critics to the painting at the time of its exhibition in that city.[20] After the painting was turned down by the Strasbourg art community— through either silence or direct refusal to purchase the work—Brion agreed to send the work to the 1858 Nantes exhibition.[21] At the conclusion of the show there, the local Société purchased three compositions: a classical theme by Jean Léon Gérôme, a landscape by Camille Corot—both of them traditional, "appropriate" themes—and the tragic narrative by Brion. Why Brion's work was singled out by the Société in Nantes is not clear, for he was, at that time, still an aspiring, relatively unknown artist. Whatever the reasons, Brion's work is important in the study of the realist movement because it signifies one of the first times that members of a local art group selected a purely realist painting that was both timely and contemporary. Brion's *Potato Harvest* remains one of the starkest, most powerful realist canvases from that early period, depicting as it does a tragic and all too common attempt by field laborers to save themselves from annihilation. Given the moralizing aspect of the painting and the narrative focus of Brion's style, the *Potato Harvest* provided ample opportunity for all levels of society—some for the first time—to view an explicit and compassionate documentation of the condition and plight of the downtrodden.[22]

The support generated for Brion's canvas may also have aided the development of realism in the provinces in still another way. In 1861, after Gustave Courbet's *The Grain Sifters* (fig. 2.3) was shown in Paris, Brussels, London, and Besançon, it was included in a regional exhibition in Nantes.[23] When the show closed, the painting was acquired by the town government and presented to the municipal museum, the first time a regional municipal government purchased a painting by Courbet.[24] In the absence of town council records, it seems unusual that this painting would have been acquired by the city of Nantes, except for the interest in realism already expressed by the acquisition of Brion's *Potato Harvest* in 1858. It is likely that members of the municipal government, aware of Courbet's importance as a contemporary painter and well versed in the painting's depiction of a common, everyday theme, regarded it as a complement to Brion's peasant scene. It also represented Courbet's personification of a work theme essential to rural life.[25] It is significant to note that by 1861 the Nantes museum—for reasons still not clear—had become one of the most important regional repositories for the appreciation and collection of realist art, purchasing paintings on its own without overt intervention by the central government, and in accordance with local taste and an understanding of contemporary realism.

Other provincial museums were also involved in the acquisition of paintings that might be considered realist, or at least proto-realist, in style. Some years earlier, in 1834, following exhibition at the annual Salon in Lille, the local *Société des amis des arts* purchased Philippe Auguste Jeanron's *Peasants from the Limousin* (fig. 2.4). This romantic-realist composition represents an important step in the encouragement of regionalist imagery, because the figures Jeanron portrayed playing musical instruments were typical provincial types. The instruments might well be those used by itinerant musicians who travelled from place to place throughout the provinces. Jeanron's use of this theme is not unusual in realist iconography and may be one reason the work was purchased from the painter. Another reason is connected with Jeanron's position in the art world; he was just becoming an established Salon painter, and his naïve, almost primitive painting style may perhaps have been considered avant-garde in 1834. Purchase by the Lille art society gave credence to that community's independent ability to select a work that epitomized new trends that an increasing number of contemporary painters were adopting. Since there is no other record of a Jeanron painting being acquired by a regional museum before the painter's "retirement" to Marseille in the opening years of the Second Empire, this purchase reveals a timely perspicacity on the part of an art society making its selection on the basis of regional themes.[26] Even as early as 1834, local patrons may have been cognizant of the value of having art works that could appeal to many; Jeanron, who was already quite famous in Paris as a proponent of radical change, was recognized as an artist whose images were capable of reaching a broad audience. This was one reason his canvas of the *Peasants from the Limousin,* which stressed regional customs and folklore, was of such value to the artistic community of Lille.[27]

By the mid-1860s the number of regular regional art exhibitions under local sponsorship had increased greatly. The problem many of the local art societies now faced was one not simply of organizing and mounting a show in the community but rather of selecting entries that would enhance the awareness of art.[28] Paintings from Paris still received first consideration in these exhibitions and continued to be purchased for municipal collections, but the recognition and support of local talent became increasingly important. The acquisition of such decidedly realist canvases as Ribot's *Cook Accountant* (fig. 2.5) in 1862, or the same painter's *The Returns* (fig. 2.6), by the Société des Bouches du Rhône is some indication of the efforts made to seek out painters and sponsor them in local exhibitions. It was not always easy to locate artists for a regional exhibition, and municipal exhibitions did not always reflect the level of quality that was represented in the Paris Salons. Even though many critics found that, given the constant support by the art society since 1850, the level of local painting in Marseille had not improved significantly, the call for a strong regionalist style also persisted there.[29]

A review of the yearly exhibitions held by art societies throughout the country reveals that, by the end of the Second Empire, regional efforts had been able to promote some realist artists and had certainly done much to raise the level of taste and to acquaint a growing number of people with an awareness of art. The decentralization of art control would not have been as successful, or realism as all-pervasive, however, if it had not been for the often single-minded enthusiasm—or speculation, if you will—of private patrons, many of whom contacted painters directly, soliciting specific themes—more often than not intimate scenes of daily life or contemporary events.

The Private Patron

Many of the private collectors who supported realist artists cannot now be identified with certainty, but the few that are known are characteristic of the new, informal relationship that was emerging between artist, art dealer, and patron during the realist period. These collectors came from a variety of backgrounds. Many who became proponents of the new realist aesthetic had earlier been collectors of either academic or romantic compositions. As they became aware of the potentialities of realism to mirror their own concerns, within a contemporary format, they often became staunch advocates of the new, popular style.

Among the early collectors of realist painting was Comte Duchâtel, a former politician who had faithfully served the July Monarchy but who, by the early 1860s, had retired to the south of France near Bordeaux. As a proponent of the *juste milieu*, Duchâtel typifies certain members of the moneyed aristocracy who, seemingly tired of supporting classic and romantic painters, turned their attention to the growing number of contemporary genre painters whose entries were being accepted at the Paris Salons.[30]

Duchâtel's interest in these themes may have been influenced by his own earlier political training and the reforms he advocated during the opening years of the July Monarchy. It is more likely, however, that he commissioned realist images depicting activities on his estate not only as an indication of his means and his position but also to call attention to his role as a responsible landholder concerned about the peasants hired to work his land.[31] When Duchâtel first began collecting art is not known; by the late 1850s his collections probably already included a number of old masters as well as works by leading figures of the nineteenth century. He is known to have favoured Italian Renaissance panels and Northern scenes, and to have owned at least two works by Ingres, *Oedipus and the Sphinx* and *The Source*, which were later given to the Louvre as part of the Duchâtel bequest.[32]

In 1861, at the close of the Paris Salon, Duchâtel purchased a work by Jules Breton entitled *Les Sarcleuses* (a canvas unfortunately now lost), which he had seen during the Salon exhibition. The painting was shipped to Duchâtel's estate, Château-Lagrange, near Bordeaux, and put on display in his home among the other compositions that he owned.[33] Duchâtel had been aware of the rising young painter for some time because of previous exhibitions in Paris and the numerous medals and favorable support in daily newspapers that Breton had already received.[34] Shortly after acquiring *Les Sarcleuses,* Duchâtel invited the artist to visit Château-Lagrange, offering him a commission to re-create a scene on the Duchâtel estate during the annual grape harvest. It was the first time in his collecting career that Duchâtel had commissioned a work directly from an artist. The relationship between painter and patron was an encouraging one, and on at least one other occasion, Duchâtel urged Breton to complete a composition recording laborers in the fields or specific types from the Medoc region.

In preparation for his first assignment, *The Grape Harvest at Château-Lagrange* (fig. 2.7), Breton visited the Duchâtel villa in 1862 and again in 1863. While there, he completed a series of preliminary drawings (figs. 2.8, 2.9) that reveal how Breton simplified his image to reflect a natural, relaxed atmosphere among the field workers. Also crucial to the completion of the final canvas, which was executed some time later at Breton's studio in his home in Courrières in northern France, was a series of photographs taken during his visit at the estate, which capture some of the figures and various postures, as well as other aspects of the composition.[35] The use of photographs to organize the final arrangement of his figures heightened the reality and truthfulness of Breton's scene. Thus, both Breton and Duchâtel were, in effect, working together to create a realistic image of a specific, annual event.

Upon its completion, *The Grape Harvest at Château-Lagrange* was exhibited at the 1864 Salon. This was the only time it was publicly displayed and the only time that other artists were privileged to see the work. Immediately after the exhibition, it was shipped back to Duchâtel's home, where it remained until it was sold at public auction in 1888.[36] Despite its relative obscurity and realist content, the painting points out a relevant aspect in the development of realism. Because of Duchâtel's sponsorship, a significant regional canvas was created that must have enhanced Breton's reputation as a recorder of contemporary life. Without Duchâtel's support, Breton might not have undertaken a painting of this type or completed it with such veracity. The history of the work exemplifies one way in which a patron newly attracted to the movement could actively influence the creation of regional realist images.

The relationship between Laurent Laperlier, a second patron, and another realist artist, François Bonvin, further illustrates the importance of the connection between painter and patron in the development of the realist movement. A government bureaucrat by profession, Laurent

Laperlier became an admirer of the eighteenth-century works of Jean Siméon Chardin and, because of that interest, a patron of the contemporary works of François Bonvin. Like Duchâtel and Breton, Bonvin and Laperlier enjoyed one another's company and shared similar interests. More than that, Bonvin often served as Laperlier's personal guide and mentor, correcting, developing, and refining Laperlier's decisions concerning acquisitions, pointing out the distinctions that separated the masters from the plethora of marketplace "works of art."[37] In turn, Laperlier's appreciation of Chardin and previous artists influenced Bonvin's study and awareness of the former masters, who were then being rediscovered—and who at that time served as models for many of the realists in enlarging and developing their own styles. Bonvin's admiration for Chardin and his continued dependence upon the eighteenth-century master for inspiration in his own work demonstrate one way in which imagery of earlier times functioned as a foundation for nineteenth-century themes derived from the life of the people.

In addition to his interest in Chardin, Laperlier became a committed sponsor of paintings and drawings by his friend Bonvin. Without Laperlier's ready encouragement and financial support, it is unlikely that the impoverished Bonvin would have been able to continue painting and drawing. During the 1850s and 1860s, Laperlier purchased a number of works by his friend—a fact documented by the number of Bonvins that Laperlier sold in 1867 when he moved from France to Algeria.[38] The relationship between Laperlier and Bonvin resembles that between Gustave Courbet and Octave Tassaert and their patron, Alfred Bruyas, in that their reciprocal appreciation went far beyond objects commissioned and represented a deep personal commitment on the part of a patron toward the well-being of an artist.[39] This relationship enabled Bonvin to continue the type of work he enjoyed most, since many of the works Laperlier purchased were small, intimate scenes that Bonvin obviously painted for his own pleasure.

Laperlier's encouragement may have inspired other collectors (who are still not known) to take an interest in Bonvin's work or in the work of other, even lesser-known artists who pursued the realist tradition. Many drawings and paintings by Bonvin, since they were small in scale, found their way into some middle-class households, where there were few other paintings to compete with them.[40] In this way, Bonvin's imagery helped reinforce the tastes and the understanding of middle-class families whose collections were not extensive or well-known but who wanted to own and display a few original works of art and appreciated Bonvin's familiar or humble domestic scenes.

Unlike wealthy patrons who wished to develop a collection or who sponsored specific artists in times of need, the captains of industry were a third type of private patron of realist art, who sought to record their economic accomplishments and to impress the public with their achievements. The new realist imagery did much to proselytize the changes and development in production and mechanization that were being brought about by industrialization. Eugène Schneider's support of François Bonhommé typifies this new, industrial patron.

François Bonhommé chose as his subjects scenes illustrative of Napoleon III's massive modernization program in the mining regions of France. He began his career by documenting events he witnessed in his daily life. By 1836, with the help of his teacher Delaroche, Bonhommé was hired to prepare a commission for the Fourchambault ironworks, an assignment that established him as an artist ready to work with contemporary entrepreneurs (fig. 2.10). Bonhommé's entry at the 1840 Salon, *The Iron-Works at Fourchambault*, confirmed his reputation as a recorder of scenes in French industrial mills and the men who worked in them. This work led to a series of commissions from other leading entrepreneurs, who responded to his special talent for accurately documenting what he saw.[41]

Like many of the realists, Bonhommé actually visited the sites he painted, and he created compositions that were didactic in format. On location, he prepared carefully detailed preliminary drawings of workers, owners, or machinery. Later he recomposed and humanized these individual studies of laborers and capitalists so that in the final canvas they appeared united in an endeavor that would enhance the well-being of the country. In an all-out governmental effort to modernize and unify the nation during the Second Empire, Bonhommé's type of realism flourished. Between 1850 and 1870 he was able to document, in watercolors of mines and factories (figs. 2.11, 2.12), the remarkable expansion of industry and to depict the skilled and unskilled classes of workers that provided the basis for this new type of mechanized economy.

Most likely, Bonhommé came to the attention of Napoleon III and private industrialists through a series of works he was commissioned to do for the Ecole des Mines in Paris about 1851.[42] Each of these murals was a significant contribution to Bonhommé's oeuvre and, to a great extent, an indication of his capacity as a realist and as an artist who created easily understood images.[43]

The majority of Bonhommé's images were privately commissioned by the young, energetic entrepreneurs who were then transforming French society. Few relationships between artist and industrialist during the Second Empire are as well documented as that between Bonhommé and Schneider. At the time Bonhommé received the commission for the Ecole des Mines, he was already corresponding with

Schneider, a major industrialist then revitalizing the town of Le Creusot from an insignificant manufactory into one of the major centers of mining and iron production in the country. Bonhommé had already received a commission from Schneider to work for him and had visited Le Creusot to make the preliminary studies that he would incorporate into paintings for his new patron.[44]

Since the artist had no political interest in the workers' cause, his compositions made no judgments about the conditions under which they lived or worked. Unlike some later naturalists, Bonhommé simply recorded the achievements of industry, painting common laborers, foremen, owners, and buildings in a series that—because of its thoroughness and meticulous detail—is comparable with other realist depictions of urban and rural life.

Through Schneider, Bonhommé received other commissions, sometimes from the government. Schneider was enthusiastic in commending the artist's ability to faithfully document the machines and activities of industrialization.[45] The relationship reflected in their correspondence is one of mutual influence and close cooperation: Schneider recognized Bonhommé's capacity to convey the new vision of energy and dynamism that was vital if France was to compete with other developing nations, and Bonhommé welcomed Schneider's support, as it provided new opportunities for his talent. In October 1852, perhaps in response to the commission for the Ecole des Mines, Bonhommé wrote to thank his mentor for all that had been done on his behalf and to confirm his proposed trip to Le Creusot to discuss with Schneider further details about the themes and figures he would include in projected works. If this letter is any indication of the manner in which Bonhommé completed the Ecole des Mines paintings, then the creation of realist images that would dramatically show France responding to changes in mining and manufacturing was, indeed, a joint effort.[46] Thus, the mid-1860s were the peak of Bonhommé's career, and his series of large water colors and gouaches of Schneider's Le Creusot symbolized the triumph of imagination fired by the energy of an enlightened capitalist.[47]

The New Maecenas Redefined

By the end of the Second Empire, support for contemporary art in France had greatly expanded. On the one hand, traditional state-supported commissions continued—to a great extent inspired by images at the Paris Salons that recorded events the government wanted documented. On the other hand, regional opportunities for artists increased as a result of renewed activity by local art societies and a growing number of municipal governments. Added to this, commissions and purchases by an eager and growing number of middle-class patrons opened the movement to many more artists than official patronage could ever have sponsored. Once these individual patrons began acting on their own, establishing contacts with many of the artists personally and independently—even those outside official exhibition circles—informal relationships were established and nurtured that further extended the avenues of patronage.

Not all the art works purchased or commissioned in this way reflected developments in the realist tradition. An increasing number, however, revealed a heightened modernity. By 1870, the middle class was the recognized supporter of realism. Patrons seeking an art that was not only direct but also easily understood and purveyed by art connoisseurs in all parts of the country continued to be attracted to the movement. Classicism and romanticism still remained important styles and still influenced artistic taste, but realism attained a position of prominence among younger patrons and traditionalists in urban and rural locales.

Among art historians, the problem still persists as to why some patrons of realism were not more fully utilized by realist artists, and why the government did not support the smaller canvases by the realists—especially those that depicted intimate, personal themes in a freer style. Was this because some aspects of realism revealed a personal approach that only appealed to individual painters and their close friends, or did the Salons require a formal style, in a large didactic format, which meant that small compositions would never be adequately seen? Size was always a factor if a painting was to create a dominant, lasting effect. If this, indeed, was the case, then state and local patronage of the arts could only be germane for large-scale compositions with a contemporary, propagandistic purpose. The smaller canvases or drawings—those created without a known sponsor—reveal that realism was also a direct and honest way of painting, which perhaps could not be channeled into preconceived exhibition or collecting patterns. The complexity of the modes of realism and the bond between this movement and contemporary society still await clarification if all aspects of nineteenth-century realism are to be understood.

NOTES

1. For a discussion of social conditions, see Léon Rosenthal, *Du Romantisme au Réalisme, essai sur l'évolution de la peinture en France de 1830 à 1848* (Paris, 1914). Not all painters subscribed to radical change; many tried

to follow the middle-of-the-road policy that Albert Boime discusses in *Thomas Couture and the Eclectic Vision* (New Haven, Conn.: Yale University Press, 1980).

2. The growing unification of France is discussed in Eugen Weber, *Peasants into Frenchmen: The Modernization of Rural France, 1870–1914* (Stanford, Calif.: Stanford University Press, 1976).

3. For a discussion of the role and importance of art societies, see Léon Lagrange, "Des Sociétés des amis des arts en France, leur origine, leur état actuel, leur avenir," *Gazette des Beaux-Arts* IX–X (1861): 102–17; 158–68; 227–42; 291–301. The evaluation of the importance of art societies and the documentation of differing private patrons remain largely incomplete because of the lack of accessible records and the anonymity of many collectors. For one aspect of state encouragement of realist painting, see Gabriel P. Weisberg, "In Search of State Patronage: Three French Realists and the Second Empire, 1851–1871," in *Art, the Ape of Nature: Essays in Honor of H. W. Janson* (New York: Abrams, 1980).

4. Rosenthal, *Du Romantisme*, p. 3.

5. For a brief discussion of Jeanron's role in realism, see Gabriel P. Weisberg, *The Realist Tradition: French Painting and Drawing, 1830–1900*, exh. cat. (Cleveland Museum of Art, 1980). Jeanron's influential position in the nineteenth century was documented in Madeleine Rousseau, "La vie et l'oeuvre de Philippe Auguste Jeanron, peintre, écrivain, directeur des musées nationaux, 1808–1877" (Thesis, Ecole du Louvre, 1935).

6. Jeanron's petition is deposited in C. 2.100, Archives Nationales. For further reference, see Rousseau, "Jeanron," pp. 29–31.

7. For a discussion of art under Louis Philippe, see Rosenthal, *Du Romantisme*, pp. 11 ff. Louis Philippe managed to retain the power behind the Ministry of Fine Arts, and, largely through his efforts, Salons became annual events. The special collections that he encouraged, such as the Spanish Gallery at the Louvre, were to be of special significance in the evolution of realism. For further information, see I. H. Lipschutz, *Spanish Painting and the French Romantics* (Cambridge, Mass.: Harvard University Press, 1972).

8. Rosenthal discusses the importance of the landscapists and genre painters in advancing new ideas.

9. The tastes of the middle class in art patronage were complex and often mirrored changing fashions. Some members of the middle class, however, became astute collectors of art and later in the century appreciated the newer tendencies. For further discussion, see Albert Boime, "Entrepreneurial Patronage in Nineteenth-Century France," in *Enterprise and Entrepreneurs in Nineteenth and Twentieth-Century France* (Baltimore and London: Johns Hopkins University Press, 1976).

10. Art critics in Paris and the provincial centers did much to foster an appreciation for specific painters. For further reference to the rise of art criticism, see Irene Collins, *The Government and the Newspaper Press in France, 1814–1881* (Oxford: Oxford University Press, 1959).

11. Rosenthal, *Du Romantisme*, pp. 20 ff.

12. Lagrange, "Des Sociétés," pp. 292 ff.

13. Both of these tendencies were viewed as attacks against the Academy. For further discussion, see Lagrange, "Des Sociétés," pp. 296 ff. When romanticism began to fade and realism was perceived as a tendency that deserved encouragement on a regional basis has yet to be determined. There were regional realists active in the 1830s (such as Jean François Monanteuil

in Le Mans and Alençon) who may have helped encourage the development of scenes of actuality far before the date usually considered applicable to realist taste in the provinces. For further reference to Monanteuil, see Weisberg, *The Realist Tradition*, pp. 55, 165, 305.

14. A search of the municipal records of the Musée des Augustins and the Archives Nationales, Paris, has disclosed no specific reason why this particular painting was sent to Toulouse. Deputies may have sponsored the sending of the painting. In discussions with the author, Jacques Vilain, Inspecteur des Musées Provinciaux, noted that often there was no specific reason why a given Salon painting was sent to a particular provincial museum. Perhaps it was simply part of the process of the mass diffusion of art objects to the people, which operated on a random basis.

15. About state policy, see Weisberg, "In Search of State Patronage." With the exception of one work by Alexandre Antigna that depicted Napoleon III's concern for flood victimes in the Ardennes regions (a painting now in the Angers Museum), there seems no clear indication of a specific state policy of selectivity for a location other than a generally held belief that the state should try to educate, or reach, the masses through local distribution of images that could be readily comprehended. In this way provincials could be educated even if they could not always read.

16. Little documentation is available on the total number of individuals who attended regional exhibitions or from what section of society most of the visitors came who studied the paintings on view.

17. Rosenthal, *Du Romantisme*, pp. 64 ff.

18. As Albert Boime has recently noted, a document written by F. de Mercey, Director of Fine Arts, to Minister of State Achille Fould in 1856 advanced the use of realism as a means of officially recording episodes that occurred during the Second Empire. See Boime, *Thomas Couture*, pp. 263–64.

19. A search of the municipal archives in Nantes by the Curator of the Museum failed to yield specific information on how the painting was purchased or even the names of local authorities who might have regarded the painting appropriate for their collection.

20. In order to find out further information on the reception of the painting in Strasbourg, it would be necessary to locate local newspapers and to search for records in the regional archives, a task the author was unable to complete in time for this publication. The pre-sale history of Brion's *Récolte* is similar to Rosa Bonheur's *Horse Fair*, which was sent to Bordeaux for exhibition, with the hope of finding a purchaser. The painting was neglected by officials in Bordeaux during its exhibition in the city.

21. For reference to the purchases made by the *Société des amis des arts* in Nantes from 1836 to 1858, see Lagrange, *Du Romantisme*, p. 110. Further details on the founding of the Nantes museum can be found in H. de Saint-George, *Notice Historique sur le Musée de peinture de Nantes* [19th century] n.d.; Theodore Guedy, *Musées de France et Collections particulièrés* (Paris, n.d.), p. 365, notes the Brion as one of the major works in the museum and, further, refers to it as "*effet bien compris*."

22. No information has been located, as yet, on the working sessions of the Nantes Société in 1858. Often these Sociétés had a representative in Paris, similar to Adrien Dauzats, who worked for the Bordeaux group, who would make contact with painters and secure their work for regional exhibitions. Nantes probably had a similar contact who communicated directly with a painter, although his name has not been identified.

23. The painting was listed as no. 183 in the Nantes catalog. See also *Gustave Courbet (1819–1877)*, exh. cat., Grand Palais, 30 September–2 January 1978, no. 43, pp. 134–35.

24. Ibid., p. 135.

25. For further reference to the purchase of this painting by Nantes, see Claude Souviron, "Documents autographes de Courbet: achat des Cribleuses de blé par le Musée des Beaux-Arts de Nantes," *Revue du Louvre*, no. 4 (1977).

26. The records of the Lille Société that would provide information on the deliberations of 1834 have not been located. For further reference to Jeanron's participation in regional exhibitions, see Rousseau, "Jeanron," p. 59. Jeanron exhibited in Caen in 1836, Amiens in 1837, and finally in Nantes in 1840.

27. Artists were beginning to investigate regional customs and folklore as part of a concerted effort to understand their country. Jeanron's *Les Petits patriotes*, a work that rivalled Delacroix's *Liberty on the Barricades*, had been purchased by the state after the 1830 Salon and sent to the Caen museum. This state purchase may have helped establish Jeanron's career or have influenced Lille to secure his work as a means of keeping their collection contemporary.

28. During this period provincial exhibitions were often used to promote secondary paintings by art dealers anxious to make a profit. The cost of transportation of art objects had also risen, making it difficult for painters to send canvases to shows without the assurance of making a sale.

29. Lagrange, *Du Romantisme*, pp. 34 ff.

30. Duchâtel was one of the men most interested in Thomas Couture's *Romans of the Decadence*. See Boime, *Thomas Couture*, pp. 135–36. A search of the biographies on Duchâtel has not revealed reasons why he shifted his allegiances from romanticism to realism. Perhaps location of letters will clarify his thinking. For a brief discussion of some private patronage questions, see Madeleine Fidell-Beaufort, "Peasants, Painters and Purchasers" in *The Peasant in French 19th-Century Art*, exh. cat., The Douglas Hyde Gallery, Trinity College, Dublin, November 1980, pp. 45–82.

31. For further reference to Duchâtel's career, see L. Vittet, *Le Comte Duchâtel* (Paris, 1875).

32. For further reference to Duchâtel's donations, see *Les Salles de peinture du Musée du Louvre* (Paris: Gaston Braun, n.d.). The Salle Duchâtel also contained works by Bernadino Luini and Hans Memling.

33. For further reference to Duchâtel's collection, see *Catalogue des Tableaux anciens et modernes . . . provenant de la collection de M. le Comte D. . . .*, Hôtel Drouot, Paris, 14 May 1888.

34. By the early 1860s, Jules Breton was considered one of the leading genre painters in the country and an outstanding proponent of regionalism. Even more so than Jean François Millet, with whom he has often been compared, Jules Breton visualized the rural traditions of northern France.

35. For further reference to Breton's use of photographs, see Gabriel P. Weisberg with Annette Bourrut-Lacouture, "The Grape Harvest at Château-Lagrange," *Arts Magazine* 55 (January 1981). While these photographs have not been located, Breton mentioned his use of them in correspondence to the Duchâtels and his wife, Elodie. It is possible that Duchâtel may have arranged to have a certain number of the photographs taken for Breton's use. The author and Mme. Annette Bourrut-Lacouture are working on a monograph on Jules Breton; he is indebted to her for her assistance on this artist.

36. It is not surprising that this painting, along with *Les Sarcleuses,* was sold in 1888, at the height of Jules Breton's popularity in many countries.

37. For further information on Laperlier and Bonvin, see Gabriel P. Weisberg, *Bonvin: La Vie et l'oeuvre* (Paris: Editions Geoffroy-Dechaume, 1979). The role of the independent art dealer in promoting realism is one area that needs investigation. Records of various firms instrumental in fostering an early interest in realism (i.e., Brame, Martinet, or Tempelaere) have unfortunately not survived, making it even more difficult to document what works passed through the art market at a given time. The documents owned by such firms as Durand-Ruel (who came to support realism quite late) and others have also proven nearly inaccessible to the author.

38. For further reference, see *Collection de M. Laperlier, Tableaux et dessins du XVIIIe siècle et de l'école moderne,* Hôtel Drouot, Paris, 11–13 April 1867.

39. Bruyas's collection in Montpellier was well known in the nineteenth century. His keen interest in Octave Tassaert, whom he tried to cure of alcoholism, merits further study, since it gave Tassaert an opportunity to continue working.

40. The collecting of many small realist paintings by anonymous members of the middle class is one of the reasons why so many of their works disappeared. The unknown collector left no record of the objects he secured from art dealers or artists, making it even harder to recover these lost objects today.

41. For further information, see Gabriel P. Weisberg, "François Bonhommé and Early Realist Images of Industrialization, 1830–1870," *Arts Magazine* (April 1980): 132–35; *The Realist Tradition,* pp. 71–73, 75, 76, 78–80, 270.

42. These works were destroyed sometime after 1900. For a discussion of them, see J. F. Schnerb, "François Bonhommé," *Gazette des Beaux-Arts* IX (January 1913): 11–25; (February 1913): 132–42.

43. The availability of murals in public buildings was advocated by some realist critics but few painters in the group acted upon this belief. The realist style was ill suited to large wall decoration, also.

44. Bonhommé considered Schneider one of his most influential patrons and did not hesitate to write him for help, a factor that suggests the two men knew each other prior to 1851. For further information, see François Bonhommé to Eugène Schneider, 2 February 1851, now in the possession of the Schneider Manufactory archives.

45. See Bonhommé to Schneider, 5 September 1852.

46. It is likely that even though the murals for the Ecole des Mines were first encouraged by the Provisional Republican government of 1848, the undertaking had to be reconfirmed under the new regime of Napoleon III, a delay that continued until late 1852. The murals were not completed until 1854–55.

47. For a detailed discussion, see Patrick Le Nouène, " 'Les Soldats de l'Industrie,' de François Bonhommé: L'Idéologie d'un projet," *Les Réalismes et l'Histoire de l'art, Histoire et Critique des Arts,* no. 4/5 (May 1978): 44 ff.

The Second Empire's Official Realism

Albert Boime 3

THIS CHAPTER OUTLINES A SIMPLE theory about a subtle conspiracy organized by the Bonapartist regime to fashion a visual style appropriate to its ideological position. Contrary to most previous studies, which have associated it with outmoded classicism, confused eclecticism, or renewed romanticism, this study suggests that the Second Empire's style was realist. Indeed, the government's taste for realism promoted the assimilation of this movement into the mainstream of modern French culture. Manet's naturalism and Monet's impressionism are incomprehensible without the profound investment of government resources in the encouragement of realism during the 1850s and 1860s.[1]

Louis Napoléon, both as prince-president and emperor, fostered this official style in several ways. He and his administration won over a younger generation of academically trained painters, encouraged the rise of alternative realist styles to rival the radical tendencies, and, through Salon criticism and high influence, managed to blunt and neutralize the realist style of the Left. The Bonapartist government aimed at a consensus realism, which meant forcing concessions from both the Academy and the painters perceived as leftists. By making academic models conform to new molds and progressive tendencies conform to traditional ones, the administration succeeded in establishing what we may call an "official realism."[2]

It will become apparent that we must clear the air of stereotypical views of the Second Empire government as an adventurous band of bumblers in the cultural realm. We owe such views largely to conservative scholars unwilling to admit governmental influence in the rise, spread, and success of an avant-garde. Yet thinkers on the Left have also deprecated the imperial regime's involvement in the beaux arts as stupid and ineffectual. Neither Left nor Right has yet understood that the Second Empire comprised a number of creative conservatives who were supremely pragmatic, flexible, and ingenious in dealing with the visual arts, and who left a lasting imprint. We may not like their methods or the results, but to dismiss their role is to distort historical circumstances. Hard-headed types like the Comte de Morny, the Duc de Persigny, the Comte de Nieuwerkerke, Romieu, de Mercey, Courmont, and even the emperor himself took active roles in producing an artistic consensus integral to the ideological aspirations of the Second Empire. No artist then working could have avoided the impact of their stewardship.

It should not seem surprising that the Second Empire preferred realism. Critics and artists had already begun to regard the alternatives, romanticism and classicism, as old-fashioned. While they persisted under various eclectic guises, their respective leaders, Delacroix and Ingres, were no longer the favorites of the dominant class.[3] At the same time, these two painters were tainted by their identification with the Legitimist and Orleanist parties now antagonistic to the new government. If Louis Napoléon's party could not tolerate for long the early radicalism of Courbet and Millet, the Bonapartists at least respected their talents and encouraged them under certain conditions. The positivist, scientific, and industrialist proclivities of the regime further disposed it to a sympathetic view of innovative realist forms, including photography, the genre-like pictures of the Neo-Greeks, Ernest Meissonier's paintings, and the animal scenes of Rosa Bonheur and Constant Troyon.[4] Above all, since the emperor's professed aim was to communicate with a broad constituency, he needed a direct form of visual communication. The Salon pictures of his civil and military exploits were frequently lithographed and engraved for distribution in the provinces, and government placards incorporated illustrations done in the official realist style.[5]

Certainly, this style was not formulated in a "smoke-filled room," nor did it spring forth fully fashioned from the head of Napoléon III. The administration began to define it, with typical pragmatism, by its practice. Already by the mid-1850s the administration had developed a fairly coherent art policy, which it invoked for overtly propagandistic themes, such as the Crimean War, and major civil events, such as the birth of the prince imperial and the emperor's visits to the flood victims of 1856. Being clearer at first about what it did not want than about what it wanted, the regime expressed this policy in essentially negative terms, but by 1863 it could declare its intentions programmatically.

I. Media Control

An intensive campaign to create this realist style was launched during the period between the *coup d'état* and the Exposition Universelle of 1855, to demonstrate a visual equivalent to the industrial and agricultural progress of the regime. As soon as the Great Exhibition of London ended in 1851, the government of Louis Napoléon projected one on a similar scale and planned to add to it works of art, a category absent from its predecessor.[6] All the organizers of the 1855 World's Fair proclaimed this innovation in international expositions and thus attested to the government's desire to see itself glorified through the fine arts as much as through its industrial products.[7] A secondary interest further related the two categories, as defined by de Mercey: "The exposure of our *chefs d'ateliers*, decorators, and industrial artists to the outstanding art productions of each people should incite their imagination, enlighten their taste, stimulate their intelligent activity, and impress their products with that character of originality and seal of nobility and high distinction which doubles their value and glorifies a nation."[8] Hence the government needed the artists' cooperation to produce examples suitable to its imperial ideal, vague as that might have been at the time. To this end the titular head of the Second Empire's art machine, Comte Nieuwerkerke, tightened Salon regulations and counseled juries to toughen entry standards.[9] Nieuwerkerke was also appointed president of the jury for admissions, and in addition to the usual number of loyal artists and museum officials chosen by the administration, key members of the imperial commission organizing the exhibition—including Prince Jérôme Napoléon, Achille Fould, Comte de Morny, and Baroche—served on this jury. All were powerful members of the emperor's court and were instrumental in the attempt at cultural hegemony. That they held some clear idea about what they wanted is demonstrated in the case of young Jules Breton when he brought his *Gleaners* and two other pictures to the barracks provisionally constructed to receive incoming entries for the World's Fair. Alfred Arago, Inspector-General of Beaux Arts and member of the awards committee, spotted them and singled them out for praise: "You will have success, much success!" Later, Breton's guardian friend at the Louvre told him that the jury had been completely won over by his *Gleaners*.[10]

Before analyzing the specifically propagandist use of the visual arts, however, I would like to review in general the Second Empire's control of the media. At the outset of his career, Louis Napoléon had to seek his allies among opponents of the Orleanist monarchy and outside the domain of conventional party politics. He had to appeal to the masses.[11] Early on, he preached against the narrow franchise of the monarchy, advocating universal suffrage, and as the inevitable ally of the republicans in 1848 he called for the restoration of the Consulate and the Republic. Even after his landslide victory in December 1848, and the plebiscite that acclaimed his *coup d'état* in 1851, he still did not consider his task complete. It was not enough to have the peasantry behind him: he wanted to attach himself to the upper classes while yet satisfying "the interests of the most numerous classes." He actually set out to forge a new ruling class from a broad constituency and to indoctrinate a younger generation to replace those whose minds had been "perverted by the revolution of 1848."[12]

Despite the fact that he now controlled France through his army and police, the fear of a republican insurrection and the anxieties of his inexperienced cabinet created a climate of insecurity, which in retrospect appears at odds with the actual state of affairs. His own fears of illegitimacy—both personal and political—contributed to this insecurity. He was obsessed with dynastic succession, and much of the Second Empire cultural propaganda aimed at identifying the regime with the Holy Roman Empire. The need to establish an aura of legitimacy predisposed Louis Napoléon and his staff to seek control over as many avenues of intellectual and cultural life as possible. The role assigned to propaganda by the regime was fundamental, and the emperor proved to be an able manipulator of public opinion.

He and his administrators controlled the press by direct and indirect pressures until almost the very end of the regime. A directive for the elections of 5 April 1869 shows the degree of governmental influence with respect to the so-called independent paper *Le petit journal*, aimed primarily at the working classes and peasantry. The directive noted that while the paper was nonpolitical it had a distribution of 250,000 copies. Millaud, its director,

> in general agreement with our press arrangements, has begun to publish a certain number of informal portraits of the ministers, principal members of the majority. . . . These portraits, very skillfully done, skirt the political question without directly touching upon it. This journal is also preparing the publication of a military novel about the First Empire, conceived in order to counterbalance the political novels of the opposition directed against the army. This novel . . . originates from the Cabinet of the Emperor.

The lithographs of individual government candidates were to be distributed at the cheapest cost by an organized cadre of image peddlers. Finally, "none of the methods of popular propaganda . . . will be neglected. . . ." While this was written near the end of the regime, the report from the Prefect of the Police to the future emperor in

October 1852 essentially states the same thing and in a more urgent tone.[13]

Journalists were hired, papers secretly subsidized, brochures published, speeches written—all to influence public opinion and measure public reaction to government policy. The government accomplished this with the "carrot and stick" approach: it used repression and suppression, cajolery, and bribery—always proceeding pragmatically rather than emotionally or vindictively. While it made effective use of political cartoons for posters in election campaigns, the government suppressed opposition cartoonists like Daumier and forced them to change from commentary on current events to social satire. Not coincidentally, Daumier turned increasingly to painting after 1852.

Louis Napoléon especially needed the press to convert the influential, the articulate, the propertied, and the intellectual communities through brochures and articles in daily and weekly political and literary journals.[14] The journals were indispensable for defining the consensus he desired. The regime reorganized the *Moniteur officiel*, the official organ, and by reducing its subscription rate substantially increased its circulation and made it a rival of several popular journals. Naturally, the *Moniteur's* official position limited it as a propaganda weapon, but it was well suited to cultivating the intellectual elite, so the new editors enlarged its literature and criticism sections and employed outstanding writers like Gautier, Champfleury, Feuillet, Houssaye, and Sainte-Beuve. Through one means or another the government gained control of *Le Pays*, *Le Constitutionnel*, and *La Patrie*, which could shape public opinion more directly.[15] While differing in form and content, they often shared the same pro-Bonapartist personnel. But Napoléon III was not content with a devoted press; he wanted to create a diversity of opinion within a consensus of approval. His remarkable formula provided for an opposition press, where differences in opinion were neither too strident nor too radical. During the period 1850–51, when the pro-Bonapartist *Constitutionnel* was one of the three largest papers in circulation, the other two, the so-called opposition papers *Le Siècle* and *La Presse*, created the illusion of a democratic press. Actually, both *La Presse* and *Le Siècle* were owned by shareholders whose main interest was a return on their investment and who were consequently vulnerable to the threat of suspension. The Comte de Morny (the emperor's half brother and indefatigable champion of the Bonapartist cause) advised several of his friends among the key shareholders about the advantages of government cooperation. As a result, the tone of *Le Siècle* became moderate and constitutional, as it avoided all direct attacks on the government. It expressed safe, liberal positions, such as praise for the 1789 revolution, rejection of aristocratic pretensions, demands for providing for the needy poor, and (after 1859) anticlericalism. The result of all this was that the government looked upon the paper as its own "republican" voice.[16]

Like the persuasive Morny, who constantly attracted talent to the Bonapartist party, Prince Napoléon actively sought liberal cooperation for the government's projects. He was close to republicans and leftists like Leroux, Reynaud, Lammenais, and even Proudhon, who later had to explain his periodic visits to the prince's residence at the Palais Royal. As deputy from Corsica, he asked for clemency for the workers arrested after the June Days, and later he even criticized the *coup d'état*. Nevertheless, he became quickly reconciled to the empire and held a number of key offices, including Minister of Algeria and the Colonies, member of the Council of State, and President of the Imperial Commission for the Exposition Universelle of 1855. The emperor used him as his liaison with the opposition, and it was through Prince Napoléon's connections and friendships that many writers of the Left were snared into writing pamphlets for the government.[17]

It is probably hard for us today to appreciate the importance of the pamphlet in indoctrination, but in an age when the main forum of communication was the printed word, it was a favorite weapon in the propaganda arsenal. The government marshalled the forces of the press to give a brochure maximum publicity. By publishing in the dailies either the whole of a brochure or excerpts, it could also promote a large circulation and increase the size of the reading audience. A speech could receive enormous publicity, but its official connection could never be denied. On the other hand, if reaction to an officially inspired pamphlet was overwhelmingly antagonistic, the government could immediately withdraw press support and, if necessary, seize the pamphlet.

Pamphleteers, usually recruited from the journalists, formed a major part of the government's "kept band"[18] of writers. Their activities often overlapped with the arts, as in the cases of Romieu, the Director of Beaux Arts following the *coup d'état*, and Edmond About, a popular art critic and author. Romieu, a son of a general under the First Empire, devoted his journalistic and literary abilities to attacking the republicans of 1848 and ingratiated himself with Louis Napoléon. In 1850 he wrote *L'ère des Césars*, and the following year he published the notorious *Spectre rouge de 1852*, both of which prepared the public psychologically for the *coup d'état*. The government subsidized both brochures and awarded him the directorship in 1852. About was a fervent Bonapartist attached to the intellectual circles around Achille Fould, Princess Mathilde, and Prince Napoléon. He was a known favorite at the Tuileries, one of the select French delegation that participated in the ceremony for the opening of the Suez Canal in 1869. Through the influence of his friends, he became involved with politics from 1857 to 1865 and wrote several brochures and articles for the *Opinion nationale* in support of the government's policies. One of the most important of these was *The Roman Question*, first serialized in the *Moniteur* and then commissioned as a pamphlet by the emperor himself. Napoléon III, Prince Napoléon, and Morny read the proofs, while Fould and Morny wrote key sections.[19]

Napoléon III's cunning ways were based upon his recognition of the media's success in molding biases, opinions, and stereotypes. He tried to create a new political consensus to educate a new generation and wean them from radical doctrine. Minister of the Interior Persigny expressed the official attitude in 1852: "The evil doctrines spread through the country by anarchic works, and the moral disorder and crimes which are the consequences, call for an energetic intervention on the part of the administration in favor of good social principles. This intervention can best be accomplished by means of publications and pamphlets encouraged and, if need be, financed by the administration. . . ."[20] The same year he circulated a letter to the prefects in connection with local elections, emphasizing the importance of undermining the old political foundations and parties and of creating a new party.[21] The cultural analogy to the new party was a new style—different from the romantic, classic, and eclectic styles identified with the previous regimes—or at least some type of revitalization of the older forms, in line with the government's bolder approach to foreign and domestic affairs.

The extortionate plans of the government were not limited to control of the press but extended to the whole of literary production. This astonishing attempt was masterminded by no less a personality than Sainte-Beuve. Like Mérimée, he welcomed the *coup d'état* and supported the Second Empire actively. While Hugo, his close friend from the romantic movement, went into exile, Sainte-Beuve trafficked with his enemies. The June insurrection unnerved him, and he believed that Louis Napoléon was the only one who could tame the "ferocious beast." In 1852 he accepted the *Légion d'honneur*, which he had twice refused under Louis Philippe. After the coup he appealed to the Constitutional Monarchists not to sulk but to join the emperor, and he transferred his own *Lundi* articles to *Le Moniteur*.

Among the papers discovered at the Tuileries after the debacle was a memorandum dated 31 March 1856, which Sainte-Beuve submitted to Mocquard, the emperor's confidential secretary.[22] The memorandum was certainly written in response to a request for a systematic strategy from an administration already cultivating a stable of writers through paternalistic support. Sainte-Beuve advised the emperor to ignore well-known professors and academicians but to aim at the rank and file—what he termed the *presse littéraire*—as if they were manual workers. He suggested three ways of dealing with the general mass of authors: (1) provide relief for indigent writers and raise their self esteem and gain their loyalty by addressing them in the name of the emperor; (2) establish an organization to award an annual prize for appropriate subjects designated by an imperial commission; (3) provide lodgings at the Louvre for representatives of the new literature and maintain direct links with them through the emperor or minister of state. Sainte-Beuve warned against communicating through the Ministry of Public Instruction, which was inevitably tied to traditional approaches. He anticipated administrative concern about democratizing the writers' corps and providing opportunities for a literary "proletariat," but he emphasized the government's power and secret intelligence "to elevate and organize it."[23] Under previous regimes, writers were motivated by simple greed, and the need to be heard and singled out from the crowd encouraged production of material antagonistic to the public authority. As a result, administrative officials developed the attitude that it was impossible to regulate this type of production. Yet nothing was easier, according to Sainte-Beuve, than to influence it decisively through government resources. Currently, literature had no *parti pris* and was in a state of hopeless disarray; the slightest move on the part of the regime would provide the focus and direction needed.[24] Sainte-Beuve stressed the advantages of an imperial prize for both poetry and prose, awarded for "national subjects, actual, neither too curious nor too erudite, but conforming to the life and instincts of modern society."

Sainte-Beuve suggested that the organization to award these prizes be called the *Académie du suffrage universel*, a term intended to confute opponents. His aim, consistent with Napoleonic thought, was "to coordinate . . . literature with the entire institutional ensemble of the Empire, and to insure that it was not left to its own resources or to chance." At the same time, this encouragement would stimulate a Second Empire style capable of serving warning to academic bodies. Their institutional constraints and rigidities disposed them to routine and casual public involvement; they would age quickly in the face of progress promoted from above and would eventually be forced to toe the line. The moment, he continued, was especially propitious: the dynastic heir so long desired by France had just been born; a glorious peace had been won, and the results had crowned all expectations. An era of unlimited prosperity and grandeur was emerging.

This astonishing document attests to the grandiose schemes of the Second Empire to establish a national style in the arts and letters. Furthermore, the methods for accomplishing this in literature are consistent with those used to subjugate the press. Sainte-Beuve's memorandum points to a consensus based on national themes and grounded in reality, and rejects both the monarchical-minded academies and avant-garde fantasies. Above all, he wanted a realist style for the government and planned to achieve it by promoting an alternative to already existing tendencies, absorbing rival organizations, and neutralizing the potential opposition.

The pattern of cultural hegemony that evolved at this time also manifested itself in the realm of popular culture. For example, the administration deemed it necessary to suppress the public singing of what were seen as subversive songs, such as the *Marseillaise* and *Ça ira*. At the same time, it came out with its own tunes like *Le peuple français à Louis Napoléon Bonaparte* and *Le Neveu de son oncle* ("Qu'il parle haut à tous les rouges!/D'un mot, qu'il fass' fermer leurs bouges!"). Songs about the first Napoleon were now revived, including the popular *Le petit caporal* and old favorites by Béranger.[25] The government also censored drama. Thus the ministry blocked an opera about the Fronde scheduled for the Académie de Musique in December 1852 because of its expressions of revolt. It regarded as potentially dangerous any theme that was based on an uprising and used the phrase "aux armes!" The administration could not sanction it for fear that the same cry might be repeated in other theatres, in café-concerts, and eventually on the street. During the same period, Musset's *Lorenzaccio*, scheduled for the Odéon, was also rejected by the imperial censors. The report claimed that the debaucheries and cruelties of Alessandro Medici, young duke of Florence, the running discussion of the obligation to assassinate a sovereign whose crimes cried out for vengeance, and even the murder of the prince by one of his relatives, presented too subversive a spectacle for the public. Another play at the Opéra-Comique, Sardou's *Capitaine Henriot*, was allowed to proceed after initial reservations. Permission was granted at the topmost layer of the bureaucracy: the hero, Henri IV, was less important for founding the Bourbon dynasty than for recalling the glorious "heritage of the throne" now occupied by the emperor himself.[26]

A final example was a presentation of twenty-five tableaux summing up the history of France at the Théâtre de la Porte Saint Martin. Here the administration offered its approval on the condition that the director agree to major revisions. Its stable of writers created a new ending, which the director, over the head of the original author, accepted. The government censors had demanded either that the play terminate before the revolution or that the final tableaux be devoted to Napoléon I. The team systematically eliminated tableaux it found objectionable and then supplied the finale showing *Napoléon I Distributing the Eagles on the Champs-de-Mars*. The commission concluded that the work had been profoundly altered in accordance with imperial "conventions," and it congratulated the director for his foresight in granting the presentation "a larger and broader interpretation, and a more French character."[27]

II. The Government Influence in the Beaux-Arts

No one would deny the Second Empire's assertion of control in the realm of the visual arts.[28] But the main proposition here concerns the government's stylistic preference, and a review of the extent and character of this control should help in clarifying that preference. The administration wanted to indoctrinate a new generation; already, in 1853, the Minister of Public Instruction founded a commission to adopt standards for teaching drawing in the *lycées*. The famous report, published in the *Moniteur* early in 1854, was written by Félix Ravaisson, who was a popular philosopher at the Court of the Second Empire. Ravaisson, who enjoyed the collaboration of Delacroix and Meissonier, systematically reviewed all the currently employed pedagogic methods and then advised a straightforward empirical approach that could serve as the basis for both the fine and the applied arts. The earliest lessons would stress geometric solids, parts of the human head, and plants. The report recommended that photographs be used as much as possible for studying the human figure and the cast.[29]

The major institutional vehicle of communication in the arts was the government-sponsored Salon exhibition, the means by which artistic output was screened and rewarded. It was intimately associated with the press, since it represented an important cultural event regularly reviewed in the newspapers. Often the reviews—which ran serially —were assembled into a pamphlet and sold on the market. Most of the art critics were talented writers who belonged to the *presse littéraire* described by Sainte-Beuve. Those who held government jobs or otherwise enjoyed close connections with the regime—such as Houssaye, who wrote generously about the court in *L'artiste*—included Gautier, About, Chesneau, and Saint-Victor.[30]

By making the Salon from 1850 to 1863 biennial (with the exception of 1853) the government reduced the opportunities of artists by one half. While the administration allowed artists to elect the jury in 1850, following the *coup d'état* it began to appropriate this function for itself: in 1852 it appointed half of the jury members, and for the Exposition Universelle of 1855 it named the entire panel. Succeeding juries remained entirely official, with Nieuwerkerke, then Director-General of Museums, named in perpetuity as ex-officio president. Trying to enlist the support of the younger generation, the administration announced in 1853 that the Medal of Honor, valued at 4,000 francs, would be designated specifically for the encouragement of young talent and exclusive of academicians and members of the *Légion d'honneur*.[31]

In 1852 Nieuwerkerke tightened up the regulations by limiting each artist to three admitted works, an innovation he justified at the awards ceremony in July: "The exhibitions held as they are, gratuitously in one of the palaces of the State . . . confer in themselves a fundamental reward upon those admitted to them." Artists "should therefore be received there by one of their most complete works and not by sketches or *ébauches* unworthy of display in a great competition opened by the State." Here the government entered directly into the process of artistic production. The rule governing exemptions was now modified as well; those who previously won a medal (heretofore exempt from jury scrutiny) could still be rejected if their work proved unacceptable. Clearly, the government was aiming for high quality for the Exposition Universelle of 1855. In 1855 the emperor founded a triennial prize of 20,000 francs (made biennial in 1859) to be awarded "to the work best capable of honoring or serving the State." His attempt that year to win over the artistic community is shown by the 40 *Légion d'honneur* decorations, 240 medals and 222 Honorable Mentions.[32]

Speeches at the awards ceremonies following the *coup d'état* further reveal the intentions of the administration. Nieuwerkerke told his audience on 20 July 1852 that the government had assumed responsibility for rewarding artists "in the name of the country," and for "discouraging false vocations and false talents who obstruct all the avenues open to art." Thus the opportunity to enter the artistic profession would henceforth be decided by Nieuwerkerke, Baroche, Persigny, Maupas, Morny, Fould, and Prince Napoléon.[33]

Persigny took the rostrum after Nieuwerkerke and apologized for the prince-president's absence: Louis Napoléon had attended an industrial exhibition at Strasbourg and was unavoidably detained. Both events, however, attested to the chief's desire to encourage all activities contributing to the glory and grandeur of the country. As Persigny declared: "If a government, which owes its origin and even its principle to the poetic sentiments of the masses, disdains the cult of the arts for the cult of material things, it will depreciate the very conditions of its existence and fail to recognize the genius of its country." Persigny then affirmed Louis Napoléon's faith in the union of art and industry and claimed that art had nothing to fear from the growing commercial and industrial expansion of modern civilization. Whatever activity French society practiced, nothing could undermine "the chivalrous and artistic aspect of the national character." Above all, the power of the government rested on "popular faith" and was independent of "party intrigues" and "factions." It appealed to the people for its art and drew its inspiration from modern society. When Nieuwerkerke reclaimed the floor, he addressed himself to the question of the jury and affirmed Persigny's remarks. He asserted that government appointees were necessary to mediate school rivalries and factions and to overcome the complacencies of confraternity whose entrenched routine vitiated progressive tendencies. Here is the language and approach of Sainte-Beuve's memorandum now transposed to the realm of the fine arts.[34]

The following year Nieuwerkerke announced profound improvement in the quality of work submitted to the Salon and advised the jury to be even more severe than before. Napoléon III's decree of 22 June 1853, which established the Exposition Universelle of 1855, specifically declared that "perfections in industry are intimately tied to those in the fine arts," and it was clear that the severe regulations were designed to project the government's taste before rival nations. This exhibition was placed under the sponsorship of Prince Napoléon, whose commission included Baroche, now President of the Conseil d'Etat; Jean Dollfus, textile magnate; Le Play, Engineer-in-Chief of Mines; Morny (who was everywhere at once and served on all major juries); Emile Péreire, President of the Conseil d'Administration du Chemin de Fer du Midi; Regnault, Administrator of the Imperial Manufactures at Sèvres; Schneider, head of the Le Creusot ironworks; Seillière, banker; Delacroix; and Ingres—fervent Bonapartists all, whose achievements were the backdrop for the technical and artistic display of France at the World's Fair.[35]

At the awards ceremony on 27 July 1853 Fould, Minister of State, promptly compared the Age of the Second Empire with previous epochs of superior cultural renovation and innovation: the Century of Pericles, the Century of Léon X, the Centuries of Augustus and of Louis XIV. While the honor of having a sovereign's name attached to an epoch is rare, Fould dared to imagine what the present epoch would be called in the distant future. He praised the overall improvement in the exhibition, and especially commended the artists for their "tangible progress in the technical side of art, in material imitation." While he expressed regret that the younger generation did not pursue "le beau idéal" with the same ardor that it brought "to the study of reality," he observed that the administration applauded the results and wanted to do justice to the remarkable productions. Nevertheless, he hoped to see, following the example of the old masters, conciliation of the ideal and reality and the union of the Beautiful "with the intelligent study of forms and scenes which the spectacle of nature presents to the eyes." (Fould had in mind a realism tempered by the ideal, in opposition to the sordid and vulgar examples of Courbet and Millet.) Next, Fould called attention to the government's extensive patronage; immense constructions were going on that would require decoration. The government would look to the chiefs of the French school for guidance, but, in addition, "more than one honorable place is reserved for the modest talent who, under the leadership of a sure guide, awaits the proper moment to jump to the first rank." Fould ended his address by reminding his audience of the coming World's Fair and the need to surpass foreign rivals.[36]

The breakdown of the prizes for that year indicated a great success for the realists: of the three Medals of the First Class, one went to Daubigny, landscapist; of the six of the Second Class, four were for genre painters, including Gustave Brion and Millet; of the twelve winners in the Third-Class category, all but two were genre and landscape painters, including Hamon, Verlat, and a female still-life artist, Octavie Paigné.

The distribution of awards in 1855 took place amid dazzling pomp; nearly forty thousand people assembled in the nave of the Palais de l'Industrie, which was brilliantly adapted by Le Play for the ceremony. Prince Napoléon opened the festivities by linking the spectacle at home with the stunning victories of the French abroad in the Crimea. Commenting on the generous number of awards, he announced that the emperor had proved again that in contemporary France "the only true nobility are the soldiers and workers who distinguish themselves." The prince emphasized the benefits of industrial expansion and the promotion of culture in emancipating society from savagery and drudgery. He noted that the overriding question of the future was how to share more equitably that which was currently the province of the few. The imperial dynasty responded energetically to the needs of the new society, whose base was universal suffrage. The World's Fair embodied the emperor's most cherished dreams in demonstrating this progress, displaying before all the nations French perfection in the methods and instruments of labor. Agriculture especially, which received the emperor's generous solicitude, stood out for its mechanical advances and their potential contribution to the national prosperity. At the same time, the field worker, the farmer, would be emancipated from the "brutal part" of rural labor.

Napoléon III then addressed the audience, declaring his peaceful intentions and emphasizing that French factories, like French art, arts of war and arts of peace, were forged alike for the benefit of all the world. The emperor capped the ceremonies by congratulating Le Play, the commissioner-general who stepped in at a late date to salvage the poorly managed exhibition, and whose participation in the final arrangements underlined the regime's intentions in organizing the gigantic enterprise.[37]

The bestowing of awards that year was complicated by the presence of a large body of foreign artists who had to be respected, as well as by the Grand Old Men like Ingres and Delacroix, who carried the banner of tradition. But Meissonier won one of the Grand Medals of Honor; Rosa Bonheur, Troyon, Corot, and Français won Medals of the First Class; Isidore Pils, Verlat, and Stevens were among the Second-Class winners; and in the Third-Class were Alexandre Antigna, Bonhommé, Breton, Bodmer, Daubigny, Luminais, Octave Tassaert, and Ziem. Realists of other countries—including the English Millais, the American William Morris Hunt, and the Norwegian Tidemand— also did quite well.

Following the 1855 Exposition Universelle there was a loosening of Salon regulations; the limit on admissions was lifted and the government fell back on a more conservative line. At the awards ceremony in 1857 the main speaker was Fould, who applauded the "rising talents." But he expressed concern that the younger generation was abandoning the tradition of their illustrious teachers in favor of the caprices of "public taste," which just then tended toward realism. Yet he also noted that the preferred themes of art emanated from the contemporary world, at the apex of which was the example of the emperor. In no other period had a government been so supportive of the arts, nor had there ever existed in the past the range of subjects now offered "in the acts of abnegation and heroism among all the classes of the nation, from the most modest to that rarefied region where the sovereign himself provides the model of total self-sacrifice!"[38] Not surprisingly, it was in this very period that the government embarked on a major series of commissions illustrating its eventful military and civil achievements and required in this program a style capable of reproducing faithfully the dress and customs of the epoch. As in his previous speech, Fould fully accepted the realist approach but wanted it tempered or softened, in line with administrative ideals.[39]

By the 1860s, the administration had a clear view of what it needed, and it began to prepare for the 1867 Exposition Universelle. Count Walewski replaced Fould, whose fall signalled a political turn as well.[40] In 1861 Walewski proclaimed that the government embodied the principle of "paternal authority," forever reconciling and protecting "tradition and invention, order and progress, discipline and originality." He commented that the crowds at the exhibition halted before new works—works that were not always irreproachable, mind you, but that revealed the spirit of innovation. This tendency was especially marked in the various landscape attempts: everywhere there was "perfection in all the genres of landscape; the young recruits march in step with seasoned veterans; women rival men in study; and those who occupied the steps of the throne do not disdain descending into the muddy arena; so many efforts crowned with success and so many skilled practitioners—that I have felt it necessary to increase the number of medals."[41] Here we find not only a taste for landscape and its derivatives, but also the intimation of a developing consensus.

This was brought home to the audience when Walewski mentioned the surprise inspection of the Salon Exhibition by the emperor and empress before it opened to the public. They spent many hours examining works and complimenting and inquiring about those artists whom they singled out as budding geniuses. Clearly no ruler better understood or protected the arts as well; not only did he purchase objects through official channels; he also studied them at close hand and chose for himself. Walewski then excited the artists among his audience by reminding them that they were now planted in the emperor's memory and could henceforth work with conviction. Once again, the conferring of awards proved favorable for all types of realists. Nieuwerkerke awarded the *Chevalier de la légion d'honneur* to Jules Breton and Alexandre Antigna, while winners in the genre and landscape categories outnumbered history painters four to three. Pils earned the Medal of Honor; Breton won a *rappel* of the First-Class Medal, while *rappels* of the Second-Class Medal were awarded to Tissier, Brion, Courbet, Verlat, and Lanouë.

The year 1863 was a landmark in the definitive formulation of the government's art program and ideology: the renewal of the restriction on admissions, the inauguration of the Salon des refusés, the reforms of the Ecole des Beaux-Arts, and the journalistic accounts all pointed to a coherent plan. Much of the regime's thinking on the question had been galvanized by the London exhibition of 1862, which demonstrated that the English had made immense progress in industrial design and now threatened France's lead in the luxury market with cheaper methods of production.[42] At the awards ceremony that year, Vaillant, an old soldier now occupying the post of Ministre de la Maison de l'Empereur et des Beaux-Arts, first gave the usual polite nod to the public taste and then endorsed enthusiastically the concept of originality. He advised all the artists who were willing to take risks for the sake of original ideas that they would find a receptive audience, because in the final analysis, "invention is one of the most precious qualities of art."[43] Vaillant also announced that the Salon would again be annual—a concession made to appease those who complained of the restriction on admissions, but also a means to receive regularly the new experiments.

Nieuwerkerke took the floor to clarify Vaillant's remarks. He observed that the Administration of the Beaux-Arts was attached to the Maison de l'Empereur, bringing it directly under the aegis of Napoléon III. He boasted that one result of this new orientation was the Salon des refusés, "an essentially liberal measure" carried out in favor of the wider community of artists and directly owing to the emperor's solicitude. The *surintendant* declared that he was following the emperor's lead in addressing himself to everyone exhibiting, those who were listed in the official catalogue and those displayed in the rooms set aside for the *refusés*. He then took up the question of the current trend; he began with the lament that the national art was moving away from "la grande peinture," but quickly added that this was nothing to get alarmed about. If, for example, the preferences of a few pushed them irresistibly to the study of landscape, their success should not cause undue anxiety over the future of high art in France. "Each epoch . . . yields to a unique movement, to an extremely dynamic pressure on minds and on taste. What is important is that in all of the directions pursued talented people attain the height of their endeavor." In short, realism was a *fait accompli* and contemporary artists had to strive to achieve excellence within this current. He declared himself open to an infinite variety of talents and original aptitudes and willing to grant the maximum liberty in the practice and direction of art. The trade-off for this generosity was that artists had to work hard and flee the "à peu-près" in all genres. Those who rejected the traditional route might seem to be "prodigal sons," only in this case the parable was turned upside down and the prodigals could return home with "their hands full."[44]

Simultaneously with its attempt to demonstrate impartiality, the government stepped up pressure on the Academy.[45] The Academy was made to order for its purposes since it was a national institution. But the Academy had usurped many of its prerogatives and behaved in an autonomous and despotic fashion. Its reluctance to fall in line completely led to a tug-of-war with the administration that was especially striking in the early 1860s. This attack was spearheaded by Nieuwerkerke, himself a member of the Academy.[46] Hints of government pressure came through the architectural competitions for the Prix de Rome of 1860 and 1862, entitled respectively: "Une résidence impériale dans la ville de Nice" and "Un palais pour le gouverneur de l'Algérie, destiné aussi à la résidence temporaire du souverain"—both, incidentally, pointing to the expansionist policies of the regime.[47]

The most dramatic episode in the conflict was the official decree of 13 November 1863.[48] Shocked critics likened it to a *"coup d'état"* in the cultural domain, and the government partisans proclaimed it the start of a new French Renaissance. Essentially, the decree represented a reaction against the influence of the Academy and the classicism it preached, and its ideological pronouncements invoked the language of the independents. Like the realists, the authors of the decree (mainly Viollet-le-Duc and Nieuwerkerke) challenged the authority of the Academy before the tribunal of sincerity and originality. At the same time, the reforms emphasized the need to unite art and industry, and introduced ateliers and modern workshop techniques into the program of the Ecole des Beaux-Arts. As Sainte-Beuve had recommended in regard to the literary establishment, the government moved in aggressively to revitalize a ready-made corporate body and make it more responsive to its ideological imperatives. The government now administered directly the pedagogical program both in Paris and in Rome through its unprecedented Conseil supérieur d'enseignement. Nieuwerkerke became ex-officio president and Morny and Gautier were appointed among the five "amateur" members. The regime also seized the occasion to install three of its favorite artists in the newly founded ateliers of the Ecole, Gérôme, Pils, and Cabanel.

The immediate effect of the reforms was to destabilize momentarily the academic system and to displace the Academy from its position as arbiter of French art. Academic classicism became one among several styles. The critic Thoré noted early in 1863 that there existed in painting two opposing currents that extended in new terms the old struggle between classics and romantics, or, more generally, "between conservatives and innovators, tradition and originality."[49] Indeed, it seemed to the public in 1863 that the administration had thrown its weight on the side of innovation, a codeword in that period for realism.

The reforms of 13 November exemplified the Second Empire's manipulation of the press. It marshalled its journalists, pamphleteers, and prominent supporters to publicize its position and discredit the campaign mounted by the Academy. Writing for *La Presse*, Paul de Saint-Victor applauded the reforms and systematically denigrated the opposition.[50] Another ardent champion of the decree was the young art critic and author Ernest Chesneau, whose brochure, published in 1864, is still a key document in the controversy that reached as high as the *Corps législatif* in January of the same year.[51] In the course of his arguments, Chesneau singled out two celebrated and vociferous opponents of the decree who he thought made strange bedfellows: the painter Ingres and the art critic Castagnary. The former was a disciple of David and guardian of the classical tradition, while the latter was a disciple of Courbet and supported the extreme realists. How ironic, Chesneau slyly commented, that they should find themselves on the same side of the fence on this issue. He derided both for their suspicions that romanticism had usurped the bureaucratic ideals and mocked Castagnary's reference to Courbet as the "glory of the French school," as well as his description of *Return from the Conference* as "one of the immortal masterpieces by the artist."[52] By his seeming disdain for romanticism and his hostility to the partisans of extreme classicism and realism, Chesneau clearly articulated the ideology of the reforms.

On 1 July 1863—four months before the November decree—Chesneau published an article in the *Revue des deux mondes* entitled "Le réalisme et l'esprit français dans l'art."[53] Like so many of the government-inspired writings, it was meant to prepare a particular segment of the public for the reforms of 1863. It contended that contemporary realism was no more than a return to the French medieval tradition, which had been diverted from its natural course by the impact of the Italian Renaissance. Chesneau emphasized the importance of the miniatures and the early manuscript illustrations as authentic documents of the life of the period. Realism had remained the key component of French taste through the centuries, Chesneau argued, and the contemporary movement could free art from the stultifying control of the "philosophic mentality." This he defined as a celebration of "moral reality" over and against "material reality." At the same time, however, he warned modern realists against going to extremes in the application of this style.

Chesneau's conception of realism was generous compared to the view of most older critics, who fully condemned the doctrine. Nevertheless, he did not recommend pure materialism but a materialism tempered by idealism. He observed Planche's unrelieved critique of realism, and yet at the same time saw that the movement continued to attract new adherents and promised to absorb all the energies of the younger generation. Faced with this contradiction, Chesneau condemned as useless any attempt to attack realism in the name of "sane doctrines"—an outmoded cliché. Since the tide could not be turned, it was wiser to redirect the current by studying it at its source.

Chesneau subtitled his article "Les frères Le Nain," and elsewhere referred to Champfleury's recent publication on the brothers, entitled "Les peintres du réel sous Louis XIII." He paid homage to the patient research of Champfleury—one of the leaders of the realist movement[54]—but objected to his extravagant praise. His attempt to absolve the Le Nains of technical flaws set a poor example for the new school, which tended to disregard solid technique and reinforced the current decline in art instruction. Sound craftsmanship ultimately took precedence over the choice of theme. Chesneau agreed with Champfleury, however, that the Le Nains were significant because they sought "absolute sincerity," and in this he foreshadowed Chardin and Géricault. Chesneau's stress on the indispensable quality of sincerity anticipates one of the leitmotifs of the decree of 13 November.

Chesneau elaborated on his idea of realism as historically essential in expressing the character of an epoch. The older artists furnished an authentic image of their times, but the present epoch would also be history one day: "shall we therefore leave it to posterity to reveal ourselves, in the domain of art, our customs, costumes, our conventions, our sentiments and our ideas? What will our descendents make of our history if we do not trace our own development, and why should they do it if we are too ashamed to do it for ourselves?" And he lamented that David was unable to complete the *Oath of the Tennis Court* for

the historical record; both he and his heir Géricault seized the initiative in painting in a style commensurate with the needs of modern
society. Chesneau then called for the Second Empire's type of realism:

> People of the nineteenth century, how many subjects are in us,
> around us; how many plays, how many facts that entreat, that
> imperiously demand the brush of the painter, the chisel of the
> sculptor! Yet painters and sculptors turn aside hesitatingly, trem-
> bling, as if they feared the ridicule before the reproduction of the
> beauties in modern life. Those who are master of their craft, who
> are endowed with an aesthetic sentiment, are afraid to compromise
> their established position and reputation by making fresh attempts;
> the others, those who would take the risk or who are taking it, are
> unable to place at the service of a vulgarity of imagination without
> parallel more than a capricious talent, one that occasionally and
> by surprise rises a little above the mediocre—but one never fully
> in control and master of self![55]

Chesneau's plea to already-established artists to experiment with
realism and his attack on hard-core realists again testified to the
consensus view of the regime and distinctly underscored official realism. Chesneau concluded that one need not despair over the future
of realism, but warned that French realism was effective only when
it could be fused with the ideal.

This article's appearance in the conservative *Revue des deux mondes*
is significant. This journal considered the Revolution of 1848 a catastrophe and was very much relieved by the *coup d'état*.[56] Once the
danger of social revolution became remote, however, it assumed a
more liberal tone. Its early bias against realism was reinforced by its
politics, and it generally identified realist tendencies with democratic
aspiration. It was only in the mid-fifties and early sixties that it began
to make concessions to the realist movement. It now identified the
growth of realism with a rising middle class motivated by practical
concerns. Planche, for example, believed that the division of property
led to a lowering of the taste for the ideal, since the bourgeoisie possessed neither the leisure nor the tradition. In any case, both Champfleury and Buchon published in the *Revue* during the mid-1850s, and
conservatives like Montégut admitted that, despite its vulgarity,
realism was valid as a reflection of its epoch. Here again it was the
historically significant side of realism that rendered it valuable. This
attitude was shared by critics of realism on both the Right and Left
during the same period.

The Second Empire's firm grasp of the ideological potential of
realism was implied already in 1856 by a rare document written by
Frédéric de Mercey, then Director des Beaux-Arts, to Achille Fould,
Minister of State:

> Not many years have gone by since the Emperor Napoléon III was called to govern France, first as President, then as Emperor, and this short period has been distinguished by many memorable deeds and glorious events. It is for art, as for history, to consecrate its memory in a striking manner. Indeed, the artist may, through the means at his disposal, give an air of reality to the fact which narrative cannot achieve, and historical painting alone may preserve the image of contemporary personages in a precise and certain manner, show them to us actively engaged, indicate the disposition of the locales, the exact style of their clothes, reproduce, in short, the physiognomy of the era whose events it traces.[57]

Except for the specific aim of this program—the apotheosizing of the emperor—this is the language of realism and compares closely to statements made by Duranty and Champfleury in roughly the same period.[58] The allusion to "the exact style" of contemporary costume especially recalls the development of an idea first articulated by Baudelaire. Courbet's own manifesto stated that he wanted to "be in a position to translate the customs, the ideas, the appearance of my epoch"—language borrowed by de Mercey for his proposal to Fould. Courbet's later declaration that "historical art is by nature contemporary" also found confirmation in the official aesthetic.[59]

De Mercey further proposed the creation of a museum to house the images commemorating "civil and military deeds." One set would depict the outstanding domestic events of the last eight years of Louis Napoléon's reign, including the Proclamation of the Empire, Queen Victoria's Visit, the Distribution of Awards at the 1855 Exposition Universelle, the Completion of the Louvre, the Marriage of the Emperor, and the Baptism of the Imperial Prince. The other set would center on the great victories of the Crimean War and would be exhibited in a special gallery. De Mercey evidently responded to a previous exchange with Fould, as he noted that the minister understood that "our epoch must not be neglected," and that there already existed a body of pictures for the new museum, including Tissier's *Liberation of Abd-el-Kader,* as well as military commissions assigned to people like Yvon and Beaucé (who researched battle locations in Africa and in the Crimea). De Mercey added that now that peace reigned, both art and industry could progress, and a new series of pictures might be commissioned. These images could include the *Visit of the Grand Corps de l'Etat to Saint Cloud during the Night of 1 December 1852* by Cabanel, the *Distribution of the Eagles* by Glaize, the *Opening of the Exposition Universelle* by Gérôme, the *Visit of the Queen of England* by Jalabert, the *Distribution of Awards at the Closing of the Exposition Universelle* by Jobbé-Duval, and land and sea battles by Pils, Yvon, Gudin, and Morel-Fatio. What was unusual in this projection was the presence of so many younger academic disciples, some of whom numbered among the Neo-Greeks. While this group made use of classical settings, the action they depicted was considered genre and the psychology related to contemporary life. They also made easy converts to the Second Empire program.

III. General Observations on Second Empire History Painting

The generation of military painters emerging during this period manifested a preoccupation with historical accuracy. While their ultimate task was to aggrandize the emperor, they often overcame this constraint through a close attention to detail. They also followed Napoléon III's lead in resisting a mythologizing character inconsistent with events, so that often he was shown in informal poses appropriate to the contemporary trend. In fact, his informality made it difficult for artists to deal with him in more idealizing media like coins and medallions (figs. 3.1, 3.2). Chesneau described the military painters in the Exposition Universelle of 1867 in terms reminiscent of the contemporary criticism of the realists: "Today our battle painters are less artists—that is, beings endowed with passion and sensibility— than chroniclers, editors of military bulletins. They report the facts and nothing but the facts."[60]

Another Bonapartist critic, Olivier Merson, devoted a major section of his review of the Salon of 1861 to subjects of contemporary history, commenting that modern dress and ideas were not antipathetic to art and that the "beau idéal" was a relative concept contingent on time and place.[61] The most important category under this heading was military painting, and the work he most admired was Pils's *Battle of Alma* (fig. 3.3). He quoted the description of the event in the Salon catalogue, which provided the exact date and time, the names of the individuals involved, and the type of maneuver executed. He complained, however, that the artist translated too literally the official bulletin, that it lacked "the blast of true combats, the bellicose energy."[62] A commonplace criticism of left-wing realism was its lack of discrimination in the selection of details and narrative features. Olivier Merson also uttered this complaint in connection with several of the military pictures at the 1861 exhibition.[63] He preferred Yvon's *Solferino* to all the rest in this category, which nevertheless portrayed the emperor on the summit of Mount Fenile, just ahead of his general staff, with "unpardonable vulgarity."[64]

Despite Olivier Merson's professed sympathy for realism, it was evident that he had not entirely outgrown the bombastic military scenes of Louis-Philippe's Galerie des Batailles. The battles of the Second Empire were less a question of hand-to-hand heroics or ad-

venturous warriors on horseback than of complicated logistical problems and long-range artillery. Indeed, the battle of Alma centered on
a telegraph station. The French had no cavalry troops, and the conflict of the Crimea anticipated the technological character of modern
warfare. Then too, the soldier of the Second Empire could no longer
be visualized as either classic warrior or delirious conqueror; he was
regarded, and even saw himself, as a pawn in a chess match who had
been moved into position on orders from a remote headquarters. In
his *Salon of 1864* About singled out Meissonier's *Battle of Solferino*
as the most distinguished work, praising especially the artist's concentration on the emperor's general staff (fig. 3.4).[65] The emperor
himself, posted two steps in front of his general staff, studied the
battle "like a cold-blooded player studies his chessboard."[66] If he
occupied a central role, his position was not at all heroic: he was a
safe distance from the battle, whose outcome was as yet unclear. Meissonier was actually present at the skirmish (he depicted himself in
the picture), and his focus on the general staff to which he was attached was revealing of Second Empire realism in its ideological
as well as aesthetic sense.[67]

Besides painting battle scenes, the emperor's stable of artists recorded his colonialist aspirations. De Mercey's report mentioned Ange-
Tissier's *Submission of Abd-el-Kader*, a work also shown at the 1861
Salon (fig. 3.5). Tissier's vast canvas depicted the moment at the
Château d'Amboise when the emperor granted the Algerian his freedom. Napoléon III has entered the room of detention, where Abd-el-
Kader was surrounded by his family and servants. The emir's elderly
mother advanced and leaned over to kiss the hand of his imperial
benefactor, who is accompanied by the Maréchal Saint-Arnaud,
Baroche, and the generals Goyon and Roguet. In the center of the
composition are two Arab children who stare at the emperor "avec une
surprise naïve," while here and there other Arabs and blacks are
scattered in the Gothic enclosure. Ange-Tissier's scene was an excellent example of the official realism used to influence public opinion.
Napoléon III stressed the civilizing influence of the empire on the
Algerian peoples, and during his regime the image of Abd-el-Kader
underwent a profound transformation.[68] When he resisted the French
forces, he was shown as a ferocious militant leader, while during the
Second Empire he came to be seen as a benign, almost saintly figure.
This corresponded to his political neutralization, which was the real
subject of Ange-Tissier's picture. The Arab entourage is represented
submitting to the new crusades under the aegis of a vaulted medieval
chapel. The ceremony was dominated by the emperor and his military
advisers; Saint-Arnaud, who was Morny's strong right arm during the
coup d'état, had earned his reputation in Algeria fighting Abd-el-

1.1   JULES BRETON, *The Gleaners*

1.2   JEAN FRANÇOIS MILLET, *The Gleaners*

2.1 ISIDORE PILS, *The Death of a Sister of Charity*

2.2 GUSTAVE BRION, *The Potato Harvest during the Flooding of
the Rhine in 1852, Alsace*

2.3 GUSTAVE COURBET, *The Grain Sifters*

2.4 PHILIPPE AUGUSTE JEANRON, *Peasants from the Limousin*

2.5 Théodule Ribot, *The Cook Accountant*

2.6 Théodule Ribot, *The Returns*

2.7 JULES BRETON, *The Grape Harvest at Chateau-Lagrange*

2.8 JULES BRETON, *Preliminary Drawing for "The Grape-Harvest"*

2.9 JULES BRETON, *Preliminary Watercolor for "The Grape Harvest"*

2.10 FRANÇOIS BONHOMMÉ,
*Employee with Shears, Workman—
Fourchambault, 1839–40*

2.11 FRANÇOIS BONHOMMÉ, *Blanzy Mines: Open-Pit Mining at Lucy*

2.12 François Bonhommé, *Workshop with Mechanical Sieves at the Factory of La Vieille Montagne*

3.1 EUGÈNE-ANDRÉ OUDINE,
*Medal: The Accession of
Napoleon III to the Empire*

3.2 EDOUARD DETAILLE,
*Napoleon III crowned with laurel
and smoking a cigarette*

3.3 ISIDORE PILS, *The Battle of Alma*

3.4 ERNEST MEISSONIER, *The Emperor Napoleon III at the Battle of Solferino*

3.5 ANGE-TISSIER, *The Submission of Abd-el-Kader*

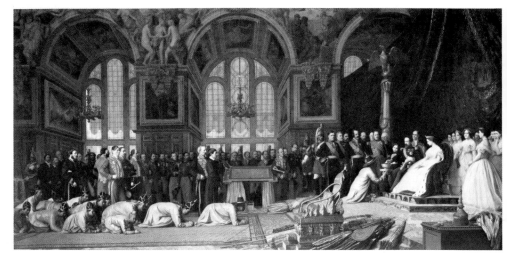

3.6 Jean Léon Gérôme, *Reception of the Siamese Ambassadors by Napoleon III and the Empress Eugenie at Fontainebleau, 27 June 1861*

3.7 Gustave Courbet, *The Burial at Ornans*

3.8 Jean Léon Gérôme, *Age of Augustus*

3.9 Gustave Boulanger, *Rehearsal of "The Flute Player" in the Atrium of the House of H.I.H. the Prince Napoleon*

3.10　JEAN-LOUIS HAMON, *My Sister is Not at Home*

3.11　JEAN-LOUIS HAMON, *The Human Comedy*

3.12 EUGÈNÉ GUÉRARD, *Théâtre de Guignol (Champs-Elysées)*

3.13 JEAN-LOUIS HAMON, *Conjuror*

3.14 AUGUSTE TOULMOUCHE, *Forbidden Fruit*

3.15 JEAN FRANÇOIS
MILLET, *Immaculate
Conception*

3.16 JEAN LÉON GÉROME, *Pope Pius IX Blessing Locomotives*

3.17 WILLIAM-ADOLPHE BOUGUEREAU, *Entrance of the Emperor at Tarascon, 14 June 1856*

3.18 LOUIS HERSENT, *Louis XVI Distributing Alms to the Poor during the Rigorous Winter of 1788*

3.19   ALEXANDRE ANTIGNA, *The Visit of the Emperor to the Slate Quarry Workers of Angers during the Floods of 1856*

3.20   HIPPOLYTE LAZERGES, *The Emperor Distributing Alms to the Flood Victims of Lyon*

3.21   ANGE-LOUIS JANET-LANGE, *Napoleon III Distributing Alms to the Flood Victims of Lyon in June 1856*

3.22   ROSA BONHEUR, *Ploughing in the Nivernais*

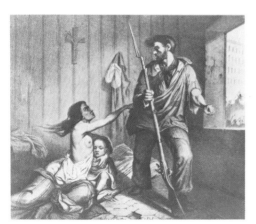

3.23   JULES BRETON,
Misery and Despair

3.24   JULES BRETON, *Hunger*

3.25 CHARLES GLEYRE, *Ruth and Boaz*

3.26 EVARISTE LUMINAIS, *Champ de Foire*

3.27 ISIDORE PILS, *Rouget de l'Isle Singing the Marseillaise for the First Time*

3.28 ISIDORE PILS, *Soldiers Distributing Bread to the Poor*

3.29 FRANÇOIS BONHOMMÉ, *Diploma for a Mutual Aid Society*

4.1 ADOLPH MENZEL,
*Chodowiecki on the
Jannowitz Bridge*

4.2 ADOLPH MENZEL,
*Commemorative Print for the
Celebration of G. Schadow's
Hundredth Birthday*

4.3 DANIEL CHODOWIECKI, *Cabinet d'un Peintre*

4.4 ADOLPH MENZEL, *Family by Lamplight*

4.5 DANIEL CHODOWIECKI, *The Death of Frederick II*

4.6 GOTTFRIED SCHADOW,
Frederick and His Whippets

4.7 ADOLPH MENZEL,
The Death of Frederick II

4.8 ADOLPH MENZEL, *Oil Sketch for
"The Dinner Conversation"*

4.9 ADOLPH MENZEL, *The Flute Recital*

4.10 WILHELM VON KAULBACH, *The Destruction of Jerusalem*

4.11 ADOLPH MENZEL, *Frederick the Great and His Men at Hochkirch, 1758*

4.12 ADOLPH MENZEL, *The Meeting of Frederick II and Joseph II, 1769*

4.13 Franz Krüger, *Parade in the Opera Square*

4.14 Eduard Gaertner, *Klosterstrasse*

4.15 JOHANN ERDMANN HUMMEL, *The Granite Basin in the Berlin Lustgarten*

4.16 EDOUARD GAERTNER, *Unter den Linden*

4.17 ADOLPH MENZEL, *Sunday in the Tuileries Garden*

4.18 ADOLPH MENZEL, *Weekday in Paris*

4.19 E. Guérard, *The Tuileries—allée des feuillants*

4.20 Adolph Menzel, *King William's Departure on 31 July 1870*

4.21   CARL BLECHEN, *Iron Rolling Mill at Eberswalde*

4.22   CARL BLECHEN, *Preparatory Study for the "Iron Rolling Mill at Eberswalde"*

4.23 ADOLPH MENZEL, *The Iron Rolling Mill*

4.24 ADOLPH MENZEL, *Memorial Sheet for Heckmann*

4.25 PAUL MEYERHEIM, *Forging the Locomotive Wheel*

4.26 MAX LIEBERMANN, *Women Plucking Geese*

4.27 MAX LIEBERMANN, *Women Cleaning Vegetables*

Kader. This humbling of the Arab chieftain is crowned by the grateful mother greeting the emperor as the savior of her son and, by inference, of the Arab peoples.[69]

Jean-Léon Gérôme's *Reception of the Siamese Ambassadors by Napoléon III and the Empress Eugénie at Fontainebleau, 27 June 1861,* executed during the period 1861–64, further exemplified the Second Empire's craving for overseas markets (fig. 3.6). The painter perceived the powerful Siamese delegation as a group of servile primitives overwhelmed by the pomp and splendor of an advanced European culture and the venerable presence of their august hosts. Gérôme's commission commemorated the visit of the diplomatic mission from P'ra Maha Mongkut, emperor of Siam, to the emperor and empress of France, who received them in the Salon d'Hercule, Château de Fontainebleau, in 1861. This meeting highlighted a broad trading and political treaty signed by both France and Siam on 15 August 1856, negotiated by the French ambassador to Siam, Charles de Montigny, who appeared at the head of the Siamese delegation together with the *abbé* Lanardie, Catholic missionary and interpreter. Mongkut, awed by Napoléon's success in the Crimean War, permitted the French navy and merchant community more privileged access than that extended to Great Britain and the United States. As a trade-off, he hoped that the French presence would serve as a bulwark against his enemies in Cochin-China.[70]

This work typifies one crucial aspect of the official realism, what I wish to term *myopic realism,* verisimilar in its painstaking detail but ringing false in the whole. It is a complex picture, revealing a thorough knowledge of traditional ceremonial and processional events, yet comparable in some ways to Courbet's radical *Burial at Ornans* (fig. 3.7); both represent official rites, are based on portrait studies, convey the indifference and even boredom of certain participants, and studiously avoid artful groupings and a central thematic and psychological focus. Courbet's picture, nevertheless, may be termed an example of *hypermetropic realism,* less veridical than Gérôme's when viewed closely but more convincing as a whole in its capacity to obtrude itself on immediate reality. Naturally, the two artists conveyed their understanding of reality from opposing ideological perspectives, but Gérôme met the demands of a dominant elite projecting absolute power, while Courbet analyzed the structure of authority and pointed to class differentiation.[71] The former did not question the structure of control with which he identified; the latter did. It is known that Gérôme nearly went mad trying to satisfy the demands of various officials who wanted to be placed as close as possible to the locus of power, the imperial throne. And while there is no central psychological focus, the kneeling delegates and their offerings are ingeniously orchestrated to direct attention to Napoléon III and Eugénie, at the far right. Indeed, Gérôme clearly lavished his energy on the gifts, which later entered the empress's collection of foreign curios and objets d'art. While Mongkut and Lanardie hoped that the gifts would give the court a representative sample of Siamese crafts and culture, Gérôme presents them as quaint objects within the dazzling setting of Fontainebleau. Thus ideological manipulation of the figures and of the accessories actually betrays the remarkable accuracy of the meticulously studied details.[72]

Gérôme's progress from a Neo-Greek phase to official realism was already marked at the 1855 World's Fair, for which he designed allegorical personifications of important maritime towns for a lighthouse exhibit and at the same time exhibited his colossal *Age of Augustus*, based on a passage in Bossuet's universal history (fig. 3.8).[73] The passage recounts the stages of Roman hegemony over the peoples of North Africa, the Near East, and Asia and notes that the Germanic tribes were checked and that universal peace was assured: "Tout l'univers vit en paix sous sa puissance, et Jésus-Christ vient au monde." Clearly Augustus was the persona of the emperor himself, with whom he was often identified in official propaganda. When we recall Napoléon III's words at Bordeaux, "L'empire, c'est la paix," and his close identification with the church in this period, the correspondence becomes even more striking. Gérôme here equated the Second Empire with the Age of Augustus and alluded to the dynastic and imperialistic designs of the new regime. Not surprisingly, the date of the commission, 30 October 1852, foreshadows by little more than a month the actual coronation of the emperor.[74] (Significantly, the director noted in the margin of the *arrêt* commissioning the picture to leave "the amount of payment open," a sign of the administration's attempt to win the full adherence of Gérôme.[75])

Gérôme was one of the original members of the Neo-Greek movement, which inadvertently contributed to Second Empire realism and to the regime's campaign to neutralize the radicals. The Neo-Greeks, who were inspired by Gleyre and included Hamon, Picou, Aubert, and Toulmouche, extended history painting into new areas by depicting the ancients in their daily life as if they were Parisian middle-class types. This captivated a bourgeois audience unable to relate comfortably to erudite classical subjects by appealing to their vanity. In addition, the Neo-Greeks often painted their subjects with a tongue-in-cheek attitude, somewhat akin to Meissonier, with whose eighteenth-century scenes they had much in common. It would seem that the Second Empire's sense of insecurity and illegitimacy was marked on the one hand by strenuous attempts to identify itself with the great dynasties of the past, and on the other by the mocking of established convention.

It required as one part of its cultural program a mechanism for ridi-
culing the erudite, the aristocratic, and the classical.[76]

The member of the court who promoted this style was Prince
Jérôme, the so-called liberal of the Second Empire hierarchy, who
went so far as to commission a mansion on the Avenue Montaigne in
the Pompeiian, or Neo-Greek style.[77] Gustave Boulanger's *Rehearsal
of "The Flute Player" in the Atrium of the House of the Prince Napoléon* shows how the prince lived out his fantasy in everyday life
(fig. 3.9). The subject is a play about antiquity, in which the roles
are enacted by the prince and his friends, including the art critic and
novelist Gautier, the dramatist Augier, and well-known professional
actors. Gautier's central position in this work attests to his actual
participation in the Neo-Greek movement. He was their ardent champion and almost always had unqualified praise for Gérôme, whose
Age of Augustus he claimed merited the painter "the number one position among the new generation."[78] A noted critic of the *Moniteur* and
a favorite at the imperial court, Gautier was the linchpin in the
government sponsorship of the young Neo-Greeks.

Next to Gérôme in this school, Gautier admired Hamon as its
"purest" representative. Starting in 1852 government patronage enabled
Hamon to devote himself full-time to the fine arts.[79] His famous Salon
work of 1853, *My Sister is Not at Home*, was bought by the empress
to decorate her apartments at Saint-Cloud (fig. 3.10). It represents
an innocuous situation involving adolescents, yet Gautier went into
raptures over it, lauding its grace, simplicity, and poetry while pointing
to its sense of actuality.[80] Another work by Hamon, *The Human
Comedy*, was purchased by the government: first shown in 1851 and
exhibited again at the 1855 World's Fair, it enjoyed a popular success
despite its somewhat puzzling subject (fig. 3.11). Hamon set his
scene in the mythical Elysian Fields, the realm of the blessed heroes
of the past, and invited his Salon audience to join the inhabitants
in contemplation of a diverting spectacle where "Love is hanged,
Bacchus is thrashed, and Minerva, who eternally settles everyone's
accounts, provides plenty of amusement for the curious passers-by
in the ideal abode. . . ." The picture's focus is an outdoor puppet show
entitled *Théâtre Guignol*, the name of a real marionette show located
at the Champs-Elysées, which inspired Hamon's pun on the Elysian
Fields.[81] Like the Italian comedy (and the Balzacian concept as well),
the outdoor entertainment was often referred to as a "petite comédie
humaine," where a few primal characters summed up the whole of
human experience. A print of 1856 depicts the actual *Théâtre Guignol*,
with its repertoire of the Commissary of Police, the Devil, and Punch-
inello (fig. 3.12). It was aimed primarily at children, but it is evident
that it fascinated adults as well. This justifies the mixed audience in

Hamon's scene, with the exception that here the adults comprise illustrious types, such as Homer, Dante, Diogenes, Alexander, Socrates,
and Aeschylus. It clearly parodies Ingres's *Apotheosis of Homer* and
mocks erudite classicism by reducing the eminent protagonists to
frivolous juveniles entranced by popular culture. At the same time, it
gives a familiar scene antique trappings; Gautier, who complimented
the work, wondered about the anachronistic appearance of the flower
girl and the woman passing the collection plate, who came straight
out of the Boulevard Italien.[82] This interfacing of actuality and
anachronism points to the administration's requirement for an alternative realism and its sponsorship of a revival of popular culture and
folk art in this period.[83]

A few years later Hamon displayed his *Conjuror*, which also enjoyed
an enthusiastic reception (fig. 3.13). Like *Human Comedy*, it built
on anachronisms, but its contemporary features were more readily
recognizable. Hamon depicted the mixed reactions of various social
types to the charlatan performing his trick. Schoolmasters and philosophers speculate on the mysteries occasioned by the conjuror's confidence game, while an astronomer with his telescope gazes at the
heavens. All of these are conjuror's in their own right and are ridiculed
by the artist. Olivier Merson, who was thoroughly captivated by this
picture, noted that the entire scene had a familiar ring: "Haven't we
seen this pot, this charlatan, this inscription ['Mort aux rats'], and
these hanging animal skins at the Place de la Bastille?"[84] Except for the
Athenian clothing, he declared, this could be contemporary Paris
with its crowds of saltimbanques and costermongers. Indeed, Hamon
shares with Courbet and Daumier their exploitation of caricature and
folk art to attack established authority, although he emphasizes the
nonpolitical and safe side of these traditions.

Merson's recognition of the motif meshes with the prints and texts
of the Second Empire that attest to the multitude of street hawkers,
peddlers, organ grinders, jugglers, magicians, and saltimbanques on
the streets of the major cities. They constituted a *lumpen* group, which
often menaced the regime with their subversive potential.[85] Hamon
defused this threat but also pointed to a deeper level of the regime's
fears concerning its legitimacy. Marx wrote in *The Eighteenth Brumaire
of Louis Bonaparte* that on 2 December the February Revolution
was "conjured away by a cardsharper's trick," and that Bonapartists of
dubious origin depended for their success on "vagabonds, discharged
soldiers, discharged jailbirds, escaped galley slaves, swindlers, mounte-
banks, *lazzaroni*, pickpockets, tricksters, gamblers, pimps, brothel
keepers, porters, *literati*, organ-grinders, ragpickers, knife grinders,
tinkers, beggars—in short, the whole indefinite, disintegrated mass,
thrown hither and thither, which the French term *la bohème*."[86]

Hamon's Neo-Greek realism, however, was consciously exploited by the administration to counterbalance the radicals. In 1861, the year of Boulanger's picture of Prince Napoléon's Pompeiian House, Merson lumped the Neo-Greeks and the realists together, noting their common preoccupation with exactitude and minutiae.[87] But he endorsed the Neo-Greek approach, claiming that it would merit a prominent place in the history of Second Empire art because it arrived just in time to neutralize the impact of the radical realists. Like Gautier, he emphasized the repugnance of the Neo-Greeks for extravagance, vulgarity, and the more flawed aspects of nature; as a result of their tastes, they found writers to glorify them and recommend them to an adoring crowd. He concluded: "It is incontestable . . . that their diversion has been very useful and their part in the victory merits a title too honorable to ever let them be forgotten or ignored." This candid statement makes understandable the government's protection of this style; not unexpectedly, Merson found that Breton had much in common with the Neo-Greeks, suggesting an even more direct relationship between the authentic radical realists and the government-sponsored realists.[88]

The critic also referred to Toulmouche in this context, an ex-Neo-Greek now painting contemporary subjects; but if he was no longer at Corinth or at Pompeii, his Neo-Greek background kept him from being submerged "amid . . . modern pressures."[89] Toulmouche's *Forbidden Fruit*, exhibited in 1865, reflected the transition to modernity while keeping the artificial character and upper-middle-class pretensions of the Neo-Greek style (fig. 3.14). When we recall, moreover, that Toulmouche advised his cousin Monet to study with his own master Gleyre, then we cannot ignore the role of the movement in early impressionism (which often depicted fashionably dressed women in moments of leisure) or, more importantly, the ultimate impact of the Second Empire patronage on the second- and third-generation realists.

The curious alliance of Gérôme and Millet for the decoration of a special railway wagon presented to Pope Pius IX by the French government is still another example of the government's strategy.[90] French engineers were commissioned to build the carriage in 1857, and the main task of construction and ornamentation was subcontracted to Emile Trélat, professor of architecture and engineering at the *Conservatoire des arts et métiers*.[91] Froment-Meurice, the emperor's silversmith, ornamented the interior, and Trélat assigned Gérôme to decorate the throne room with a frieze of the Apostles and to execute two designs for the vaults of the carriage showing the Pope blessing steamships and locomotives.[92] He then charged Millet to do a painting of the *Immaculate Conception* for the oratory of the wagon, a subject of topical concern since Pius IX had promulgated the controversial doctrine of the Immaculate Conception in 1854 (figs. 3.15, 3.16).[93] While the papal response to Millet's work seems to have been luke-warm, the conjoining of these two artists in the semiofficial commission further reflects the novel art policies of the Second Empire. On the one hand, it encouraged the academic painter to portray modern subjects, and on the other, it lured a radical painter into doing tradi-tional and even conservative themes.

Almost everyone in this era was affected by the railway boom.[94] Both the state and the business community contributed to railway capital formation. The government stimulated railway speculation and subsidized railroad entrepreneurs. Railroad expansion stimulated the rapid growth of the iron industry with enormous orders for rails, bridge framework, railway stations, locomotives, and rolling stock. Various artists such as Thomas Couture and his pupil Edouard Manet seriously considered the railroad as a subject for contemporary painting. But perhaps the most impressive testimony to the mental climate came from Sainte-Beuve, the government's propagandist in the realm of literature. In a letter of 22 April 1862 to the writer Charles Duveyrier, he wrote:

> I was talking the other day to Courbet; he is a solid, energetic fellow who also has ideas, including what is I think the important one of creating a monumental form of painting in tune with modern society. . . . His idea is to turn the big railway stations into churches for the painter's benefit: those great walls could be covered by all kinds of highly suitable subjects, such as previews of the main sites through which the traveller will pass; portraits of great men associated with cities in the line of route, picturesque and moral themes, industry and metallurgy—in short all the "saints and mira-cles" of modern times.[95]

Sainte-Beuve hoped that Duveyrier could mediate between Courbet and the Péreire brothers—railway and credit tycoons—to translate this concept into reality. Sainte-Beuve flattered Duveyrier, calling him a maternity doctor for men and ideas, and urged him to help develop and clarify Courbet's ideas. "In short, aid him so that he can aid you."

This letter is especially interesting when we recognize that Duveyrier was one of the pamphleteers for the Second Empire and a member of the *Société des gens de lettres*—the organization through which Sainte-Beuve advised the emperor to gain control of the literary establishment.[96] His pioneering work in advertising and promotion brought him to the attention of Prince Napoléon, who introduced him to the emperor. The ex-Saint-Simonist Duveyrier was commissioned to do several pamphlets, including *L'avenir et les Bonaparte*, which pre-pared the public for a "liberal" empire.[97]

Sainte-Beuve's plans for organizing writers also included close contacts with artists. His secretary, Jules Troubat, knew Champfleury intimately, and through him Buchon—both close friends of Courbet's. In fact, Champfleury was a protégé of Sainte-Beuve's, and it was he who got Sainte-Beuve to hire Troubat. Champfleury was also a member of the *Société des gens de lettres,* and Troubat claimed that through him Sainte-Beuve mediated between the apostles of realism and the critics.[98]

The Second Empire skillfully manipulated a combination of press, Salon reviews, and imagery. One of Napoléon III's favorite propaganda devices was the "whistle stop" tour throughout the countryside.[99] It was a novel idea made possible by the railway expansion; during the *ancien régime* the kings had visited towns hard-hit by natural disasters, but no previous ruler had used the tour so systematically or made such a planned effort to develop personal contacts with his subjects. Louis Napoléon often employed this type of propaganda in areas where leftist opposition was strong or where there was a previous history of radical opposition. The local officials, notified of his trips ahead of time, curtailed potential protest, organized groups, prepared gala celebrations and fireworks, reviewed the troops, and even distributed government-subsidized gifts to the poor.

Government officials confirmed the tours as an effective way of increasing regional loyalty to the regime. Reports of the local *procureurs généraux* and the prefects frequently commented upon the favorable impression created by these visits. During the floods of 1856, the *procureur général* of Douai reported that the emperor's visits "have had a great effect here; they have resulted in new conquests, particularly among the popular classes." The propaganda value of these tours was not confined to the towns and regions visited by the emperor and empress. Newspapers, pamphlets, and placards throughout France reported their movements in detail; they emphasized the enthusiastic crowds and the gifts that the emperor gave to workers along his route.[100]

Napoléon III used the "official" realists to publicize these events. The 1857 Salon was especially rich in Second Empire realism; in addition to the innumerable battle pictures commemorating the victories in the Crimea, there were a number of works depicting domestic events such as the emperor's visits to the various regions hard hit by the flooding of the Rhône and Loire rivers in the summer of 1856. The portrayal of the emperor amid combat and domestic crisis revealed him as a compassionate ruler at home as well as a victorious leader abroad. To this end the administration exploited both the Prix de Rome laureates and the semi-independent artists such as Antigna, Janet-Lange, Lassalle, and Moullin, as well as a number of others who painted subjects on their own initiative when they sensed a sure sale.[101]

Perhaps the most unexpected example of Second Empire realism is by Bouguereau, whose *Entrance of the Emperor at Tarascon, 14 June 1856* perfectly manifested the taste of the regime (fig. 3.17). The painter had been given a letter of introduction to the prefect of the department of the Bouches-du-Rhône, charging him with furnishing Bouguereau with all the facilities he required.[102] Bouguereau visited the flood site, sketched the mayor and others who were present, and made drawings of the surrounding landscape. Newspaper reports were also used, which noted how the emperor reached Tarascon and was conducted in a boat guided by two oarsmen, accompanied by Rouher, Minister of Public Works, and generals Niel and Fleury.[103] Despite the ruinous conditions, every house was decorated, and people shouted "Vive l'Empereur!" while extending their arms in blessing.

Bouguereau faithfully reported the details of the scene, including the man on the rooftops lifting his hat to salute the chief of state, and observed accessories like the old mattresses. From the *myopic* point of view everything is rendered convincingly and accurately, but the emperor dominates the scene, and, as in the Gérôme, one senses the ideological manipulation of those who greet Napoléon III. The flood victims run to him as a savior, and his Christlike role is accentuated by the spire of the Tarascon cathedral, which Bouguereau has situated just above his head. Still, in terms of verisimilitude, it is an advance over earlier portrayals of royal alms-giving, such as Hersent's *Louis XVI Distributing Alms to the Poor during the Rigorous Winter of 1788* (1817) (fig. 3.18).[104] Playing on the traditional images of Christian charity, Hersent managed to give the king a "sacred" position directly in the center, isolated from the rest. Bouguereau's ruler, on the other hand, is off-center and in close touch with the oarsmen and the crowd of victims. At the same time, he assumes a more informal pose with one foot poised on the rim of the boat, and his dress is a field uniform rather than ceremonial garb. While both pictures show moments of real hardship for a rural population, Bouguereau's emerges as a more authentic image of emergency conditions.

Finally, however, the implications of charity-giving are similar in the two cases. Both protagonists are shown taking money from a purse and distributing it to an adoring populace, who reveal their social status by bowing reverently. Charity had traditionally substituted for equitable social programs, but it made sense only when it appeared in the guise of a special favor and under special conditions. The dispensation of benevolence was most effective during natural catastrophes, when even able-bodied workers could be deprived of their livelihood. Then the recipients could show themselves grateful to the delivering agency and acknowledge their subordination. Both the emperor and the empress were great believers in alms-giving and paternalistic gestures in return for submission at the work site. Since relief was a favor, it was best to have it administered under the aegis of the church by the Sisters of Charity, or in the secure presence of high-ranking military and civil officials.

The emperor's visit to Tarascon was also consistent with the strategy of the tours; the town represented a major agricultural market with a strong leftist tradition.[105] In the elections of May 1849 over 30 percent of the electors voted for radical slates. While Tarascon voted overwhelmingly for the empire in 1852, there was always a potential for an organized group that could be called upon in a moment of crisis. This was particularly true for Trélazé, near Angers in the department of Maine-et-Loire. Two of the seven works depicting the tour to the floodlands showed the emperor visiting the slate quarries of Trélazé, one by Moullin and the other by Antigna (fig. 3.19). While Moullin's picture is presently lost, the Salon catalogue carried a lengthy description. The painting depicted a vast lake formed by the flood waters; the ridges of the slate quarries were barely glimpsed. The emperor arrived after his visit to Angers; he advanced alone in the middle of a crowd of slate workers, who received him "with an immense and prolonged cheer." In appreciation of his visit, four slate splitters demonstrated their skill by laying open a thick block and dressing a piece of slate. Duly impressed, the emperor smiled and handed out a large amount of money to the laborers.[106]

Significantly, the only major insurrection against the Second Empire occurred in this region in the previous year—1855. During the period 1853–55 the population of Trélazé suffered dearly from low wages and the high cost of bread, which was maintained at artificial price levels by a monopoly of local grain merchants. The slate workers were particularly affected, since their average daily wage of 2.58 francs—well below the average of the Parisian laborer—could not keep pace with inflation. They were ill organized in contrast with the owners and the managers of the slate quarries, who often owned the farmland as well. The conditions in 1855 did not permit the slate worker to live on his salary, and in desperation a number of socialists, republicans, and dissatisfied Bonapartists organized a branch of the secret society known as the *Marianne*. During the night of August 26 and 27, a body of six to seven hundred workers, mainly from the slate quarries, staged a coup against the arsenal of Trélazé and then attempted to take over the town hall at Angers. The coup failed and bitter repression followed: many of those arrested were deported to Cayenne and to several fortified prisons, where they eventually died.[107]

The insurrection convulsed the government, which tried to blame the uprising on a gang of socialist hoodlums bent on no other aim than simple robbery. Meanwhile, newspapers reported that the government was striking successfully at the organization of the *Marianne*.[108] That the emperor's trip to this region was carefully orchestrated in conjunction with this event is demonstrated in a *Moniteur* article of 13 June 1856:

> No sooner had he arrived at Angers than the Emperor crossed by boat over the various flood areas and immediately made for the slate quarries, where an immense crowd of workers, their wives and children assembled on the heights to greet him. At the sight of His Majesty, the cry of *Vive l'Empereur!* let loose from all their mouths with an enthusiasm that cannot be described: these workers, *formerly led astray,* recognize and acclaim as their best friend he who has braved the danger to aid them and console them. After having left the token of his munificence . . . the Emperor departed amid universal blessings.[109]

Antigna (fig. 3.19) labored to translate the official fantasy in accordance with the need for realism in detail, but, understandably, he could not resolve all the complexities. The emperor is situated slightly off-center, and this time one of the generals distributes money to the crowd. Napoléon III stands as if in a contrite position, while before him are a group of slate workers reacting with contrasting gestures of enthusiasm, inquiry, and defiance. Behind him are the faithful: his retinue of military and civil officers, the Archbishop of Angers, and several local officials. In contrast to the Bouguereau, there is a striking sense of ambivalence in the presentation, directly owing to the actual circumstances in the area.

One clue to Antigna's dilemma is the image of the wounded veteran of the Crimean campaign in the center middleground. His downward cast makes him conspicuous amid the fervent swarm around him. At the trial of the Mariannistes at Trélazé, one of the defendants equated the revolutionaries with the heroic victors at Sebastopol, which so infuriated the presiding magistrate that he imposed strict silence on the court.[110] Antigna evidently had difficulty juggling his imagery to satisfy the tension between imperialism abroad and repression at home. Antigna extended official realism in the direction of radical realism, setting the scene in a lugubrious landscape relatively unaffected by the hierarchy of social rank. While he was influenced by Courbet's *Burial at Ornans*, Gautier could comment that Antigna "does not systematically seek out ugliness like M. Courbet, but he does not flee from it when he meets it."[111]

The emperor moved south on his tours, visiting Lyons, Arles, and

Avignon—areas of traditionally strong radical activity. His trip to Lyons especially was widely publicized, with the local accounts exemplifying the official combination of observed detail and blatant propaganda:

> It is literally impossible to say how enthusiastic the reception was for His Majesty on the entire route of his itinerary: the cries of *Vive l'Empereur!* resounded from everywhere . . . the entire population has made a point of thanking the sovereign for the happy thought which brought him to us, bearing consolations and hope. . . . At each step, the Emperor encountered the suffering victims ruined by the flood, who beseeched him for aid; His Majesty was accompanied by General Niel, his aide-de-camp, who held a sack of gold, and he plunged an open hand into it and gave to all the unfortunates a first aid destined to sweeten their present afflictions.[112]

Three artists painted the scene in Lyons, seemingly preoccupied with the specifics of time and place, as in the case of Lazerges, who depicted the emperor on horseback in the *cours Morand* (fig. 3.20). Lazerges was anxious to get the details of Napoléon III's uniform correct and went to considerable lengths to obtain the original for study.[113] He also interviewed Rouher, who had accompanied the emperor on the tour. His first sketch, however, projects the ruler in a traditional pose of heroic dominance. Janet-Lange's version was described in the catalogue with an extract of an article published in the *Moniteur* (fig. 3.21):

> [The Emperor] contemplated all these disasters with a look of profound sadness and appeared visibly moved; nothing can explain what passed between the sovereign of France and this poor people. . . . The Emperor was without guards and almost without retinue in the midst of this multitude of workers. . . . Poor women, poor children pressed around his steed; the Emperor halted with an extreme gentleness and benevolence, and appeared to gravitate by choice to the weakest. He had a leather sack attached to his saddle in which he plunged each instant, distributing his bounty himself. The population, electrified by their encounter with the sovereign in the midst of their misfortune, regarded him as a consoling angel; it burst out in enthusiastic acclamation much easier to understand than to describe.[114]

Thus the content of the official newspaper had a direct complement in official realism—in those paintings of contemporary history controlled by the Second Empire.

IV. Other Examples of Second Empire Visual Control

This final section will present other individual cases of government intervention to demonstrate how widespread government control was at the time. As in other areas of political life, the government wanted to wean the younger generation from radical tendencies and induce loyalty to the Bonapartist regime. The Great Divide was the Revolution of 1848, and while it may be argued that the natural progression of events alone would have modified and redirected the activity of artists, it is certain that government action accelerated the process.

Thomas Couture was working on the Second Republic's major commission, the *Enrollment of the Volunteers,* when the *coup d'état* broke out. Shortly afterwards, he received a visit from the Duc de Persigny, who condemned the work as a "tableau de démagogues." Couture subsequently negotiated with the regime to soften the effect and efface the image of Liberty; in return, he was promised, but never received, a commission to decorate the Pavilion Denon in the Louvre with large-scale paintings glorifying the Second Empire. The centerpiece of the cycle would have shown the *Empire Relying on the Church and the Army to Suppress Anarchy.* The scheme also made a place for the emasculated *Enrollment,* which would have been ornamented on the borders with imperial eagles. The government did award him the commission for the *Baptism of the Imperial Prince,* a major event heralding the continuation of the Napoleonic dynasty and signalling closer ties with the papacy in the mid-1850s. The work typified consensus realism in its photographic depiction of the sovereigns, members of the court, military personnel, and the papal envoy, but added the allegorical complement of Napoléon I occupying a lofty place in the transept of Notre Dame. Objections were raised by the emperor's own entourage that this suggested the ruler's inability to stand on his own two feet. Nevertheless, the work attempted a synthesis of Second Empire ideology in celebrating its awesome diplomatic and military prestige in 1856.[115]

Even Rosa Bonheur's animal imagery was affected by the changing political conditions. She painted a forceful picture for the Republican government, *Ploughing in the Nivernais* (fig. 3.22). While based on the opening chapter of George Sand's bucolic *La mare au diable*—the first of the author's series of pastoral novels that later meshed with the Bonapartists' desire for a revival of folk culture—it showed an image of enormous power controlled for the working of the land.[116] As in the majority of her works, animals dominate the human; but in *Nivernais* the oxen move in accordance with a specific task here accentuated by the processional character of the action. The Nivernais region was not particularly fertile, but its animal husbandry was well known throughout France. The breed of the *nivernais-charollaise* cow and the oxen of Morven enjoyed a wide reputation, and it was appropriate that Bonheur's depiction of labor in this locality centered on the driving team of oxen. This glorification of labor was identified with a region with a well-organized Left, one of the few rural areas that not only took up arms against the *coup d'état* but opposed it with stiff resistance.[117]

By 1853 Bonheur exhibited her panoramic *Horse Fair* together with a *Vaches et Moutons*, which was purchased by the Duc de Morny. *Horse Fair* was in many ways an homage to the horse fanciers of the Second Empire; Morny, for example, was an expert on horses who belonged to the fashionable Jockey Club and cut quite a figure at the Steeplechase. The animals in the picture were a specific type, *la percheronne*, the native French breed from Normandy. The *percheronne* was thus identified with a highly conservative region and carried national and patriotic associations. Napoléon III was especially fond of the breed; the imperial stable was filled with them, and they were employed to draw coaches and the imperial posting service, which supplemented the railway in some parts of the country. Brigades of the posting service always followed the court to Compiègne, Fontainebleau, and other parts of the provinces. Indeed, the government demand for these horses raised their price on the market. The *Horse Fair* therefore glorified the Second Empire, just as the earlier work manifested a closeness to the young Republican regime.[118]

At this moment, conservative critics positioned her as an alternative to coarser realism: Delaborde, who refused even to mention Courbet's name, noted that Bonheur's picture was set in a specific time and place and drew for its substance on actuality, yet it was nonetheless an authentic work of art. It was not simply an affair of horses or workpeople in blouses, but a scene animated with passion, where the elements of nature were ennobled.[119] As opposed to the *Nivernais*, the animals were not shown at work but on display; their function was to contribute to the opulence of the imperial court. Significantly, it was this regime that conferred upon Rosa Bonheur the first *Légion d'honneur* ever awarded a woman in France.

The career of Jules Breton is a singular example of the government's impact. He was identified with the Revolution of 1848 and early focused his attention on the plight of the poor.[120] He exhibited *Misery and Despair* at the 1849 Salon and *Hunger* at the following Salon (figs. 3.23, 3.24), where Millet's *Sower* and Courbet's *Stonebreakers* were also shown. By 1852 he was in touch with the Neo-Greeks Gérôme and Toulmouche. His outlook began to change in this period, and he turned with loathing from lugubrious subjects. While still in touch with his radical friend Delalleau, he completed a *Return from the Harvest*—a transitional work whose skying in the Salon of 1853 severely shamed him. This decided him to visit the Comte de Morny, to whom Breton's representative in the Chamber of Deputies had recommended him. He prepared his *Gleaners* for the Exposition Universelle of 1855, which was spotted prior to the opening by Alfred Arago, Inspector of Beaux-Arts, who assured him of success (cf. Bezucha, fig. 1.1). Breton, whose reminiscences published near the end of his life treated the peasants from his village condescendingly, softened the theme of rural labor, which Millet and Courbet sought to expose in all its drudgery. He based his work partly on the master of the Neo-Greeks, Gleyre, whose *Ruth and Boaz* furnished a biblical setting for field work (fig. 3.25). Above all, Breton designed his composition to emphasize the presence of the "garde-champêtre," the rural policeman supervising the gleaners. While the artist drew nostalgically upon his native village of Courrières for inspiration, the *garde-champêtre*—benevolent as he may appear—embodied state authority in preserving the principle of private property and guarding the imperial forests. His friendly-looking expression puts a benign front on authority, while at the same time assuring the bourgeois Salon audience that rural life is subject to control. This was not a unique feature in Second Empire painting: in 1861 Evariste Luminais exhibited *Champ de Foire* (an image of a horse fair strongly influenced by Rosa Bonheur), where a rural *gendarme* at the far left maintains the public order (fig. 3.26). According to the reviewer of the Salon, "the *gendarme*, no less peaceable than a peace-maker, dominates the gathering and the silver braids of his respected tricorn [sic] hat appear resplendent in the eyes of the reassured public."[121]

The question of gleaning rights was hotly debated in 1854 and discussed in the press and in parliamentary debate. Once a feudal prerogative, the new landowners objected to gleaning as an infringement of private property that encouraged the poor to expect a "free lunch." Strict rules governed gleaning to prevent theft of an already-secured crop and to screen gleaners for eligibility. Gautier especially admired Breton's work, enjoying the fact that the gleaners were regimented, "these poor Ruths who will probably not find their Boaz at the end of the day."[122]

Breton made one very revealing confession about his career: he was astonished that success came so quickly to him; that the greatest art critics of the time said the most extravagant things about his pictures. They kept seeing Virgil, Ruth, and Theocritus in his work, and he in turn strove to live up to their claims. He noted that the art critic Paul de Saint-Victor especially liked him, and that he often served on Salon juries.[123] Saint-Victor, a fervent Bonapartist, is perhaps most remembered for his vicious attacks on Millet: his enthusiasm for

Breton says a great deal. Breton's personal position coincided with the government's artistic policy; he criticized both Courbet and Millet for their extremism. Other government critics like Gautier and Chesneau contrasted Breton and Millet as the chiefs of opposing camps, praising the former unreservedly and citing the vulgarity of the latter. Chesneau saw in Breton the true artist who exacted from his models "a nobility of gesture, an elegance of contour, a majesty of lines," embellishing nature and making rural life more sympathetic and appealing to a city audience for whom the peasant often had a frightening aspect.[124]

Isidore Pils gained fame in 1849 as the painter of *Rouget de l'Isle Singing the Marseillaise for the First Time* (fig. 3.27). In 1852 the government commissioned his *Soldiers Distributing Bread to the Poor* (fig. 3.28), a work meant to portray the military in a friendly light in the wake of the *coup d'état*. Gautier, true to form, picked right up on the government's intention and lauded the act of the soldiers sharing their own frugal repast with the needy. He called the soldiers "very sweet, very tender, very sympathetic," characterizing them as "Saints Vincent and Paul in yellow trousers," who serve soup to starving children with "maternal kindness." He commented that Pils showed troopers "under a human aspect" and made them as lovable and admirable as heroes in combat.[125] Ironically, Pils soon established his reputation with a series of realist battle pictures ordered by the government; these reveal the novel side of contemporary military operations like trench warfare, artillery emplacements, and sophisticated logistics.

Pils's *Soldiers Distributing Bread* was one of four pictures at the Salon of 1852 centering on the theme of charity, a special preoccupation, as we have seen, of Napoléon III and Eugénie.[126] Pamphlets destined for workers stressed this concern: the *Clémence et bienfaits de Sa Majesté Napoléon III*, from around 1853, consisted of excerpts from the *Moniteur* attesting to the generosity of the emperor. One story told of how Napoléon III gave money to injured construction workers; another was the perennial favorite about how the young Louis Napoléon returned home without shoes and almost naked after giving his clothes to a needy family. This was the subject of a painting by Lassalle in the Salon of 1857.[127] Empress Eugénie's visits to hospitals and prisons were also advertised to illustrate the imperial family's concern for workers and the unfortunate. Not surprisingly, the only form of workers' organization encouraged by the Second Empire was the mutual aid societies set up to help members during periods of illness or incapacity. The numbers of these organizations and their membership increased significantly during this period, nearly tripling. These organizations were totally subjugated to government control, and it

was understandable that Bonhommé's design for a diploma for a
mutual aid society in 1852 showed the prince-president in the center
of improvident workers, women, and children—paternalistic images
exactly like the ones for the 1856 tours (fig. 3.29).[128]

Mme. Carette, an intimate of the Second Empire court, noted the
great energy invested by the government in philanthropic and charitable institutions.[129] Asylums, hospitals, orphanages, nurseries, and
schools multiplied, many coming under the direct patronage of the
empress. Pils's *Prayer in the Hospice*, revealing the child-care function
of the Hôpital Saint-Louis, reflects the administration's attachment
to charitable institutions administered by such religious orders as
the Sisters of Charity. The open primer on the floor affirms that the
education and socialization of lost waifs, orphans, and delinquents
were safely under the auspices of the church. Pils's painting was purchased by Empress Eugénie in 1853 and donated to one of her
favorite institutions, the *Hospice des enfants trouvés*.[130]

Bonvin established a reputation for compassionate studies of poor
people and sympathetic portrayals of paternalistic institutions socializ-
ing the poor. He was in close touch with Courbet and Champfleury
and at first antipathetic to the *coup d'état*. Just prior to the plebiscite
of December 1852 the prince-president asked to see him and personally
designated the painter to execute *L'école régimentaire* for the Palace
of Saint-Cloud. Exhibited in the 1853 Salon, it was a monumental
picture containing fifty-three figures.[131] After this date, Bonvin displayed loyalty to Bonaparte, and the stoicism of his best work declined.
He turned increasingly to still-lifes and scenes of religious piety, and
received official commissions fairly regularly through the 1850s. In
1859 the ministry secured his *Interior of a Tavern*, a peaceful scene
in a cabaret where workers are "drinking, smoking, and *reading*."[132]
It should be recalled that cafés were often political clubs, with the
owner the organizer, and constituted a potential threat to the regime.
While each public house in an area would have its own political
nuance (and the *patron* subscribed to the newspapers desired by the
clientele), it was the remnants of the Left that made most effective use
of the local pub. Bonvin's untroubled interior, where workers indulge
in benign leisure activities and do not communicate with each other,
would have expressed the administration's ideal. In actuality, the
scene was based on Bonvin's experience, since the cabaret belonged
to his father, an ex-soldier under Napoléon I.[133]

Since the Second Empire actively encouraged development in
industry, there were artists who openly propagandized the achievements of the regime and the energy of the new entrepreneurs. One of
these artists was François Bonhommé, a painter who had strong ties
with the Left, as suggested by the images he created at the time of

the 1848 Revolution. One of these was his popular lithograph exhibited in 1849 showing the invasion of the National Assembly by the
radicals Blanqui, Barbès, and Huber—part of the prelude to June.
At one time, Bonhommé wanted to publish a series of worker images
under the title of *Soldiers of Industry*, in which he concentrated on
the individual character of factory or mine workers. With his republican ties undermined by the events of the period, Bonhommé disappeared from public visibility between 1849 and 1851, only to reappear
at the Salon of 1852 as an advocate of the prince-president.[134]

In 1852 Bonhommé received the commission for the mutual aid
society diplomas. From then on he exhibited regularly at the Salon,
receiving a third-class medal at the prestigious World's Fair of 1855.
Well-supported by the regime, Bonhommé tempered his liberalism
to become the official painter of the newly industrialized economy.
He urged the administration—including the emperor himself—to retain
him on the order of the military painters so that he could document
the imperial industrial triumphs and the life of the veterans of the
Crimean and Italian campaigns as they reentered the labor force.[135]
He flattered the emperor, claiming that the ruler's encouragement of
industrial progress and regard for the working classes inspired his
aesthetic concern for "technical truth." Bonhommé declared that French
artists must portray the working classes for the sake of "the posterity
and history of the Imperial reign, on the battlefield and in the camps,
and also in industrial life, on the terrain of pacific conquests where
Imperial France hosts the nations."

Bonhommé enjoyed the support of ranking officials of the regime,
including Morin, the brilliant civil engineer and director of the
Conservatoire des arts et métiers, and Eugène Schneider, the tough-
minded director of Le Creusot. Bonhommé's work was displayed in
government technical and administrative institutions like the Ecole
des mines, the Conservatoire des arts et métiers, and the Palace of
the Conseil d'Etat. In a letter to the administration in 1862 he proposed
a tour image of the emperor visiting the site of new mine activity
at Passy and requested government support for a trip around the
country to paint the major strategic harbors and honor the country
"by exposing to the view of the French public the strenuous efforts
of the Imperial regime to upgrade the navy until it is worthy of the
grandeur of the Empire."[136]

As Gabriel Weisberg notes, Bonhommé served Schneider as the
official painter of the industrial complex at Le Creusot.[137] He did his
first studies of Le Creusot in the mid-1850s and continued through
most of the next decade. In 1867 he exhibited two watercolors at the
World's Fair showing views of the Schneider manufactory about ten
years apart, thus documenting not only the incredible growth of the

enterprise but also the remarkable industrial expansion of the Second Empire. At Le Creusot Bonhommé concentrated on recording machinery and factory structures; he no longer painted close-ups of individual workers but showed them either swallowed up in the vast expanse of industrial terrain or as insignificant appendages to the mechanical apparatus of the factory interior.[138]

Still another painter who established close ties with the Second Empire was Meissonier. Already established by the end of the July Monarchy through the patronage of the haute bourgeoisie, he manifested profound realist tendencies in *Souvenir de guerre civile*, exhibited at the Salon of 1850–51. During the ensuing period he received regular visits from Morny, who purchased at least three of his six Meissoniers between 1852 and 1854.[139] *Une rixe*, a genre scene set in the seventeenth century, was a hit at the 1855 World's Fair and was purchased by the emperor for the unprecedented sum of 25,000 francs. By the end of the decade, the emperor was inviting Meissonier to join his military campaign in Italy to gather material for painting the *Battle of Solferino*. At the same time, Meissonier projected a series of pictures illustrating the momentous events of the First Empire.[140]

Meissonier earned his reputation under the July Monarchy mainly for his combination of eighteenth-century French subjects and seventeenth-century Dutch technique, a synthesis ideally suited to the taste of his patrons (who generally collected both centuries) and one that reflected the regime's eclectic outlook. He also added his own special traits of self-identification with the subjects (sometimes taking himself as a model in the sketches), so that they appeared as contemporary people acting out a role. The year 1848 jolted him from his complacency: a partisan of the conservative republicans, he perceived himself as a dutiful citizen and loyal soldier when he enlisted as a captain of artillery in the National Guard to help crush the June insurrection. He ordered the firing of the cannon as if acting out another fantasy, but when he saw the combatants in his own unit killed and viewed firsthand the effects of his salvo on the barricades, he gained an insight into the falseness of his position and the nature of the conflict that the Right glamorized as a struggle for "law and order." He tried to expiate his guilt by shifting his horror and resentment onto another officer, one totally indifferent to the bloody sight before him, which included innocent victims accidentally killed in and around their habitations. When the conservative mayor of Paris, Armand Marrast, asked the officer if all the corpses were insurgents, he replied: "I can assure you, Monsieur le Maire, not more than a quarter of them were innocent."[141]

Meissonier's *Souvenir de guerre civile* was based on this experience. His heretofore sublimated realism could now be openly expressed.

He originally entitled the work "Juin" and planned to exhibit it in the Salon of 1849, but memories of the event were all too fresh, and he was persuaded to withdraw the entry. When it was shown at the following Salon, however, it had not lost its power. Critics on both the Left and the Right were overcome by its relentless realism, which reduced dead people to the state of inert paving stones and treated the entire scene like a pile of debris or refuse. The reformist critic Sabatier-Ungher compared the treatment to the objectivity of a daguerreotype and related it to the matter-of-fact attitude of certain historians who coolly recorded statistics of victims of some catastrophe in one sentence and then passed quickly to the next with some trivial anecdote. In this sense, Meissonier preceded Courbet in recording death with a lack of emphasis, dramatic contrast, and a circumspect selection of detail.

Above all, critics were astonished by Meissonier's lack of artifice, as in the case of the conservative Peisse, who declared that the work prevented an aesthetic distance—that its realism kept thrusting itself at the spectator. Finally, neither the Left nor the Right could see mirrored some ideological content with which they could identify, that could be formalized in visual terms. Despite his own conservative disposition, Meissonier penetrated one of the social deceptions of the dominant class. He neither heroized nor morally degraded the victims; this was not a neutral statement or one that refused to take sides, but rather a depiction of reality that defeats art, that denies art its capacity to distance us from reality. Thus this work is unusual for a conservative in being both *myopically* and *hypermetropically* true.

Alexander Herzen, a Russian exile in Paris during the June Days, heard drunken National Guardsmen sing "Mourir pour la patrie," while other youths, fresh from the country, bragged about how many insurgents they had shot. Later, when he articulated more fully his disillusionment and no longer dreamed of the good society, Herzen claimed that it was possible to combat only specific falsehoods that were encountered close up. Marx, on the eve of 1848, wrote: "All that was solid and established crumbles away, all that was holy is profaned, and man is at last compelled to look with open eyes on his condition of life and true social relations."[142] Certainly, Meissonier gained a momentary insight into these "social relations" during the terrible June Days.

Thus the Meissonier of the *Souvenir* was a potential threat to the Second Empire ideology and had to be brought into the fold; accordingly, we find Morny entering the scene during the pivotal years 1852–54. Morny purchased *Les bravi*, which hung at the Salon of 1852; *Young Man Reading while Dining*, on exhibit in 1853, and *Amateur Studying Drawings*, which was purchased the following year. These revert to his earlier style, which now again received the official stamp of approval, although even here the critical events of the period affected his themes. *Bravi*, depicting two hired assassins waiting expectantly behind a closed door, was unusual in his work for its implied violence and carried an allusion of the real threat of assassination in the wake of the *coup d'état*. Members of the Left were systematically hounded, and in turn Bonapartists feared reprisals against the prince-president. Several such attempts were made in 1852, including bogus ones designed to shore up sympathy for Louis Napoléon. Meissonier's picture, while set in the time of Henri III, conveyed specific hints of the heated aftermath of 1 December.[143]

According to the *Economist* of 29 November 1851, the stock exchanges of Europe regarded Louis Napoléon as "the sentinel of order"; Meissonier's many single figures of guards, musketeers, sentinels, and even off-duty soldiers served as efficient reminders that the imperial army—whose barracks were everywhere—was continually present to suppress the "hydra-headed monster of anarchy." While his single guardsmen wear the costume of earlier epochs, he was ultimately pressed into the service of contemporary official realism. Saint-Victor and other Bonapartist critics went after him in the 1850s for his limited repertoire, then praised him enthusiastically for his *Battle of Solferino* when it was exhibited in 1864. About's remarks recalled somewhat the effect of the *Souvenir;* he commented that the dead Austrian troops had been "reduced to the state of scrap." But now the stark realism served the ideals of the Second Empire; the emperor observes from atop the hill the impending defeat of the enemy. At the same Salon, Meissonier exhibited, as a kind of pendant to *Solferino, The Retreat of 1814,* where Napoléon I is shown retreating after his setback in Laon in March of that year. *Solferino* was thus the antithesis of this work and pointed up Napoléon's legacy of military genius to his triumphal nephew. The *Solferino* commission actually grew out of an earlier (1849) government assignment to do a typical *Reader,* but the artist kept delaying the project to get a higher price, and in this the later administration seems to have acquiesced. By 1856 Meissonier received a commitment of 20,000 francs and now aspired to greater things; Napoléon III invited him to Solferino and he abandoned his old genre style in favor of a modern battle picture. This transition marked another stage in the government's manipulation.[144]

Finally, those artists who can be identified as radical realists, Jean-François Millet and Gustave Courbet, must be considered in light of their contact with the Second Empire regime. Millet was at first perceived as a partisan of the extreme Left in the aftermath of 1848; the *Sower,* with its monumental character and rough-and-ready technique, was identified as the "Modern Demos" (the Greek designation for populace, symbolizing by inference solidarity with the contemporary rural laborer). But Millet's friend and eventual biographer Sensier worked for the Ministry of the Interior during Louis Napoléon's period and mediated between the government and the painter. Sometime in 1852 Sensier went to the office of Romieu, director of fine arts and author of *Spectre Rouge*, and left there Millet's domestic picture of *Two Women Sewing*. After investigating Millet's political affiliations, Romieu awarded the painter a state commission. In the summer of the same year, Gérôme paid Millet two visits and praised his work (recall also their collaborative effort in the late 1850s for the papal railway carriage). For the next two Salons Millet produced more traditional pieces: in 1853 his *Harvesters Resting* reminded Gautier of Michelangelo. Saint-Victor pointed out the ugliness of the types, but his criticism was unusually muted, and he characterized the work as a "Homeric idyll translated into patois." Meanwhile, Sensier obtained government subsidies for his protégé, who began preparing his exhibit for the World's Fair of 1855. Millet delivered one of his mildest peasant themes to date, *Man Grafting a Tree*. The source was Virgil, the types relatively idealized; the warm color and light were diametrically opposed to the effect of the *Sower*. The mother and her infant appeared as Madonna and Child, and the theme itself symbolized the prosperity of the family tree. This work was generally well received by government critics: Gautier praised it effusively and was happy to see these peasants—and with them their succeeding generations—"resigned" to their lot.[145]

Following the Exposition Universelle, Millet vacillated between the aggressive and idyllic poles of his production. The *Angelus* of 1855–57 (not shown at the Salon) amplified the theme of the pious peasant, while the *Gleaners* (cf. Bezucha, fig. 1.2) revived the cutting edge of the *Sower*. *Gleaners* came in for mixed criticism: Saint-Victor in *La Presse* objected to their "gigantic pretensions" and was disappointed to find that Millet, instead of refining his style like Courbet, reasserted his belligerent tone. About, however, seemed to see in it from afar a religious image and commended its serenity. About and Saint-Victor, who were close friends, obviously played a cunning game: the former took the high road and encouraged those aspects of Millet acceptable to official ideology, while the latter took the low road and attacked the features that were odious to the regime.[146] Unlike Breton's *Gleaners*, which stressed government control of gleanage, Millet's figures appear to act independently of any agency. They command the visual space and act in concert, literally and figuratively encroaching on the terrain.

Except for *Man with the Hoe*, which was exhibited in 1863, Millet's

critical fortunes steadily improved. Yet the *Man with the Hoe* struck
the critics differently from the threatening figure of the *Sower*. His
cretinous look especially disturbed them. This is a complex picture
to unravel, but one that may have struck the official critics as further
to the right in its implications than current government policy. The
year 1863 saw the inauguration of the so-called Liberal Empire (recall
now the art reforms of that year), and even though government candidates continued to roll up large majorities in rural districts, the state
sought to appeal to the interests, rather than play upon the fears, of
the rural sector. The government now felt secure enough to reach
this portion of the electorate through reason rather than emotion; it
assumed a rational, conservative peasant who understood that his
interests were best guaranteed by Napoléon III. Ironically, it was the
moderate republicans who assumed an uneducated and stupid peasantry. Their spokesperson Jules Ferry, who wrote the pamphlet *Les
élections de 1863*, attacked the peasant's political unintelligence. In
this sense, Millet's doltish laborer reflected the attitude of the frustrated
opposition. Chesneau, the government critic, reacted to Millet's cretinous types by commenting that they were relevant only to a tiny minor-
ity of peasants whose numbers were dwindling each day.[147]

At the same time, there began in the 1860s a reinterpretation of
Millet's work in the context of Christian stoicism and the acceptance
of one's lot.[148] Conservative critics joined forces to effectively neutralize
its political potential. Later, the magnates in France and the robber
barons of America who collected his work applied their interpretation
to embrace the whole range of lower classes (including urban), understanding Millet's images as embodying the ethics of hard work
and resignation. Sensier admitted the distressing lack of forehead
in the *Man with the Hoe*, but declared that the structure of the man's
body was solid, his limbs well fashioned and proportioned, and that
altogether he was capable of sixty more years of productive labor.
His passion and primary function was "to pick the soil and clear the
lands, with no ambition for anything else."[149] This position was seconded by Théophile Silvestre, a sophisticated Bonapartist critic who
received a regular subsidy from the emperor's private purse. Silvestre's
study of the artist, published in the progovernment paper *Figaro* in
1867, traces his style to the stolid peasantry of his native Gréville, a
politically conservative region where the rural laborer spent his life
"serving the earth" as proudly as he manned the imperial army. He
compared Millet's pictures favorably to the pastoral authors and associated his work with the evocations of Merovingian Gaul. For Silvestre, *Man with the Hoe* epitomized eternal rustic resignation.[150]

Silvestre praised Millet further for being a "master of nature rather
than its slave," the opposite condition of the people he depicted. The

artist's freedom inhered in the dehumanization and servitude of the subject, and thus the critic could justify Millet's elevation to the ranks of the exploiters through his transformation of the peasant model into "the immutable type of penury and rustic dejection." The progressively abstract interpretation of Millet's imagery is seen in Silvestre's revisionist critique of earlier evaluations and his view of *Man with the Hoe* as not simply a peasant but "a portrait of the peasantry." Silvestre's article dates after Millet's turn in critical fortune at the Salon of 1864, when his benign *Shepherdess and Flock* was unanimously praised. Sensier advised Millet to examine the picture carefully in preparation for later works, since it "really pleased everyone."[151] About wrote that no one could find fault with such a masterpiece, "where everything is true without realism."[152] And the same year Millet accepted a commission to do an allegorical cycle of the Four Seasons for a banker's townhouse, which he executed in an academic style. Finally, in 1868, thanks in large measure to the efforts of Silvestre, Millet received the *Chevalier de la Légion d'honneur*.

Like Millet, Gustave Courbet developed ties with the Second Empire that led to modifications in his style and content. His *Stonebreakers* and *Burial at Ornans*, shown at the Salon of 1850–51, were identified with the extreme Left. These *hypermetropically* true pictures upset and threatened members of the dominant class by raising consciousness of class differentiation in the countryside and called attention to the peasant as a new political force. Like Meissonier's *Souvenir*, they asserted their realism over and against predictable aesthetic patterns. The robotlike *Stone-breakers*, perceived by leftist critics as "human machines," were alienated in a double sense—from their own drudgery as represented in the picture and from the actual spectator's wish to see them conform to a conventional aesthetic and social ideal. The *Burial* was seen as one monumental caricature, and Courbet's parade of the rural social structure, with its implicit and explicit political nuances, as well as the marked indifference of the *notables* to the sacred ceremony, all added to the discomfort of the critics. The next year—just prior to the opening of the 1852 Salon—the ubiquitous duc de Morny stepped in to purchase Courbet's *Demoiselles du Village*. The critics were relieved to see that this picture showed some amelioration of his style, but roundly attacked it for its intimation of an aspiring rural bourgeoisie and for what they perceived to be basic technical flaws. The following year his *Bathers* scandalized critics by the amplitude of its protagonist, but his *Spinner* was praised; even the first was admired for its landscape setting, and there were lamentations that Courbet was squandering a brilliant talent.[153]

Around October of the same year, Courbet wrote to his patron Bruyas (who purchased both the *Bathers* and the *Spinner*) about a luncheon date with Nieuwerkerke, the all-powerful *surintendant des beaux-arts*. Courbet noted that the engagement had been arranged by the two "sell-outs" Chenavard and Français, and that the sole intention of the *surintendant* was to convert him to the government's position. Nieuwerkerke told Courbet that the administration hated to see him going alone, that he could win its full support if only he would tone down his approach and "mix a little water with [his] wine." Nieuwerkerke confessed that the regime had great respect for Courbet's talent and pointed out that he ought not assume an adversarial relationship with it. Indeed, the government wanted to see him produce his greatest example for the forthcoming World's Fair of 1855, and he, Nieuwerkerke, would personally steer it through channels. Courbet's reply to Nieuwerkerke, as he related it to Bruyas, was filled with righteous indignation. He opposed himself as an individual one-man government to the collective government of Napoléon III and shouted that the bribe insulted the entire community of artists. Nieuwerkerke finally went to the door in disgust but turned back one last time to remind Courbet: "Note well that it is the government and not I that has invited you to lunch today!"[154]

What was the result of this blatant attempt at bribery? The main picture preoccupying Courbet in the ensuing period was his notorious *Atelier*, subtitled "A Real Allegory Summarizing the Last Seven Years of My Artistic Life"—that is, from the year of the 1848 Revolution to the year of the World's Fair. While this picture and *Burial at Ornans* were rejected by the admission jury, the government supported Courbet's private exhibition of these and other works not far from the entrance to the official show. The jury, moreover, did accept eleven other works by Courbet for the Exposition Universelle, including the *Stone-breakers*. In any case, the *Atelier*, far from posing a threat like the previous pictures, manifested the impact of the government's efforts to modify the style of the radical realists. It might be more appropriately subtitled "An Allegory Summarizing My Bourgeoisification During the Last Seven Years."[155]

First, this is a truly academic picture, in that it centers on a single dominant figure flanked on either side by well-defined groups. It recalls David's *Leonidas* or any number of conventional history paintings invoking the frieze-principle, with a hero occupying the compositional center. Indeed, at the World's Fair itself there were several major variants of this pattern, including Hamon's *Human Comedy*, Couture's *Romans of the Decadence*, Chassériau's *Tepidarium*, and Müller's *Last Roll Call of the Revolution*. Of course, one of the original sources of this convention was the triumphal and commemorative monuments of antiquity, later translated into scenes showing the ruler surrounded by a courtly entourage. Napoléon III's own propaganda pictures stem from this tradition. Thus Courbet's arrogant centrality corresponds to his remark to Nieuwerkerke that he, too, was a government.

Second, Courbet's painting ranges him directly among the dominant class. His version of the Human Comedy is divided into two distinct groups; on the right is a privileged class who serve his cause and provide for his support, while on the left are those who are condemned to the margins of society, the parasites, the exploited, "those who live on death." There is no question as to which group he identifies with; he wears the fashionable jacket of his patron Bruyas, as seen in the comparison of his self-portrait study for the *Atelier* and his portrait of Bruyas in *The Meeting*. The striped collar and piping are identical in the two cases, and it may be concluded that the rustic garb of Courbet in the latter picture is part of a pretense. The Grand Bourgeois also used the language of the Stock Exchange to describe his relationship with his patrons: he called them *"actionnaires,"* or shareholders in Courbet, Inc. It is no coincidence that in this very period Courbet speculated on the stock market, investing heavily in railway shares. The result, however, was disastrous, and his financial losses threw him into a profound depression during 1855, which prevented him from working.[156] Courbet's mentor, the sociologist Proudhon (also portrayed on the right side of *Atelier*), was himself preoccupied with the Bourse in this period. Proudhon's friend and biographer, Sainte-Beuve, wrote that Proudhon tried to get railroad concessions for friends in 1853–54 and asked for help from Prince Napoléon. He also advised English capitalists who sought to finance railways in Switzerland. It was in this period that Proudhon decided to publish, although anonymously at first, the popular potboiler *The Manual of the Stock Exchange Speculator*, consisting of a mass of statistical information on all the leading companies whose shares were listed on the Bourse. Courbet must have read the work, because his letter to Champfleury borrows its terminology. Proudhon declared that the public of the Bourse, similar to the world of production, divides itself into two categories, the *exploités* and the *exploiteurs*. The first—the more numerous —consists of the "*vile multitude*, the rubbish heap of porters, domestics, *rentiers*, petty bourgeois, hard-working but greedy." They see the Bourse as a lottery, while the clever *exploiteurs* deal with the market more prudently and earn a steady profit.[157.]

The very title of Courbet's painting indicated his entrepreneurial attitude. The term *atelier* meant not only a studio but also a small factory, designating a location where mechanical and artisanal activity of every kind was carried on under the direction of a chief called the *patron*. And what is Courbet producing in his atelier? A landscape, now an artificial production removed from nature, or the prime source of realist inspiration. This signalled a new direction; in the next few years he turned out numerous commercial landscapes and hunting scenes inspired partly by the English artist-entrepreneur Edwin Landseer. Champfleury wrote at this time that it disturbed him to witness Courbet's concessions, that he was becoming increasingly pre-occupied with the sentiments of his patrons. This observation was seconded by conservative critics who noted that Courbet was gradually humanizing his work, while the more liberal Thoré regretted through-out the 1860s Courbet's renunciation of his social commitment. Finally, in 1866 *Woman with a Parrot* earned him universal esteem from the Second Empire gang, and no one was more pleased to see it than two figures already mentioned in this essay. One was Sainte-Beuve, who raved about it in the company of Troubat and the chaplain of Princess Mathilde, and the other was Edmond About, who suggested that Courbet now quit his modest studio and live like the true Renaissance Man in a sumptuous Parisian town house.[158]

Thus, even in the case of the two most dominant realists of the period—Millet and Courbet—the power and influence of the Second Empire managed to affect the way they worked and their choice of theme and style. While the methods employed by the regime of Napoléon III were varied, and are certainly not unique by standards of other periods or centuries, the fact that such a systematic control of the arts was at work just when the seeds of modernism were being sown is worth examining in detail. The government managed to blunt and neutralize the political potential of the radical realists, while at the same time elevating their own realist approach on the basis of the innovations of their regime. The Second Empire correctly saw that the only way that it could remain in power was to cultivate popu-lar support; to do this meant that the government had to manipulate the press and the visual arts so that their message was clear and the populace able to grasp their achievements. To this end they spared no expense to cultivate a propaganda milieu that molded public opinion. By establishing their own brand of realism, they furthered a mode of contemporaneity that was closely tied to the technological and expansionist policies of the regime and ultimately glorified the French nation—features that would be assimilated by the avant-garde during the Third Republic. Finally, the Second Empire established a precedent for pervasive control of the media, which became the hallmark of authoritarian regimes in the twentieth century.

NOTES

I wish to express my gratitude to the following persons for their con-tributions to the formulation of this chapter: Edward Berenson, Julius Kaplan,

David Kunzle, Janet Leonard, Edward J. Olszewski, Michael Orwicz, O. K. Werckmeister, and Stephen Yenser. Gabriel Weisberg was a marvel of patience and understanding during the finalizing of this paper, and his suggestions and scholarly input are felt throughout. I am especially grateful to Nicos Hadjinicolaou for his constructive reading and acute insights, and for his moral support and encouragement, which kept me going under pressure.

1. To cite only one critical example: the Salon des refusés. See A. Boime, "The Salon des refusés and the Evolution of Modern Art," *Art Quarterly* 32 (1969): 411 ff. Reflecting the Second Empire's sympathy for realism, the Salon des refusés encouraged the aspirations of the second-generation realists.

2. G. Weisberg, "The Realist Tradition: Critical Theory and the Evolution of Social Themes," in *The Realist Tradition* (The Cleveland Museum of Art, 1981), p. 14. For the relative character of realism and its application to specific historical epochs, see N. Hadjinicolaou, "L'exigence de réalisme au Salon de 1831," *Les réalismes et l'histoire de l'art, Histoire et critique des arts,* no. 4-5 (May 1978): 21 ff. The close connection between the government and the arts is seen in one critic's comment that Nieuwerkerke's salon had as many generals and deputies (MPs) as artists. See E. Gebaüer, *Les beaux-arts à l'exposition universelle de 1855* (Paris, 1855), p. 114, discussing François Biard's picture (Catalogue du Salon, No. 2561). See also L. Nochlin, "New York, Brooklyn Museum: The Realist Tradition," *Burlington Magazine* 122 (1980): 263 ff.

3. C. Baroche, *Second Empire: notes et souvenirs* (Paris, 1921), pp. 356–57; H. de Viel-Castel, *Mémoires,* 2 vols. (Paris, 1942), I, 238–39. This attitude coincided with that of the champion of the realists, Castagnary. See J. Castagnary, *Salons, 1857–1879,* 2 vols. (Paris 1892), I, pp. 105–106.

4. D. G. Charlton, *Positivist Thought in France During the Second Empire 1852–1870* (Oxford, 1959), pp. 5 ff; R. C. Binkley, *Realism and Nationalism 1852–1871* (New York and London, 1935), pp. 41 ff. For the interest in photography, see *The Second Empire: Art in France under Napoleon III* (Philadelphia Museum of Art, 1978), pp. 401 ff. The court had its official photographer, Comte Olympe Aguado.

5. D. I. Kulstein, *Napoleon III and the Working Class; A Study of Government Propaganda under the Second Empire* (San Jose, 1969), p. 78. Realism, of course, was not the exclusive concern of the Beaux-Arts program but rather constituted a major component of the official Salon style. Members of the imperial family privately relished eighteenth-century imagery, as well as the erotic pictures of a Cabanel or a Galimard. Galimard's *Léda,* purchased by the emperor from the Salon of 1857, provoked a lively scandal (Catalogue du Salon de 1857, No. 1092, "La séduction de Léda"). Proudhon, Courbet's friend, was shocked by it and does not even bother to mention the name of the painter. See P.-J. Proudhon, *Du principe de l'art et de sa destination sociale* (Paris, 1865), p. 262. The imperial family also stimulated the medieval fantasies of Viollet-le-Duc, but this reflected their desire to secure legitimacy through identification with the great dynasties of the past. Second Empire medievalism was mainly expressed through architecture, but there was a conservative type of religious painting tied to the government's renewed links with the church. The eighteenth-century taste —even when translated by a Chaplin—was related to the old decor of the imperial palaces and the personal preference of the empress. See E. A. Vizetelly, *The Court of the Tuileries 1852–1870* (London, 1912), pp. 159

ff.; S. O. Simches, *Le romantisme et le goût esthétique du XVIIIe siècle* (Paris, 1964), p. 3; *Positivist Thought in France*, pp. 12, 14, 67 ff.; Boime, *Thomas Couture and the Eclectic Vision* (London and New Haven, 1980), pp. 266 ff., 298.

6. M. Z. Brooke, *Le Play: Engineer and Social Scientist* (London, 1970), p. 60.

7. Archives Nationales F²¹ 519, de Mercey's draft for a report; *Exposition universelle de 1855*, Catalogue du Salon de 1855, Prince Jérôme Napoléon's speech of 29 December 1853, p. xiii.

8. F. B. de Mercey, *Etudes sur les beaux-arts*, 3 vols. (Paris, 1855–57), III, 192–93.

9. Catalogue du Salon de 1853, Paris, 1853, pp. 9 ff.

10. J. Breton, *La vie d'un artiste* (Paris, 1890), pp. 226–27.

11. P. de la Gorce, *Histoire du Second Empire*, 7 vols. (Paris, 1899–1905), I, 53, II, 106 ff.; T. Zeldin, *The Political System of Napoleon III* (London, 1958), p. 5.

12. B. A. Granier de Cassagnac, *Souvenirs du Second Empire*, 3 vols. (Paris, 1879–82), II, 84–85.

13. *Papiers et correspondance de la famille impériale*, 3 vols. (Paris, 1870), I, 27 ff. See also the report from the Prefect of Police to the soon-to-be emperor in October 1852 (ibid., III, 283): "The Empire is accomplished, it will be proclaimed, but it is necessary that it be done soon, that it be done tomorrow; for the sake of everyone concerned it must be done to put a halt to the rumors and threats of criminal assault, to close the door forever on ambitious types who conspire in the shadows, to bring home the doubtful, convince the indifferent persons, and to seal forever the attachments which are certainly sincere but which may still anticipate the possibility of a change in regime. Finally, it must be done to perpetuate the great enterprise of the Emperor. . . ."

14. Kulstein, *Napoleon III and the Working Class*, pp. 38 ff.; also the excellent study by N. Isser, *The Second Empire and the Press* (The Hague, 1974). See also I. Collins, *The Government and the Newspaper Press in France 1814–1881* (Oxford, 1959), chapters X, XI, pp. 118 ff., 136 ff.

15. Kulstein, *Napoleon III*, pp. 45 ff.; Isser, *The Second Empire*, pp. 19 ff.

16. De La Gorce, *Histoire*, II, 82–83; Kulstein, *Napoleon III*, pp. 58 ff.; Isser, *The Second Empire*, pp. 25 ff.

17. De La Gorce, *Histoire*, I, 118; Kulstein, *Napoleon III*, pp. 125 ff.; Isser, *The Second Empire*, pp. 27–28.

18. Kulstein, *Napoleon III*, pp. 80 ff.; Isser, *The Second Empire*, pp. 15 ff. I am using Professor Robert Herbert's happy turn of phrase here.

19. Isser, *The Second Empire*, pp. 86 ff. As an illustration of press manipulation in connection with the brochures, we may note that *Le Siècle*, informed by About, claimed that the pamphlet was authorized by the government, while *Le Pays* denounced this claim as erroneous, declaring that the government did all it could to prevent the pamphlet (which had been published in Brussels) from being circulated in France. Later, About wrote *La Prusse en 1860* in collaboration with Fould and Napoléon III, yet at the meeting with the German princes at Baden-Baden in June 1860, the emperor attacked About's views and lamented its publication.

20. Ibid., pp. 15–16.

21. Zeldin, *The Political System of Napoleon III*, pp. 16–17. Persigny early signaled to the prefects the need to gain support of the masses in favor of Bonapartist candidates. A draft of his letter of 1852 for local elections

sums up the government's policy: "It matters little that a few notorious enemies should be elected to the *conseil général*, what matters is that there should be no canton where the hand of the government has not at least sapped the foundations on which the old influences rested. . . . Overthrow the hold of the old influences on the minds of the people. . . . Do not fear to fight against the old parties . . . our business above all is to create a [new] party."

22. *Papiers et correspondance de la famille impériale*, I, 257 ff.

23. A. Poulet-Malassis, *Papiers secrets et correspondance du Second Empire* (Paris, 1877), pp. 315, 345.

24. Sainte-Beuve observed that most working writers already belonged to the *Société des gens de lettres*, an organization that, for modest dues, admitted all authors who published at least one volume. Its leadership, however, was weak, and the steering committee scarcely had the opportunity to consider the material interests of hard-up colleagues. The *Société des auteurs dramatiques* was somewhat more specialized but differed from the other in name only, and the two could be easily fused. The emperor, with his ingenious gifts of persuasion, would win them over handily, as he had done in the case of other kinds of laborers.

25. Isser, *The Second Empire*, p. 11; P. Barbier and F. Vernillat, *Histoire de France par les chansons*, 8 vols. (Paris, 1957–59), VIII, 74–75, 76 ff., 88, 127 ff.; Poulet-Malassis, *Papiers secrets*, pp. 200 ff. The administration's deep concern with popular songs and its peculiar approach to culture is seen again later on, when during the so-called Liberal Empire the problem of the *Marseillaise* came up. The *Eldorado*, a popular café-concert, asked for permission to allow its performers to sing the national anthem. The bureaucrat who prepared the report noted that there were two opinions on the case within the government ranks. One faction thought that the government should give a positive authorization and thereby eliminate the rebellious potential of the song. The opposing government faction advanced the opinion that, given the present state of mind, the proliferation of performances of the *Marseillaise* in public places "would be a new and dangerous source of stimulation. Its exclusively revolutionary character is only too well known and accepted to hope that the generosity of the government would neutralize its impact." It was the latter view that ultimately prevailed.

26. Poulet-Malassis, *Papiers secrets*, pp. 202 ff.

27. Ibid., p. 205.

28. E. P. Spencer, "The Academic Point of View in the Second Empire," in *Courbet and the Naturalistic Movement*, ed. G. Boas (New York, 1967), pp. 64 ff.; P. de Chennevières, "Le Comte de Nieuwerkerke," in *Souvenirs d'un directeur des beaux-arts* (Paris, 1883–89), 2d part, pp. 92 ff.

29. F. Ravaisson, "De l'enseignement du dessin dans les lycées," *Le Moniteur universel*, 18–19 January 1854.

30. J. C. Sloane, *French Painting Between the Past and the Present* (Princeton, N. J., 1951), pp. 24 ff.; H. C. and C. A. White, *Canvases and Careers* (New York, 1965), pp. 95–96.

31. C. H. Stranahan, *A History of French Painting* (New York, 1888), p. 265.

32. Catalogue du Salon de 1853, pp. 10–11; Catalogue du Salon de 1857, p. xxxiii. For views of the government at the Salons, see Sloane, *French Painting*, pp. 44 ff.

33. Catalogue du Salon de 1853, p. 11.

34. Ibid., pp. 7–9, 11.

35. *Exposition Universelle de 1855,* Catalogue du Salon de 1855, pp. vii ff.

36. Ibid., pp. xlv ff.

37. Catalogue du Salon de 1857, pp. xxx ff., xxxviii; Brooke, *Le Play,* pp. 60–61. Le Play was an engineer who taught at the Ecole des mines and later became a sociologist who did pioneering field work among the Parisian and foreign working classes and peasant populations. His work was biased by his desire to find the "ideal," morally upright working-class and peasant family and to elevate this type to the norm under the Second Empire. His "consensus" type characterized still another example of Second Empire propaganda and its influence on contemporary social science.

38. Catalogue du Salon de 1859, pp. viii ff.

39. Ibid., p. ix. By 1857 the government assumed a negative stance to bring the younger generation into line with its view of realism. Fould was gratified in 1859 to find that while no great genius had yet emerged, there was an absence of those "presumptuous singularities which a false taste inspires." There was more study, less haste; fewer *ébauches* were presented as serious efforts. The return to sane conditions reflected the emperor's solicitude and the administration's policy and merited the praise of the "enlightened public." That year Daubigny, an imperial favorite, earned a *rappel* of the First-Class Medal, and Breton and Armand Leleux received *rappels* of the Second-Class Medal.

40. Zeldin, *The Political System of Napoleon III,* p. 104.

41. Catalogue du Salon de 1863, pp. viii ff.

42. Archives Nationales F[21] 486, draft for a report to the minister of state (1862) outlining the progress of the English: "The International Exhibition at London demonstrates a quite remarkable progress in the taste of English manufacturers. Those English products which are based on design, if they have not yet surpassed our analogous manufactures, are making giant strides toward them. . . ." See also A. de Beaumont, "Les arts industriels en France et l'exposition de 1863," *Revue des deux mondes,* 1 September 1863, pp. 196–97; A. Boime, "The Teaching Reforms of 1863 and the Origins of Modernism in France," *The Art Quarterly* I (1977): 5, 9.

43. Catalogue du Salon de 1864, pp. viii, x.

44. Ibid., pp. xiii–xiv.

45. Already in 1854 Auguste Couder, member of the Academy and government partisan, proposed at one of the Academy's weekly meetings as topics for the Prix Bordin: "On the Influence of the Graphic Arts on Industry," and "On the Influence of Journalism on the Fine Arts." Both themes showed the major preoccupations of the government in its desire to direct the course of the arts. See Bibliothèque de l'Institut. Académie des Beaux-Arts. *Procès-Verbaux, January 1851–December 1855,* Séance of 19 August 1854. The final selection, "De l'influence des arts du dessin sur l'industrie," was announced in 1856. See L'Institut. Académie des Beaux-Arts. *Séances publiques,* vol. 13 (1854–58), Programme . . . 7 October 1854, pp. 13 ff. The conditions stipulated that essays had first to analyze those qualities which distinguished the products of French industry and to seek out their roots; then to indicate the advantages resulting from these qualities both for the honor of the nation and for its resources; and finally to propose suggestions for helping preserve France's high place in industry, for strengthening it, and for encouraging fine artists to inspire with their example the industrial sector of the economy that contributes to industrial expansion. Clearly, this was an unusual project for the Academy and especially for the launching of a new prize.

46. Boime, "The Teaching Reforms," pp. 2–3, 27 (notes 15–16); "An Unpublished Petition Exemplifying the Oneness of the Community of Nineteenth Century French Artists," *Journal of the Warburg and Courtauld Institutes* 33 (1970): 345 ff.

47. J. Guiffrey and M. J. Barthélemy, *Liste des pensionnaires 1663–1907* (Paris, 1908), pp. 121, 124.

48. Boime, "The Teaching Reforms," pp. 1 ff.; M. Ivens, "La liberté guidant l'artiste," *Les révoltés logiques*, no. 11 (Winter 1979–80): 48 ff.

49. T. Thoré, *Salons de W. Bürger*, 2 vols (1870), II, 375–76.

50. P. de Saint-Victor, "l'Académie des Beaux-Arts et les réformes," *La Presse*, 8–9 January 1864. Saint-Victor was a confirmed Bonapartist and was later made Inspector-General in the Ministry of Fine Arts. See Sloane, *French Painting*, p. 225.

51. E. Chesneau, *Le décret du 13 novembre et l'Académie des Beaux-Arts* (Paris, 1864). Chesneau, a protégé of Nieuwerkerke and of Saint-Victor, worked at the Louvre and wrote for *Le Constitutionnel* starting in 1863. He collaborated with Duveyrier—one of the other government pamphleteers —on the *Grande Encyclopédie* and wrote an essay on Morny's collection as well as a luxury edition of the imperial collection at Compiègne. In 1869 he was appointed an Inspector of Fine Arts. Chesneau dedicated his book on Carpeaux to Nieuwerkerke, drawing attention to their more than twenty years of "constante amitié." See Chesneau, *Le statuaire J.-B. Carpeaux, sa vie et son oeuvre* (Paris, 1880), pp. i–ii. Also Sloane, *French Painting*, pp. 49, 219.

52. Chesneau, *Le décret*, pp. 14 ff.

53. Chesneau, "Le réalisme et l'esprit français dans l'art," *Revue des deux mondes*, 1 July 1863, pp. 218 ff.

54. Ibid., pp. 229 ff. My understanding of Champfleury's brand of realism has been greatly aided by Clark's brilliant analysis: see T. J. Clark, *Image of the People* (Greenwich, Conn., 1973), pp. 53 ff.

55. Chesneau, "Le réalisme," p. 237. Still further indication of a concerted effort on the part of the government—inspired critics to prepare the public for the reforms is Sainte-Beuve's article on Champfleury in the *Moniteur* on 5 January 1863. Anticipating several of the arguments of Chesneau, Sainte-Beuve insisted on the charm of realism for serious minds but emphasized that it needed to be "refreshed" by "*style*" and feeling. Further: "You (i.e., reality) also need . . . a certain something which fulfills and completes you, which corrects without falsifying you, which elevates you without making you lose contact with the earth, which gives you all the spirit possible without ceasing for a moment to appear natural, which leaves you still recognizable to all, but more luminous, more adorable and more beautiful than ordinarily in life—in short, that which is called the *ideal*." See C.-A. Sainte-Beuve, "Les frères Le Nain. Peintres sous Louis XIII par M. Champfleury," in *Nouveaux lundis*, 13 vols. (Paris, 1864–78), IV, 137–38.

56. T. E. Duval, Jr., *The Subject of Realism in the "Revue des deux mondes" 1831–1865* (Philadelphia, 1936), pp. 46 ff.

57. Archives Nationales F^{21} 487, "Rapport à Son Excellence le Ministre d'Etat" [1856].

58. Champfleury, *Le réalisme* (Paris, 1857), p. 275; E. Duranty, "Notes sur l'art," *Réalisme*, 10 July 1856; "Esquisse de la méthode des travaux," *Réalisme*, 15 November 1856; "M. Max Buchon et le réalisme," *Réalisme*, 15 December 1856.

59. G. Riat, *Gustave Courbet, peintre* (Paris, 1906), p. 133; *Courbet*

raconté par lui-même et par ses amis, ed. P. Cailler, 2 vols. (Paris, 1950), II, 205.

60. Chesneau, *Les nations rivales dans l'art* (Paris, 1868), pp. 224–25.

61. O. Merson, *La peinture en France* (Paris, 1861), pp. 63 ff.

62. Ibid., p. 81.

63. Ibid., pp. 66, 69 ff.

64. Ibid., p. 87.

65. E. About, *Salon de 1864* (Paris, 1864), pp. 74 ff.

66. See the excellent study by C. C. Hungerford, "Ernest Meissonier's First Military Paintings: 1: 'The Emperor Napoleon III at the Battle of Solferino'," *Arts Magazine* 54 (January 1980): 89 ff. Also Boime, "New Light on Manet's *Execution of Maximilian,*" *The Art Quarterly* 36 (1973): 178.

67. O. Gréard, *Jean-Louis-Ernest Meissonier, ses souvenirs, ses entretiens* (Paris, 1897), pp. 39 ff., 242, 260, 262.

68. Merson, *La peinture,* pp. 66 ff.; D. Bernasconi, "Mythologie d'Abd-el-Kader dans l'iconographie française au XIXe siècle," *Gazette des Beaux-Arts,* 6e per., vol. 77 (1971): 51 ff. (Bernasconi incorrectly attributes the painting to Horace Vernet [ibid., p. 56, fig. 10].)

69. Naturally, the civilizing influence of the colonists converts the "heathen," and thus it is that French Christians could ask for and receive the protection of Abd-el-Kader during the massacres in Damascus in July 1860.

70. M. Etienne-Gallois, *L'ambassade de Siam au XVIIe siècle* (Paris, 1862), pp. 181 ff.; C. Meyniard, *Le Second Empire en Indo-Chine* (Paris, 1891), pp. 228 ff., 262 ff., 265 n., 403 ff., 443 ff.; G. M. Ackerman, *Jean-Léon Gérôme* (Dayton Art Institute, 1972), pp. 54–55; Philadelphia Museum of Art, *The Second Empire,* pp. 307–308.

71. No mention of the political implications of Courbet's work in the Salon of 1850–51 can omit reference to the landmark study by T. J. Clark, *Image of the People: Gustave Courbet and the 1848 Revolution* (Greenwich, Conn., 1973). It has fundamentally altered the way we perceive Courbet and perhaps the entire nineteenth century as well.

72. See Meyniard, *Le Second Empire en Indo-Chine,* pp. 316 ff., 319–20, for the implications of the gifts from the perspective of the Siamese (although actual reference is to 1856 rather than to 1861). Gérôme, of course, was the paradigm of the younger generation of academic painters carefully cultivated by the regime. During 1848 he was a moderate republican, participating in the contest for an image of the Republic but also serving in the National Guard during the June Days. The commission for the Siamese delegation opened the doors to him at Compiègne, where he often designed charades and staged *tableaux vivants* for the court. While working on the commission he married the daughter of Goupil, the famous art dealer and print publisher who also happened to be a fanatical Bonapartist. Gérôme developed a reputation for depicting ethnic types, but it should be noted that he sometimes ran diplomatic errands during his voyages to the Near East. Napoléon III made concerted efforts to maintain and increase the French influence in this area, and Gérôme's photographic approach suited the more modern colonizing techniques of the emperor than the blushingly romantic and exotic images of Delacroix.

73. C. Moreau-Vauthier, *Gérôme, peintre et sculpteur* (Paris, 1906), pp. 100 ff.; T. Gautier, *Les beaux-arts en Europe,* 2 vols. (1855–56), I, 218 ff.

74. Archives Nationales F²¹ 83: Dossier "M. Gérôme, tableau: Le Siècle d'Auguste, 30 8bre 1852, 20,000 francs."

75. The final price, 20,000 francs, was a small fortune for the twenty-eight-year-old artist.

76. Gautier, *Les beaux-arts*, II, 35 ff.; P. Petroz, *L'Art et la critique en France depuis 1822* (Paris, 1875), pp. 164 ff. One of their favorite targets for satire was Ingres: see Moreau-Vauthier, *Gérôme*, p. 100 and 100n.

77. *The Second Empire*, pp. 63–64, 259–60; Merson, *La peinture*, pp. 23 ff.

78. Gautier, *Les beaux-arts*, I, 218.

79. Hamon's first job was at the Sèvres' manufactory, where he worked as a potter and a decorator during the years 1848–52. In 1852 the government's purchase of *The Human Comedy* freed him to work full time as a Salon artist. See E. Hoffmann, *Jean-Louis Hamon* (Paris, 1903) (preface by Gérôme), pp. 58 ff., 64–65. But he continued to work independently on porcelain in the shop of Deck and later moved in the circle of Bracquemond. This would suggest that the taste for "Japonisme" is related to the decorative aims of the Neo-Greek movement and forges another link between Gleyre's first-generation disciples and the second, who became known as the impressionists.

80. Gautier, *Les beaux-arts*, II, 42.

81. J. Breton, *La vie d'un artiste* (Paris), pp. 257–58; Hoffman, *Jean-Louis Hamon*, pp. 70 ff., 89, 92; *The Second Empire*, pp. 313–14.

82. Gautier, *Les beaux-arts*, II, 44.

83. M. Schapiro, "Courbet and Popular Imagery," *Journal of the Warburg and Courtauld Institutes* 4 (1941): 175–76; R. Ponton, "Les images de la paysannerie dans le roman rural à la fin du 19e siècle," *Actes de la recherche en sciences sociales*, No. 17/18 (November 1977): 62 and 62n.

84. Merson, *La peinture*, pp. 198–99.

85. T. J. Clark, *The Absolute Bourgeois: Artists and Politics in France, 1848–1851* (Greenwich, 1973), pp. 120–21; G. Duby and A. Wallon, *Histoire de la France rurale*, 4 vols. (Paris, 1976), III, *Apogée et crise de la civilisation paysanne, 1789–1914*, p. 360.

86. K. Marx, *The Eighteenth Brumaire of Louis Bonaparte* (New York, 1969), pp. 18, 75.

87. Merson, *La peinture*, pp. 183 ff.

88. Ibid., pp. 188–89.

89. Ibid., pp. 190–91.

90. For the background on this project, see the excellent piece by G. M. Ackerman, "Three Drawings by Gérôme in the Yale Collection," *Yale University Art Gallery Bulletin* 36 (Fall 1976): 8 ff.

91. E. Moreau-Nélaton, *Millet raconté par lui-même*, 3 vols. (Paris, 1921), II, 47 ff.

92. Gautier, who saw the designs in 1858, wrote: "The pope, a railway carriage!—Strange juxtaposition of terms, which sum up so well the present epoch: the old spirit and the modern spirit, the immutable tradition blessing infinite progress." See Gautier, "A travers les ateliers," *L'artiste* 62 (1858): 18. Strange juxtaposition indeed! The Pope, Pius IX, was the same reactionary who promulgated the doctrine of the Immaculate Conception and the Syllabus of Errors, who condemned material progress and the open society. The original order for the wagon came down from the Società Pio-Latino, which built a railroad from Rome to Frascati within the Papal States. The

pope only permitted a few short lines in papal territory for fear that larger lines would contribute to political unification of Italy. That his concerns were related to events in France is certain: the following year Napoléon III assisted the *risorgimento* by defeating the Austrians at Solferino and Magenta, and his approval of the annexation of part of the papal territory to the new Kingdom of Italy unleashed a violent campaign against him on the part of conservative Catholics at home and abroad. Pius IX's benediction on industrial progress and the cooperation of the French in the production of his special gift wagon must have been seen by both sides as a gesture of friendly persuasion. Certainly, it was a concession on the part of Pius IX to the industrial expansion promoted by Napoléon III.

93. Baunard, *Un siècle de l'église de France, 1800–1900* (Paris, 1901), pp. 160, 228–29.

94. G. P. Palmade, *French Capitalism in the Nineteenth Century* (Newton Abbot, Devon), pp. 122 ff., 155.

95. Arts Council of Great Britain, *Gustave Courbet 1819–1877* (London, 1978), p. 36; *Courbet raconté par lui-même*, I, 163–64.

96. Isser, *The Second Empire*, pp. 34 ff., 61–62, 123 ff.

97. C. Duveyrier, *L'avenir et les Bonaparte* (Paris, 1864).

98. J. Troubat, *Une amitié à la D'Arthez* (Paris, 1900), pp. 31 ff., 270, 153 ff., et passim.

99. Kulstein, *Napoleon III*, pp. 69 ff.

100. Ibid., pp. 72–73.

101. Archives Nationales F^{21} 83, Dossier: "M. Génod, peinture. Inondations de Lyon, 17 8bre 1857, 2000 francs. Musée de Lyon (Rhône)." Génod wrote to the Minister of State on 9 October 1857 to persuade the administration to purchase his *Une scène des inondations des Brotteaux*, which he referred to as "Cette oeuvre toute gouvernementale," and further reminded the minister that he was a professor at the Ecole impériale des Beaux-Arts at Lyons. A second letter, dated 10 October, proved to be the clincher: "As professor of an imperial school, I wish only to have the honor to show Lyons as well as my students that the Emperor's government knows how to appreciate the works of a Lyonnais master."

102. Archives Nationales F^{21} 66, Dossier: "M. Bouguereau, peinture. Entrée de l'Empereur à Tarascon, 14 juin 1856, 5000 francs (Musée de Tarascon, Bouches-du-Rhône)," rough draft of a letter dated 14 June 1856 to the prefect of the department of the Bouches-du-Rhône. See also M. Vachon, *W. Bouguereau* (Paris, 1900), pp. 85–86.

103. See the Salon catalogue entry under Lassalle, Catalogue du Salon de 1857, No. 1585. Also E. F. Fleury, *Souvenirs*, 2 vols. (Paris, 1897), I, 345 ff.

104. See R. Rosenblum's discussion in *French Painting 1774–1830: The Age of Revolution*, Réunion des Musées Nationaux, 1975, pp. 492–93.

105. L. A. Loubére, *Radicalism in Mediterranean France* (Albany, 1974), p. 52.

106. "Partie non officielle," *Le Moniteur universel*, 10 June 1856; Catalogue du Salon de 1857, Nos. 58 and 1976; Musée des Beaux-Arts d'Orléans, *Jean-Pierre Antigna* (Orléans, 1978), No. 18.

107. For the insurrection at Trélazé and the *Marianne*, see the following: "Faits divers," *La Presse*, 2 September 1855; "Tribunal de police. Correctionnelle d'Angers. Affaire dite des carrières," *Le Constitutionnel*, 23 September 1855; F. Attibert, *Quatre ans à Cayenne*, ed. L. Watteau (Brussels,

1859), pp. xxv, 5 ff.; H. Chabanne, *Evasion de l'Ile du Biable* (*Guyane française*) (Paris, 1862); *Guerre à l'ignorance* (Pouilly-sur-Loire [Nièvre], 1867); F. Remi, *La Marianne dans les campagnes* (Auxerre, 1881), p. 53; F. Simon, *La Marianne, société secrète au pays d'Anjou* (Angers, 1939), pp. 41 and 41 n, 46, 49 ff., 79 ff., 83 ff., 101 ff., 118; J. Maitron, *Dictionnaire biographique du mouvement ouvrier français*, 3 vols. (Paris, 1964–66), I, 116–17, 166–67; II, 372–73; III, 277, 396; M. Agulhon, *Marianne au combat: L'imagerie et la symbolique républicaine de 1789 à 1880* (Paris, 1979), p. 17. For an arch-conservative view of the *Marianne*, see the anonymously published *La Marianne, ou la Jacquerie de toutes les époques* (Paris, 1856).

108. "Cours et tribunaux.–Société secrète.–Ramifications de la Marianne dans La Nièvre.–Onze prévenus," *La Presse*, 31 August 1855; "Tribunaux," *Le Siècle*, 6 August 1855; "Tribunal de police. Correctionnelle d'Angers. Affaire dite des carrières," *Le Constitutionnel*, 23 September 1855.

109. "Partie non officielle," *Le Moniteur universel*, 13 June 1856. Emphasis mine.

110. *La Marianne, ou la Jacquerie*, p. xi.

111. Gautier, *Les beaux-arts*, II, 102.

112. Quoted in "Faits divers," *Le Moniteur universel*, 6 June 1856.

113. Archives Nationales F²¹ 91, Dossier: "M. Lazerges, peinture. L'Empereur au cours Morand, Lyon, 4 juin 1856, 5000 francs"; de Mercey's draft of letter to Lazerges dated 25 March 1857; and letter from Thélin to de Mercey, 15 March 1857. Thélin was the treasurer of the "Cassette particulière de l'Empereur."

114. Catalogue du Salon de 1857, No. 1424.

115. Boime, *Thomas Couture and the Eclectic Vision* (London and New Haven, 1980), pp. 225, 263 ff.

116. Archives Nationales F²¹ 16, Dossier: "Mlle R. Bonheur, peinture. Animaux dans un pâturage, 2 juillet 1848, 3000 francs." The work was completed in 1849. In his report to the minister on 18 April 1849, Inspector of Fine Arts Garraud called the painter number one in the animal field and emphasized that "the animals in it are treated in a very remarkable style and the entire work expressed a genuine feeling for nature." See also H. Bacon, "Rosa Bonheur," *The Century Magazine* 28 (1884): 835.

117. P. Larousse, *Grand dictionnaire universel du XIXe siècle*, 17 vols. (Paris, 1866 *et seq.*), XII, 459, article "Paysan."

118. Vizetelly, *The Court of the Tuileries*, pp. 300 ff., 304–305, 309–10. For further information, see Albert Boime, "The Case of Rosa Bonheur: Why Can't a Woman Be More Like a Man?" *Art History* 4 (December 1981): 384 ff.

119. H. Delaborde, *Mélanges sur l'art contemporain* (Paris, 1866), pp. 81–83.

120. Breton, *La vie d'un artiste*, pp. 194, 197, 199, 206.

121. A. M., "Salon de 1861," *L'Illustration* 38 (31 August 1861): 136.

122. Ibid., pp. 214–15, 226–27; Weisberg, *The Realist Tradition*, pp. 82 ff.; Gautier, *Les beaux-arts*, II, 62. Breton felt proud of the fact that he had eliminated the traditional biblical reference from his work—that he did the first modern picture of gleaners. Yet he certainly idealized rural chores; he preferred crepuscular moments when figures could be silhouetted and the effects of labor diluted. Discussing his *Weeders*, he recalled the original twilight scene that inspired it: "It was like a natural transfiguration of the

humblest of labors." He added further that never before did he understand so clearly "that work is a prayer." See Breton, *Un peintre paysan* (Paris, 1896), p. 111.

123. Ibid., p. 281.

124. Chesneau, *Les nations rivales dans l'art*, p. 306. The different attitudes of Breton and Millet on the question of work is related to their class backgrounds. Although both came from conservative well-to-do families, Millet's father was a farmer who worked the land, while Breton's father managed estates and workers for an aristocratic landowner. Breton's discomfort in the presence of poor people and indigents is revealed in his childhood memories of a trip he made with his father to collect payment from wood-cutters and lumber merchants. See Breton, *La vie d'un artiste*, pp. 93 ff., 98.

125. Gautier, *Les beaux-arts*, II, 23–24.

126. See G. Weisberg, "In Search of State Patronage: Three French Realists and the Second Empire 1851–1871," in *Essays in Honor of H. W. Janson* (New York, 1981), pp. 606 ff.

127. Kulstein, *Napoleon III*, pp. 54, 83–84, 74; Catalogue du Salon de 1857, No. 1584.

128. Weisberg, "François Bonhommé and Early Realist Images of Industrialization 1830–1870," *Arts Magazine* 50 (April 1980): 133; Kulstein, *Napoleon III*, pp. 85–87.

129. A. Carette, *Souvenirs intimes de la cour des Tuileries*, 3 vols. (Paris, 1889–91), I, 283 ff.

130. Weisberg, *The Realist Tradition*, p. 112; Kulstein, *Napoleon III*, p. 54; Vizetelly, *The Court of the Tuileries*, p. 167.

131. See the monumental study of G. Weisberg, *Bonvin* (Paris, 1979), p. 49.

132. Thoré, *Salons de W. Bürger*, I, 114–15.

133. Weisberg, *Bonvin*, pp. 67–68.

134. Weisberg, "Bonhommé," pp. 133–34.

135. Archives Nationales F²¹ 65, 120; J. F. Schnerb, "François Bonhommé," *Gazette des Beaux-Arts*, 4e ser., 9 (January 1913): 11 ff.; (February 1913): 132 ff.; K. Janke and M. Wagner, "Das Verhältnis von Arbeiter und Machinerie im Industriebild: Rekonstrucktion einer Bilderfolge zur Schwerindustrie von François Bonhommé," *Kritische Berichte* 5–6 (1976): 5 ff.; L. Nochlin, *Gustave Courbet: A Study of Style and Society* (New York, 1977), pp. 111 ff.; P. Le Nouëne, "Les soldats de l'industrie de François Bonhommé: l'idéologie d'un projet," *Les réalismes et l'histoire de l'art, Histoire et Critique des arts*, N. 4/5 (May 1978): 35 ff.; Weisberg, "Bonhommé," pp. 132 ff.; *The Realist Tradition*, pp. 71 ff.

136. Archives Nationales F²¹ 120, letter from Bonhommé to Courmont, 8 April 1862.

137. Weisberg, "Bonhommé," pp. 134–35. For the relationship between Schneider's position in society and his taste, see Boime, "Entrepreneurial Patronage in Nineteenth-Century France," in *Enterprise and Entrepreneurs in Nineteenth and Twentieth-Century France*, ed. E. C. Carter II, R. Forster, and J. N. Moody (Baltimore and London, 1976), pp. 137 ff. Schneider typifies the new breed cultivated by the Second Empire; the son of a notary, he served his apprenticeship in a bank and as manager of a local iron factory. Then with his brother as the financier and negotiator, he laid the foundations of the great complex of Le Creusot, which became the leading

producer of locomotives, steel rails, machinery, and armaments in France. He represented Le Creusot in parliament during the period 1852–70 and held the appointed offices of minister of agriculture, commerce, and public works (during the presidency of Louis Napoléon), and later, president of the Legislature. The government named him to committees for the organization of the World's Fairs and revered him as the founder of an immense industrial complex.

138. This approach is expressed in his own descriptions of pictures of Le Creusot prepared for the Ecole des mines: "1er tableau: le marteau pilon, machines et figures; 2eme tableau: vue générale du Creusot, exploitation figures; 3eme tableau: forge de laminoirs à rails, figures." See Archives Nationales F[21] 65, letter from Bonhommé to Tournois, 16 June 1857, and the accompanying sketches.

139. Morny started buying Meissonier's work in 1852: see C. C. Hungerford, "The Art of Jean-Louis-Ernest Meissonier: A Study of the Critical Years 1834 to 1855," Ph.D. diss., University of California, Berkeley, 1977, pp. 312–14, Nos. 43–44, 46, 50. For Morny's direct contact with the painter (although at a later date), see Gréard, Jean-Louis-Ernest Meissonier, p. 287. Three of the seven works Meissonier exhibited in the World's Fair of 1855 belonged to Morny. For studies of the Souvenir de guerre civile, see Clark, The Absolute Bourgeois, pp. 24 ff.; Hungerford, "Meissonier's Souvenir de guerre civile," Art Bulletin 61 (1979): 277 ff.

140. Hungerford, "Ernest Meissonier's First Military Paintings: II: '1814, The Campaign of France,' " Arts Magazine 54 (January 1980): 98 ff.

141. Gréard, Jean-Louis-Ernest Meissonier, p. 218.

142. For Alexander Herzen, see R. N. Stromberg, ed., Realism, Naturalism, and Symbolism: Modes of Thought and Expression in Europe, 1849–1914 (New York, 1968), pp. 1 ff.; Marx quoted by Nochlin, Realism (Harmondsworth and Baltimore, 1971), p. 60.

143. M. de Maupas, Mémoires sur le Second Empire (Paris, 1884), pp. 526, 530–31; I. de Saint-Amand, Napoléon III and his Court (New York, 1898), pp. 55 ff. La rixe, also unusual in its tumult, enjoyed a great success at the 1855 World's Fair. It shows two men putting an end to a fight in a cabaret. The central character, who steps in between the two rowdies and disarms the one at the right, bears a distinct resemblance to the emperor himself. We may recall that at this moment he was not only insuring peace at home by suppressing all factionalism but also waging war in the Crimea and intervening between Turkey and Russia. No wonder that he and Prince Albert—his ally in the Crimea—loved this work; the emperor bought it for 25,000 francs—astronomical for a genre picture—and then presented it to Albert as a gift.

144. Naturally, the relationship between the first Napoléon and his nephew was earnestly advertised at the outset of the Bonapartist campaign, but it was gradually modified to demonstrate that Napoléon III could stand on his own two feet. The meaning of the pendants by Meissonier is anticipated in the following statement by a Bonapartist apologist: "Un jour viendra peut-être où, au point de vue des intérêts de l'humanité, le plus beau titre de gloire de Napoléon Ier, ce sera d'avoir eté le precurseur de Napoléon III." In C. Sosthène-Berthellot, Essai sur le caractère et les tendances de l'Empereur Napoléon III (Paris, 1858), p. 339. For the Solferino commission and its background, see Hungerford, "Solferino," pp. 89–90.

145. A. Sensier, *La vie et l'oeuvre de J.-F. Millet* (Paris, 1881), pp. 187–88; Moreau-Nélaton, *Millet*, I, 108–109; R. Herbert, *Jean-François Millet* (Arts Council of Great Britain, 1976), pp. 82–83; Gautier, *Les beaux-arts*, II, 57–59.

146. See R. Cortissoz, *John La Farge* (Boston and New York, 1911), pp. 75 ff., for Saint-Victor's circle of Bonapartist writers, including About, Gautier, and Sainte-Beuve. Also About, *Salon de 1864*, p. 255.

147. Chesneau, *Les nations rivales*, pp. 307–308. For a superb study of the peasant in life as well as in art, see the catalogue by J. Thompson, M. F. Beaufort, and J. Horn, *The Peasant in French 19th Century Art* (The Douglas Hyde Gallery, Trinity College, Dublin, 1980).

148. J. C. Chamboredon, "Peinture des rapports sociaux et invention de l'éternel paysan: les deux manières de Jean-François Millet," *Actes de la recherche en sciences sociales*, No. 17/18 (November 1977): 6 ff.

149. Sensier, *La vie et l'oeuvre*, p. 238. See also Herbert, "City vs. Country: the Rural Image in French Painting from Millet to Gauguin," *Artforum* 8 (February 1970): 45 ff.

150. T. Silvestre, *Les artistes français*, 2 vols. (Paris, 1926), I, 185 ff., 193. For his connections with the government, see Poulet-Malassis, *Papiers secrets*, pp. 92–95. Silvestre considered Napoléon III as the "Père et sauveur de la patrie," and claimed that the Second Empire replaced the Second Republic "pour le salut de notre pays."

151. Sensier quoted in Herbert, *Jean-François Millet*, p. 142.

152. About, *Salon de 1864*, p. 162.

153. For Courbet's presentation of the social structure of the countryside and the responses of the Parisian audience, see Clark, *Image of the People*, pp. 140 ff.; P. Mainardi, "Gustave Courbet's Second Scandal: 'Les demoiselles de Village'" *Arts Magazine* 53 (January 1979): 95 ff. Clark's and Mainardi's thesis is confirmed in part by the review in the *Messager* of 25 February 1851, where the critic notes on Courbet's *Burial:* "Quant à la laideur prétendue du bourgeois d'Ornans, elle n'a rien d'exagéré, rien de faux; elle est vraie, elle est simple. C'est la laideur de la province, qu'il importe de distinguer de la laideur de Paris." Quoted in Merson, *La peinture*, p. 214. Merson uses the quotation to preface his discussion of Lambron's *Réunion des amis*, a work also having for its subject a funeral ceremony with a bizarre cast of characters. Merson, however, places the artist and his presentation midway between the Neo-Greeks and the radical realists Courbet and Millet. (Ibid., pp. 213, 215 ff.).

154. *Courbet raconté par lui-même*, pp. 79 ff.

155. For the official correspondence on Courbet's show, see Archives Nationales F[21] 521A, letter from Prefect of Police to Minister of State, 1 May 1855, Minister of State to Prefect, April 1855, and between de Mercey and Prefect, 26 April 1855. See also Archives Nationales F[21] 2793, "Exposition universelle des Beaux-Arts, 1855," for the Procès–Verbaux of the Admission jury, sessions No. 10, 13 for Courbet's entries (no deliberations but list of rejects and admits). The *Meeting* seems to have been problematic for the jury, but was finally accepted because it belonged to the wealthy and influential Bruyas. See also Archives Nationales F[21] 520, where the *Atelier* is subtitled "résumé d'études, de 1848 à 1855." ("Notice des ouvrages," No. 5840.)

156. Troubat, *Une amitié*, p. 110; Riat, *Gustave Courbet*, pp. 144–45. Courbet bought shares in the "Chemins de fer autrichiens," a firm registered on 22 February 1855 and subsidized by the government.

157. P. J. Proudhon, *Manuel du spéculateur à la Bourse,* 5e. ed. (Paris, 1857); pp. 177–78. The "Chemins de fer autrichiens" is listed on pp. 432–33, while the term "actionnaires" pervades the entire book. For an alternative view on the relationship between Courbet and Proudhon and the way it affects the *Atelier,* see J. H. Rubin, *Realism and Social Vision in Courbet and Proudhon* (Princeton, 1980).

158. Troubat, *Une amitié,* pp. 181–82, 181n.

Aspects of Berlin Realism

From the Prosaic to the Ugly

Françoise Forster-Hahn **4**

The Debate between Goethe and Schadow:
The Prosaic Spirit of Berlin Art

THE FUNDAMENTAL RIFT BETWEEN "idealistic" and "realistic" art that characterized most art criticism in Germany throughout the nineteenth century was first explicitly debated when Goethe reviewed the Berlin Art Exhibition of 1802.[1] Three years later Goethe elaborated his aesthetic further in *Winckelmann und sein Jahrhundert* (1805), where he very clearly distinguished between an idealistic and a realistic or "characteristic" trend in art, classifying Johann Joachim Winckelmann, Karl Friedrich Lessing, Anton Raphael Mengs, and Asmus Jacob Carstens under the first, and the critic Alois Hirt and the artist Johann Gottfried Schadow under the second category.[2] For Goethe, the idealistic concept embraces all artists who submit to the standards of classical antiquity and therefore regard beauty as the highest purpose of all art, whereas those who defend the realist concept rank the "characteristic" above beauty. Goethe not only defines these two diametrically opposed principles in theory but—in accordance with this aesthetic—recognizes the same divergent tendencies in the practice of art. More important, he attaches a clear value judgment to these two opposing concepts, ranking the idealistic point of view above the realistic, because the highest form of beauty does not exclude the characteristic but rather ennobles it.

When Hermann Riegel published his *Geschichte des Wiederauflebens der deutschen Kunst* (1882)[3] he essentially followed Goethe's system of classification, recognizing the historical roots of nineteenth-century German art in these two antithetical views, which developed almost simultaneously at the turn of the eighteenth century. The majority of German nineteenth-century critics and artists conformed with this value judgment equating the realistic or characteristic with the prosaic, trivial, and ugly, while identifying the idealistic with supreme beauty, the noble, and the sublime. This dominant belief in the essentially idealistic nature of art was mainly responsible for the complete separation of art and the aesthetic sphere from the political and social structure. Hence, "the temple of art"—to use one of the favorite metaphors of the century—was elevated high above the realities of contemporary life.

The antithesis of these two radically different approaches to art emerged in public debate for the first time when Goethe criticized Berlin art four years before the publication of his Winckelmann essay. Goethe published his critical review of the Berlin Art Exhibition of 1802 in the *Propyläen* and Schadow responded in the journal *Eunomia*, attempting to defend the "prosaic" spirit of Berlin art.[4] In his essay "Flüchtige Übersicht über die Kunst in Deutschland," Goethe made the following harsh judgment about art in Berlin:

> Besides the individual merit of well-known masters, there seems to be at home in Berlin naturalism with its demand for reality and usefulness, and the prosaic spirit of the time manifests itself there most of all. Poetry is displaced by history, character and the ideal by portrait, symbolic treatment by allegory, landscape by views, general humanity by the narrowly patriotic. . . .[5]

In his own defense, Schadow responded to the individual and specific criticisms, replying to each one of them with what he thought were the true elements of the state of art in Berlin. Though Schadow's essay is by no means a fully developed theory of realism, his analysis contains some major ideas that we have now come to understand as the essential principles of a realist aesthetic. His statements are neither didactic nor programmatic but rather form a detailed series of responses to the specific critical points Goethe had raised and directed at the essence of Berlin art. In his opening remarks Schadow takes up the criticism of naturalism being most at home in Berlin. By giving his own definition of the term, he turns the negative meaning Goethe had implied into an altogether positive statement: "A naturalist is someone who practices an art without having learned it from another master (professor) or in a school. . . ."[6] As to the accusation that naturalism demands reality and usefulness, he counters:

> This, in my view, means: that one prefers here such works of art which have been portrayed faithfully and honestly after a given

model; or: every work of art is treated here as a portrait or likeness.
I would be glad if we possessed a characteristic sense of art and
though this is regarded in the *Propyläen* as belonging on the bottom
rung, it is nevertheless the only one that will enable us Germans
to produce works of art in which one would see us as ourselves.[7]

This demand for creation of art based on a faithful observation
of nature (the model) rejects all imitation of art, Greek or French.
Schadow emphasizes the precise knowledge of how to make art,
because such an almost craftmanslike professional attitude is the
only way toward a truthful representation of nature. His aim is the
specific and individual, not the general and ideal. In landscape painting, he ranks the Dutch higher than Poussin;[8] among the English artists,
he favors Hogarth because of the "Englishness" of his art, and he
appreciates the "energy" of contemporary British caricatures. Since
he himself published caricatures against the French, he was well
aware of the critical powers of ridicule.[9]

Again and again Schadow polemicizes against the imitation of art.
Because art should be specific and individual, Schadow argues, it is
always also patriotic. He sharply contradicts Goethe's contention that
there cannot be any patriotic or national art since all art and science
are rooted in a general, timeless humanity. Goethe, who defended the
idealism of the classical tradition, was unable to reconcile with this
ideal the individualistic and specific traits of Berlin art, which was
more directed toward a faithful representation of historical and contemporary reality. A generation later Adolph Menzel used the term
"authenticity" to describe this rational and scientific approach to
art.[10] Though Schadow's statements do not yet form a lucid program
or theory, his main ideas point toward a realist aesthetic and honestly
reflect the practice and production of art as well as the prevalent taste
in the Prussian capital.

The Local Tradition

When Edmond Duranty analyzed the roots of Menzel's art, he immediately pointed to the local tradition and recognized both Chodowiecki and Schadow as the two most important artists who had
mainly shaped the very specific character of the city's art, Berlin's
"early realism."[11] Menzel himself paid tribute to Chodowiecki when
he executed a life-size portrait of the older artist for the *Versammlungs-
lokal* of the *Verein Berliner Künstler* in 1859, depicting him leaning
against the wooden railing on the Jannowitz Bridge, sketching after
nature, his gaze attentively aimed at a spot outside the picture itself
(fig. 4.1). Significantly, Menzel did not paint the traditional image
of the artist at work in his studio but chose a situation that captures

him in his local urban environment, at a moment when he is concentrating on his studies after nature.[12] Five years later, in 1864, Menzel paid homage to the other great artist of the Berlin tradition, Gottfried Schadow. To celebrate his hundredth birthday on 20 May 1864, Menzel composed a commemorative print (fig. 4.2),[13] in which the dark tailor's workshop of Schadow's father and the infant artist in his cradle are surrounded by his major monuments: the statues of Frederick the Great are on the left, the one of General Zieten is in the right foreground, and the funerary monument of the young Count von der Mark serves as a unifying backdrop. In the decorative border Menzel assembled the names of artists whom Duranty had called "la famille de la vérité, de la philosophie morale et de l'observation."[14] Though critics today would hardly see Watteau, Mengs, or Piranesi in that tradition, Schlüter, Chodowiecki, and Hogarth certainly stand for an art founded on faithful observation and moral purpose.

Art in Berlin was, indeed, directed toward the sincere representation of the material world and was more intensely rooted in the artist's own experience than aimed at the imitation of the classical tradition or the timeless ideal. The austerity of Prussian life was well expressed in Chodowiecki's modest but matter-of-fact prints; his descriptive and reportage-like scenes of contemporary and historical reality earned him the name "the German Hogarth," and indeed, he had learned a great deal from his namesake. The simplicity and intimacy of his engraving *Cabinet d'un Peintre* of 1772 (fig. 4.3),[15] which shows the artist drawing in the company of his family, established a tradition that Menzel later continued with his etching *Family by Lamplight* of 1843 (fig. 4.4).[16] Chodowiecki's historical illustrations (fig. 4.5) are of convincing documentary character because he depicted his subjects in a telling moment and with such psychological insight that these small prints easily bridged historical distance and became popular interpretations of the past. As no trace of idealization embellishes his historical scenes, no ornamental extravagance or frivolity distracts from his sincere and often humorous descriptions of contemporary bourgeois life. It was this genuinely bourgeois and democratic nature of his art that made it an inspirational source for the later generation of German realists.

When Schadow countered Goethe's reproach that naturalism was at home in Berlin, he responded that he understood these critical remarks to mean that "every work of art was being treated here as a portrait or likeness." In his own sculptures he attempted to reconcile the timeless ideal of the prevailing neoclassical taste with his own personal belief in an art based upon observation of nature and aimed at the specific and individual. In Berlin the controversy between the idealistic and naturalistic approaches to art had crystallized in the so-called costume controversy, in which partisans of both sides debated whether an historical or political figure should be portrayed in classical garb or in contemporary costume. In his own design for a monument of Frederick the Great, Schadow had first envisaged an equestrian statue in idealized classical garments but later opted for a design that would show the king in contemporary dress. In his *Monument of General Zieten* (1774), Schadow had already decided for historical accuracy by portraying Zieten in his uniform and emphasizing the individual and biographical traits in the historical scenes around the pedestal rather than by "elevating" the portrait with allegorical figures. The narrative scenes testify to a profound study of history and to the artist's realist tendencies, which prompted him even in the execution of a public monument to express the individual and characteristic. While in his *Statue of Frederick the Great* at Stettin (unveiled 1793), he depicted the king in his general's uniform but added to it some symbolic attributes in order to portray him both as soldier and king, in 1822 he created an entirely private and personal image in the small bronze *Frederick and His Whippets* (fig. 4.6). As he wrote to his son Ridolfo, he had modeled the half-size figure as a pastime; he described it as "prosaic," now using the term to indicate scrupulous observation of nature and a precise characterization of the individual.[17] Schlüter's *Heads of Dying Warriors* for the façade of the Berlin Arsenal (1698–1700), Chodowiecki's documentary prints, and Schadow's sculptures, with their perceptive psychological insight, indeed form the impressive local tradition of an art founded on the sincere study of reality and essentially bourgeois in its nature.

Toward a New History Painting

It is this local tradition that inspired Menzel in his own ardent search for "authenticity" when he began to illustrate Franz Kugler's biography of Frederick the Great in 1839.[18] *The History of Frederick the Great,* "written by Franz Kugler, drawn by Adolph Menzel," is not only a milestone in the development of central European wood-engraving and book illustration; it is first and foremost a decisive step toward the realization of an entirely new conception of depicting history. Menzel must have been well aware of the innovative nature of these small illustrations, since he based all of the paintings that he executed during the 1850s on these black-and-white wood engravings (fig. 4.7). When Menzel first exhibited his paintings of the life of Frederick the Great, *The Dinner Conversation* (1850; fig. 4.8)[19] and *The Flute Recital* (1852; fig. 4.9),[20] they were severely criticized and immediately relegated from the rank of history painting to the category of historical genre. Menzel did not depict the king in "world historic" moments but rather in his private life, in such telling scenes as the one showing him in animated conversation with Voltaire. He conceived of Frederick as the philosopher on the throne, the enlightened monarch who paved the way for bourgeois freedom, the father of his people. Seen in the context of the tense political atmosphere in the years immediately preceding the revolution of 1848, the choice of subject matter, the scientific study of it, and the direct close-up views of "daguerreotypical"[21] precision reveal the artist in step with the progressive forces of his own time. When Menzel actually began to translate the illustrations into the medium of formal history paintings, the political outlook had radically changed, from optimistic hope before the revolution to the disappointment of its failure. Therefore his history paintings met with neither understanding from the critics nor acceptance from the state, because he did not elevate his subject into the timeless realm of permanence but rather created scenes of a highly momentary character, incisive fragments cut from historical reality.

Menzel created the counterconcept of a new realist history painting, confronting the monumental idealism of the cycles that Peter Cornelius and Wilhelm von Kaulbach designed in Berlin during these same years. Once more the old conflict between idealism and realism crystallized in the definition of history and its appropriate visualization. William IV, the "romantic" of the Prussian kings, had given Cornelius and Kaulbach commissions for important public works. Cornelius arrived in 1840 and began to execute the large cartoons for the never-completed fresco cycles of the cathedral and the camposanto. Kaulbach decorated the stairwell of the New Museum from 1847 to 1863. With theatrical staging and in a highly eclectic style, Kaulbach depicted the highlights of human history and—like Cornelius—painted the "idea" of great world-historic developments (fig. 4.10). Neither Cornelius nor Kaulbach represented concrete events but removed historical reality into the distant sphere of a well-ordered hierarchical system of idealized images, elevated and intellectualized by traditional allegorical motifs. It was against this ideal, monumentalized vision of history favored by Berlin authorities and destined for the city's public buildings that Menzel projected his own scrutinized close-up images of the past.

In his dramatic nighttime scene of *Frederick the Great and his Men at Hochkirch 1758* (1856; fig. 4.11),[22] he depicted the surprise raid on the Prussians by the Austrian Army. The hasty and disorderly counterattack by the Prussians fills two-thirds of the picture, the crowding of the scene being emphasized by the cropping of the frame and the overall direction of soldiers and weapons toward the left, aiming at an enemy that cannot be seen. In the background, in the middle of the melee, appears the king himself on horseback, an almost demonic figure in whose intense face the overwhelming tension of the moment seems to be concentrated. Soon after its completion, in 1858, Menzel sent this painting to the *deutsche allgemeine und historische Kunst-Ausstellung* in Munich, where, according to one critic, it not only caused a violent controversy but also became the banner and rallying point for the new realist tendency. This critic—like most others—found fault with the dim lighting, the rather small figure of the king crowded in the middle ground, and, above all, the confusion resulting from the fact that the artist had only painted "one-half" of the scene, namely the attack on an invisible enemy. The decline of history painting, which he saw as degraded from the ideal to the human level, was, in his view, a parallel to modern historical scholarship, whose authors understood history no longer "as the results of general ideas, but always as a consequence of specific (individual) personalities."[23] If the artist represented this individual historical figure in a precise, telling, momentary situation rather than imbuing the scene with some transcendent permanence, he could not hope to have his work accepted as serious history painting. The *Hochkirch* canvas thus was consigned for many years to a small antechamber in the Berlin palace, where the pages washed the teacups for His Majesty. Only much later, after Bismarck had energetically turned the wheel of Prussian history toward the formation of the German Empire, did the last kaiser have the painting installed above his desk, demonstrating his awareness of the political power of art and showing himself attuned to the ideas of the new era.[24] Now that the newly founded empire was in desperate need of historical and national identity, both the figure of Frederick II and Menzel's images were immediately interpreted in a fiercely patriotic sense.

But in 1857 Menzel's next large history painting met with the same fate as the *Hochkirch* canvas. He painted *The Meeting of Frederick II and Joseph II* (fig. 4.12)[25] on commission of the "Verbindung für historische Kunst," choosing the moment when Frederick II met the young Austrian emperor for the first time in the bishop's palace in Neisse, where the king was staying at the time. The king has come down the staircase to greet Joseph, who has left his entourage behind, a group almost completely immersed in the darkness of the vaulted staircase. The illustration in Kugler's book does not yet reveal the dramatic intensity of the painting, in which the physical closeness of the two monarchs forms the structural and psychological focal point of the scene. Why did Menzel choose this scene for a large painting? Kugler stresses in his text how much Joseph admired Frederick's policies because he, too, was filled with the ardent desire to "pave the way for freedom of the human mind."[26] Menzel painted the moment of their first encounter because to him it seemed to symbolize the ideas of the Enlightenment, peace, and freedom. A Berlin critic, however, saw in it only "a warning example of artistic aberration. Menzel paints without a trace of that higher characterization which would betoken in the person in question a representation of an historical idea."[27] The critics and the public alike were unable to accept this innovative form of history painting; nor did they see its equally progressive message.[28] In a letter of these years Menzel commented on the artistic situation. He was well aware that all new art was "partisanship" and that such large official exhibitions as the one in Munich in 1858 were "a wide arena for all dogmas." "Everybody who follows in whatever branch of intellectual production the direction of his own disposition without asking around, can above all be sure of only one thing: condemnation from the side of long-established authority. . . ."[29]

No wonder that his largest history painting, *Frederick the Great's Address to His Generals before the Battle at Leuthen* (1859),[30] which was also the most innovative in painterly terms, remained unfinished. For years it was stacked in his studio—with some of the faces rather brutally scraped out of the completed parts—and nothing could persuade Menzel to finish this canvas. Meissonier admired the unfinished canvas in Berlin and was inspired by it to begin his own cycle of Napoleon paintings, starting with *The Campaign in France 1814*, which depicted the retreat of Napoleon's army. In 1861, while at work on his *Leuthen* canvas, Menzel received the commission to commemorate the *Coronation of William I* at Königsberg on 18 October 1861.[31] After all the criticism of his historical paintings, this commission is even more surprising because he had not gained a reputation for contemporary scenes. His only earlier painting of contemporary history remained an entirely private work, the *Funeral of the Fallen of the March Revolution*. This painting commemorated the revolution of 1848 and represented the one hopeful moment of those turbulent days when the king had virtually been regarded as a prisoner of the people. When Menzel became disillusioned with the revolution, he left the painting unfinished. The *Coronation*, a state commission and a public work, meant the end of the artist's innovative interpretation of Prussian history, which was now replaced by a truly incisive, yet often ambivalent, documentation of the present. Once again the local tradition of Berlin's early realism, reflecting the essentially bourgeois and democratic tendencies of the city, proved to be the most inspiring force.

The Urban Environment

So intense was the interest in, and identification with, the urban environment and its "metropolitan" life that Franz Krüger (1797–1857) transformed even the official representation of royal parades into

popular scenes of bourgeois participation. In 1824, Krüger received
a commission from Grand Duke Nicholas of Russia, son-in-law of the
Prussian king, to paint the *Parade in the Opera Square*, which had
taken place on the occasion of his visit to Berlin in 1822 (fig. 4.13).[32]
The commission was certainly intended not only to commemorate
the military spectacle but also to celebrate the union of the two royal
houses and the political alliance between Russia and Prussia. At the
parade, the grand duke appeared in Prussian uniform to present to
his father-in-law the sixth Brandenburg Cuirassier Regiment, of which
he was commander. For five years, from 1824 to 1829, Krüger worked
intensely on this major artistic enterprise, making numerous preparatory sketches after life and individual drawings of portraits and uniforms, with each detail carefully studied for its authenticity. In 1830
the painting was exhibited at the Berlin Academy and later was publicly shown in the Winter Palace at St. Petersburg, where it met with
great popular success.

The idea of depicting a military parade was not a new one in
Berlin. Ten years earlier the local artist Anton Schrader had painted
a parade in front of the Royal Palace, and in 1822 Charles Vernet's
Fahnenweihe Preussischer Regimenter auf dem Marsfeld zu Paris
(1814) had been exhibited at the Berlin Academy. Thus Krüger, until
then primarily known for his objective, cool, and yet attractive portraits, as well as his paintings of hunting scenes and horses, could
turn to earlier models of formal representations of royal and military
power. How then did Krüger tackle his task? To get a wide overview
of the scene, he situated himself at a window of the arsenal overlooking
the square of the opera house and a portion of *Unter den Linden* in
the background. The parade takes place in the morning; bright sunshine illuminates the northern side of the square: represented are
Schinkel's guard house, only recently built, Rauch's monuments and,
visible in the background, the upper portion of the university building.
The southern side of the square is alternately dipped in shade and
light: visible are the Palace of the Princesses in the left foreground, cut
by the frame, followed by the bronze statue of Blücher, the opera
house, and the library. The entire front of the public buildings leads
diagonally into the deep space of the scene, which is closed off by
the trees of the Linden Alley. From there the regiment led by Nicholas
on horseback approaches the king, who is seated on a white horse
reviewing the parade. While the royal onlookers are placed in the
shade in front of the *Prizessinnenpalais*, appearing as small, anonymous-looking figures, the milling crowd opposite, in the right foreground—brilliantly illuminated by the sun—attracts all the attention
of the viewer. "Tout Berlin" has assembled here, and all those who
played a prominent role in the cultural life of the city can easily

be recognized. The singer Henriette Sontag is standing upright in a carriage with Paganini at her side, both framed by the green foliage of the trees. In front of her—closer to the viewer—stand the director of the Academy, Gottfried Schadow, the architect Karl Friedrich Schinkel, the sculptor Christian Rauch, and many more. While the royal and military participants in the parade actually were all present, this group of proud citizens is entirely fictitious. Paganini was not even in the city at the time and visited Berlin only in 1828, when Krüger was at work on the painting. Nevertheless, the casual grouping and individual characterizations give this scene convincing reality. In contrast, the main protagonists, the Prussian king and the Russian grand duke, appear as small figures without any specific personal features—they are recognizable only by their uniforms and their position during the very moment of the parade that Krüger chose to paint. The military spectacle is, indeed, taking place in the central part of the composition, but, because of their distance from the viewer, the two main figures are in no way rendered conspicuous. Closest to the viewer is the group of prominent and proud citizens. The lively and animated effect is achieved not only by the exact psychological portrayal of each individual but also by the depiction of different social classes and the fact that each person seems to turn toward a different direction—some actually moving toward the viewer outside the painting and thus creating the illusion that the viewer himself is part of the event. Compositional structure with a strong emphasis on creating deep space, unifying atmospheric light, and the movement of the crowd all reinforce the impression of an urban rather than a military scene. Thus the artist turns his royal commission for a formal painting of a military parade into a portrayal of contemporary urban life in Berlin. He transforms a very specific historical event of propagandistic political purpose into the proud display of those Berlin citizens who have given the city its architectural and intellectual shape!

In his view of the *Klosterstrasse* (1830; fig. 4.14),[33] painted two years after the *Parade*, Eduard Gaertner (1801–77) continued the local tradition of integrating into views of the city portraits of those who played a vital role in shaping its urban layout and cultural life. We see at the right the so-called *Beuth'sche Gewerbeinstitut* built by Schinkel in 1827–29, toward the back, the tower of the Parochial Church, and to the left, on the opposite side of the street, in the shade, the so-called storehouse, where the sculptor Rauch had his studio. Integrated into the busy flow of daily street life are the portraits of Rauch standing in front of his studio and the painter Franz Krüger on horseback in the middle of the street, greeting the artist of this painting, Gaertner, who walks towards him from the right side. To the right, in front of "their" building, are the patron Beuth (with cap) and his architect Schinkel in black top hat. The sky is overcast; a diffuse sunlight falls onto the façades at the right, while the shadows cast by the houses on the left side of the street form a pattern of dark and light areas on the street itself. The depth of the composition, the sharp precision of the architecture, the atmospheric light, and the individual characterization of the figures in the foreground all create the illusion of an almost photographic realism. Yet what seems to be a random view of a segment of the city is far more than a mere reproduction of its architecture: by placing the figure of Krüger prominently in the center, Gaertner paid homage to the older painter, whose art he greatly admired. And by integrating into the architectural portrayal of the city a number of its most prominent artists, Gaertner transformed the traditional *vedute* into a telling cultural and historical document that testifies to the essentially bourgeois character of Berlin's realism.

A year later, in 1831, Johann Erdmann Hummel (1769–1852), professor of perspective at the Berlin Academy, commemorated one of the great local events of that year in a series of four paintings. *The Granite Basin in the Berlin Lustgarten* (fig. 4.15)[34] shows the placement of the large granite basin—seven meters in diameter and cut from one single block—in front of Schinkel's Old Museum, a building that remains invisible in the painting. The highly polished basin, elevated on a temporary construction, is the focus of the composition, which is framed at the left by the old cathedral and in the background by the Royal Palace. The bright sunshine cuts buildings and people sharply from their surroundings and stresses the firm contours defining all objects. The somewhat stiff figures standing around the basin are reflected in its shiny surface, thus appearing twice in the painted scene. As Krüger and Gaertner did not just depict anonymous passers-by, Hummel included specific portraits: to the left, *Baurat* Cantian, the site planner, and at the right, Hummel's two sons and a cousin. Thus, the artist emphasized the civic nature of the occasion when the most central of public squares—surrounded by the Old Museum, the cathedral, the Royal Palace and the arsenal—was given a significant new accent with the granite basin.

For one of his major works, *Unter den Linden* (1853; fig. 4.16),[35] Gaertner chose a view of the splendid main boulevard of Berlin framed by some of the city's most famous buildings and monuments. Gaertner faced the opposite direction from the view Krüger had used for his painting of the *Parade in the Opera Square* years earlier. Perhaps the most prominent feature in Gaertner's painting is Rauch's *Monument of Frederick II* (1840–51) in the right foreground, followed by the opera house. On the opposite side, we see in the left foreground, cut by the frame, part of the old academy building, then the university and the arsenal. As in all his views of the city, the people appear as small figures, because the conceptual and compositional scale is determined by the architecture. The very idea of giving a "view" imposes the distance between us and the topographical site depicted in the painting. Gaertner created topographically concise images of the city, in which the solid permanence of the buildings overpowers the scenes of human activity. Though this contrast is somewhat reconciled by the unifying atmospheric light and the verisimilitude of street life, the emphasis is on topographical accuracy and not on the human condition. The people, who are about their daily business, are included but remain entirely subservient to the architecture.

Only a more radical realist was able to shorten the distance between us and the image of the city. A new analytical understanding of the modern city was needed to capture, in innovative scenes, the changed conditions of urban life. When Menzel painted his close-up views of the modern crowd, topographical accuracy was no longer of any significance. His most radically novel paintings of city life were all the result of his visits and experiences in Paris. Menzel visited Paris for the first time on the occasion of the World Exposition in 1855, where he may well have seen Courbet's one-man show and come into contact with the then controversial ideas of a new realist aesthetic. We know little about this first stay in the French capital, but one of the most innovative contemporary scenes of the period, the *Theâtre Gymnase*, was painted right after his return to Berlin in 1855.[36] It seems that the experience of Paris set free his own artistic imagination and confirmed him in his search for "authenticity." Menzel returned to the French capital in 1867 to see the World Exposition and was drawn there again the following year, when he exhibited several works at the Salon. Immediately upon returning to Berlin, he painted *Sunday in the Tuileries Gardens* (1867; fig. 4.17)[37] and *Weekday in Paris* (1869; fig. 4.18).[38] In *Sunday in the Tuileries Gardens*, Menzel captured in a close-up view the pleasures and pastimes of the people of Paris, a milling crowd that is made up of all social classes and generations. As in Krüger's *Parade*, diagonals lead into the background to create pictorial space that accommodates the multitude of diverse types, whose movements point into different directions, often toward the viewer and out of the painted scene. The cropping by the frame, the density of the moving crowd, and the distinct sharpness of each individual motif in conception and artistic detail all create a fragmentary scene of highly momentary character. The title and scene of the painting seem to indicate that Menzel was inspired by Manet's *Concert in the Tuileries Gardens*, which he may have seen in 1867. The differences, however, between these two park scenes also reveal

Menzel's more radical conception: Manet composed a group portrait of his friends in a modern setting and arranged the homogeneous assembly in a well-structured composition, parallel to the picture plane. Menzel takes a slightly elevated viewpoint and, by cutting deep diagonal alleys leading into the background, creates a pictorial organization that is congenial to the diversity of his crowd. Critics have always been irritated by the number of caricatural elements that disturb the harmony and balance of the scene. These satirical components have their source in popular graphics, such as E. Guérard's lithograph *The Tuileries—allée des feuillants* of 1856 (fig. 4.19), which provided artists with an uninhibited visualization of city life. It is precisely this "extreme faithfulness" or "ugliness"—the loss of harmony—which makes up the broad and essentially independent and unprejudiced view of urban life that can only be experienced in a multitude of individual fragments. In *Weekday in Paris,* Menzel captured the bustling atmosphere of a workday in the city, integrating not only a myriad of individually observed details but also the building activities that changed the architectural and urban fabric of the city. And yet, despite the precision of observation, the artist did not render an accurately chosen topographical site but fused into a convincing image of the metropolis fragments "cut from reality" and his own painfully modern experience of the changed conditions of human life, of fragmentation and alienation.

Their almost identical size and, even more so, the dialectical relationship of their themes indicate that the artist regarded these two paintings as a complementary pair: one depicting leisure, the other work. Though each one of them seems to represent with photographic realism (which was, incidentally, the criticism most often advanced against them) a specific part of Paris, the numerous sketches done on the spot prove the composite nature of these compositions. Menzel's belief in a rational understanding of the world prompted him to approach his art with a scientific rigor and a tireless effort to study the minutest detail. While he analyzed in his sketchbook and, later, in drawings after the model each individual detail, he struggled to comprehend the whole. Menzel seems to have held a powerful inner vision of the complete work while he synthesized these individually studied details into the image on canvas. He no longer executed studies of the entire composition, and contemporary witnesses described in amazement this creative process that was based on scrupulous observation of nature and an arrangement of these observations from the artist's memory. One critic friend compared Menzel's method to mosaic work. His montagelike procedure is, indeed, so convincing that contemporary critics singled out the extreme verisimilitude and often equated it with ugliness. French critics were more perceptive, and Duranty immediately recognized Menzel's unique ability to capture a modern crowd in which each individual was characterized according to his social class and generation and yet was part of the common movement.[39]

Like his two paintings of Paris, *King William's Departure on 31 July 1870* (fig. 4.20)[40] was painted a year after the event, in 1871, "from memory," commissioned by the Berlin collector Magnus Herrmann. Menzel depicted the moment when King William I left the capital to join the army, just about two weeks after the outbreak of the Franco-Prussian War. The king, accompanied by Queen Augusta, is driven in an open carriage along *Unter den Linden*, toward the Brandenburg Gate. The row of apartment houses to the right is decorated with black-and-white and black, white, and red flags fluttering in the wind. A little boy in the foreground is selling newspapers; the couple standing on the black cast-iron balcony are Herrmann's daughter and her husband, the landscape painter Albert Hertel, who was a close friend of Menzel's. Because the agitated crowd fills the largest portion of the painting, occupying the fore- and middle ground, the tiny figure of the king is almost completely obscured. The king's carriage is placed off-center, and while most of the people are looking or waving toward the monarch, there are others who turn away, disrupting the general direction of the crowd's movement. As in Krüger's *Parade* of 1829, the psychological center of attention—the king himself—is relegated to the middle ground and moved away from the center of the composition. The specific historical event now seems almost incidental, a mere pretense for the urban street scene in which the citizens of Berlin play the dominant role. But, in retrospect, the artist must have realized what a particularly fateful moment he had depicted. By the time Menzel was working on this canvas, the king had almost certainly returned as emperor of the newly created Reich. By choosing to paint a portrait of the crowd, the painter turned authentic documentation of this fateful event into sociological analysis.

The World of Industry and Labor:
The Art of Menzel and Liebermann in the 1870s

Those artists searching for a new pictorial language to express the drastic changes brought about by the industrial revolution and its effects on the human environment not only focused on urban themes but also recorded the transformation of the landscape. They depicted the powerful intrusion of industry into nature and the changes of the countryside caused by rapid industrialization. Carl Blechen's (1798–1840) *Iron Rolling Mill at Eberswalde* (1835; fig. 4.21)[41] finds its counterpart in Menzel's *Berlin-Potsdam Railroad*.[42] Blechen depicted

one of the first centers of the metal industries in the Mark Brandenburg, basing his small painting on a series of drawings that he had
made as preparatory studies (fig. 4.22). While in the drawing he describes industrial reality by focusing on the pile of cannonballs and
barrels in the foreground, he changes his viewpoint for the painting so
that it now includes the Finow canal with an idyllic boat scene.
Menzel painted his *Berlin-Potsdam Railroad* in 1847, nine years after
this first railroad in Prussia had opened. The sweeping curve of the
railroad tracks through the vast empty space links the silhouette of
the city along the horizon with the train in the foreground, stressing
the dynamic movement of the locomotive, which seems to rush toward
the viewer. Topographical accuracy, the expression of speed, and
the documentary character of the painting all make it a much more
realistic scene than Turner's *Rain, Steam and Speed* of just a few years
earlier. The same year that Blechen painted his *Iron Rolling Mill at
Eberswalde,* Alfred Rethel (1816–59) depicted *Hartkort's Factory*
in Wetter at the Rhur river.[43] Rethel poignantly called his work "portrayal of a landscape with industrial buildings" (iron foundry, iron
rolling mill, and blast furnace). Rethel, who was commissioned by the
entrepreneur, did, indeed, paint a portrait of industry, rendering the
industrial plant in close detail. Stripped of all idyllic elements, this
painting seems to be the first true depiction of an industrial site in
Germany, a portrait of an industrial plant in the strictest sense of
the term. But, like most of his contemporaries, Rethel showed only
the industrial site; he did not go inside the factory to paint an authentic
image of industrial labor. In many prints and watercolors and some
paintings of this early industrial period, artists portrayed factories
and mining areas, but they emphasized the architectural setting and
the dramatic lighting effects, while the workers appeared as small
anonymous figures in the relatively few scenes that depict labor.

It may be no coincidence that as early as 1852 Menzel's friend and
early critic Friedrich Eggers had pointed out the world of industry
as an appropriate theme for contemporary painters in an article *On
Themes for Genre and Landscape Painters* in the *Deutsches Kunstblatt.*[44] In this essay, the author advocated modern subject matter by
describing the iron works of Borsig in Berlin in exuberant tones that
betray his optimistic belief in technological and scientific progress. In
this rather romantic vision of industry, the author associates the image
of the modern workers with the figures of the cyclops, thus conveniently
overlooking social reality by elevating the subject into the realm of
mythology. Menzel himself was not entirely free from these conventions
when he first dealt with the subject of heavy industry.

In 1869, three years before he began to work on his monumental
painting *The Iron Rolling Mill* (1872–75; fig. 4.23),[45] he had been

commissioned to produce a memorial sheet—a small gouache painting—
on the occasion of the fiftieth anniversary of the Heckmann firm in
Berlin. In its odd combination of allegorical decoration and realistic
scenes of the iron foundry, the *Memorial Sheet for Heckmann* (fig.
4.24)[46] adheres to the nineteenth-century tradition of images celebrating industrial enterprise. Free of any restrictions, Menzel developed
the theme of the iron rolling mill on a large scale three years later,
in 1872. He painted this canvas—measuring 158 × 254 cm—for the Berlin banker Liebermann (uncle of the painter) and most probably
proposed the novel subject himself. In a letter to the director of the
National Gallery in Berlin, the artist himself gave a detailed description of the scene in order to correct the original catalogue entry for
future editions. He described the rolling of railroad tracks at Königshütte in Upper Silesia: "One looks at a long row of rollers, the first
of which is about to receive the bloom that has been taken from the
furnace. The two workers who have brought it up are occupied with
making the bloom glide under the cylinder by pushing up the shaft
of the wagon, while three others strive to direct the bloom with tongs."[47]
The workers on the other side are ready to return the bloom so it
can be rolled through the next cylinder, and so on, until the rail leaves
the production line. The small figure of the supervisor watching the
puddling furnace is not in the center but relegated to the middle
ground. Menzel was also very specific about the precise moment that
he chose: it is shortly before the shift change. While in the left background a group of workers washes up, others in the right foreground
are eating their lunch, which a young woman has brought in a basket.

Menzel made hundreds of preparatory sketches and studies, many
of them at Königshütte, where he spent several weeks in 1872 at a
time of economic crisis and violent conflicts between industry and
labor. He worked on his canvas intensely for three years, and when
news about this unusual theme for a monumental painting reached
the press, the comments were unequivocal: one did not think it
worthy of Menzel's talents to waste time on the representation of sooty
workers![48] The correspondence between the museum director and the
ministry that had to approve the acquisition of the painting, as well as
contemporary criticism, leaves no doubt about the controversial subject
matter. Most critics and the public alike conveniently overlooked the
social reality of the scene by reconciling the disturbing confrontation
with the image of the mythological Cyclops. Menzel's simple title
"The Iron Works" was transformed into "Modern Cyclops."

In contrast to artists who painted similar scenes of industry—for
example, Bonhommé in France—Menzel was free from the customary
restrictions imposed by commissions from industrialists. During the
early 1870s, Menzel's friend Paul Meyerheim also painted images of

industry, but he did so for the mansion of one of Berlin's pioneer entrepreneurs. In six murals for the loggia of Borsig's villa, Meyerheim recounted the production of locomotives, starting with the descent of miners and ending with the engine being hoisted on board ship. The idealized youthful workers in Meyerheim's *Forging the Locomotive Wheel* (1873; fig. 4.25)[49] contrast sharply with Menzel's "sooty workers." Stark ideological differences emerge from the comparison of Meyerheim's anecdotal narrative, replete with allusions to the Borsig family, and Menzel's unvarnished representation of the workers. If Meyerheim celebrates the entrepreneur and industrial progress, Menzel neglects the final product and focuses instead on the consequences of modern manufacturing for human life.

When Menzel began to work on his *Iron Rolling Mill*, the twenty-five-year-old Berlin artist Max Liebermann (1847–1935) painted his first major work, *Women Plucking Geese* (fig. 4.26).[50] In May of 1872 he exhibited the painting in Hamburg, sold it for 1000 *Thaler*, and with the proceeds traveled to Paris, where he saw for the first time paintings by Millet, Courbet, and Ribot. Shortly thereafter, in the autumn of 1872, he painted in a very short time his second scene of workers, *Women Cleaning Vegetables* (fig. 4.27).[51] In the first painting Liebermann depicts a group of robust older women in a dimly lit room plucking geese; in the second one he places the women who are cleaning vegetables for canning into a rigid pictorial arrangement, which matches the monotony of their work. No anecdotal element alleviates the earnestness of the scene; no sentimentality softens the oppressive atmosphere of collective work. Both paintings immediately earned the young artist such titles as "painter of dirt" and "apostle of ugliness." One critic who commented on the *Women Plucking Geese* praised the artist's technical ability and his truthfulness to life, but the brutality of the subject—plucking living geese to obtain down feathers— represented for him only the ugly, the ordinary, and the dull, and to such a degree that he almost shuddered looking at the scene. The straightforward honesty with which Liebermann uncovered the rather brutal exploitation of animals for the comfort of the well-to-do caused such a shock that it took another twenty years for Liebermann to gain recognition in his hometown.

In the last decade of the nineteenth century, the conflict between the traditional aesthetic values of the past and the necessities of the present, the new social function of art in modern society, drew an even sharper line between authority and opposition. The controversies of the 1890s, which had their roots in the 1870s, erupted in a vital burst of the naturalist movement in literature and the theater and ultimately led to the foundation of the Berlin *Secession* in 1898, whose president Liebermann became the following year. In 1890 August Strindberg published a defense of realism on the stage in a Berlin journal. His programmatic statement on the meaning and purpose of realism in the theater applies equally to the visual arts:

> The Realists have been accused of seeking the ugly. . . . We Realists have been accused of worse, namely of being Naturalists.
> This is a title of honor for us! We love nature, we turn away in disgust from the new social conventions. Because we hate what is contrived and recherché, we like to call all things by their name, and we believe that the present society will collapse, unless the most noble consensus, on which all societies rest, is restored: honesty itself.[52]

At the end of the century, when Gerhart Hauptmann's play *The Weavers* was prohibited in Berlin by the government, and Käthe Kollwitz published her first accusing prints of social conditions, the old controversy between idealism and realism still divided the established from the progressive forces. The prosaic was now called "the ugly," and the critical content and politically explosive nature of such art was well understood by the government. At the beginning of our own century, this tradition of disrespect and criticism of social and artistic conventions would be continued and forcefully voiced by the expressionists and the artists of the New Objectivity, who replaced the more cautious and often ambivalent attitude of the nineteenth century with a pungent ideological language.

NOTES

1. Hermann Grimm gives an extremely lucid analysis of this debate by explaining the development of realism and realist art as the result of life in the large cities of central Europe; cf. *Goethe und der Bildhauer Gottfried Schadow, Sonderabdruck aus der Vierteljahrschrift für Litteraturgeschichte*, [1888], pp. 13–14.

2. *Winckelmann und sein Jahrhundert. In Briefen und Aufsätzen herausgegeben von Goethe* (Tübingen, 1805). Cf. also Herman Riegel, *Geschichte des Wiederauflebens der deutschen Kunst zu Ende des 18. und Anfang des 19. Jahrhunderts. Ein Beitrag zur Geschichte der allgemeinen Wiedergeburt des deutschen Volkes*, 2d ed. (Leipzig, 1882), pp. 181–82.

3. Cf. also Herman Riegel, *Peter Cornelius. Festschrift* (1883).

4. *Propyläen* 3, II: 167. Gottfried Schadow, "Über einige in den Propyläen abgedruckte Sätze Goethe's, die Ausübung der Kunst in Berlin betreffend," *Eunomia, eine Zeitschrift des neunzehnten Jahrhunderts, herausgegeben von Fessler und Rhode* I (1801). Reprinted in Julius Friedlaender (ed.), *Gottfried Schadow, Aufsätze und Briefe nebst einem Verzeichnis seiner Werke*, 2d ed. (Stuttgart, 1890), pp. 44–55. Previously published by Friedlaender, who discovered Schadow's essay, in 1864 (Düsseldorf) as a separate supplement to the first edition of *Aufsätze und Briefe*.

5. Translations from both Goethe and Schadow are my own, here quoted after Friedlaender, *Schadow* (1864), p. 5.

6. Ibid.

7. Ibid., p. 6.

8. Ibid., pp. 12–13.

9. Ibid, p. 18.

10. H. Wolff, *Adolph von Menzel: Briefe*, intro. Oskar Bie (Berlin, 1914), p. 27.

11. Edmond Duranty, "Adolph Menzel," *Gazette des beaux-arts* XXI (1880): 202.

12. Konrad Kaiser, *Der frühe Realismus in Deutschland 1800–1850. Gemälde und Zeichnungen aus der Sammlung Georg Schäfer, Schweinfurt*, exhibition Germanisches Nationalmuseum Nürnberg, 1967, no. 178. The painting, oil on canvas, measures 197 × 113 cm.

13. Elfried Bock, *Adolph Menzel. Verzeichnis seines graphischen Werkes*, Berlin, 1923, no. 392.

14. Duranty, in *Gazette des beaux-arts* (1880): 202.

15. Wilhelm Engelmann, *Daniel Chodowiecki's Sämmtliche Kupferstiche*, Berlin, 1926, no. 75.

16. Bock, *Menzel*, no. 1132.

17. Hans Mackowsky, *Die Bildwerke Gottfried Schadows*, intro. P. O. Rave (Berlin: Deutscher Verein für Kunstwissenschaft, 1951), p. 248.

18. For an analysis of Menzel's historical scenes, cf. F. Forster-Hahn, "Adolph Menzel's 'Daguerreotypical' Image of Frederick the Great: a Liberal Bourgeois Interpretation of German History," *The Art Bulletin* LIX, no. 2 (June 1977): 242–61.

19. Formerly, Berlin, Nationalgalerie. The painting, oil on canvas, measuring 204 × 175 cm, was destroyed at the end of World War II.

20. West Berlin, Staatliche Museen Preussischer Kulturbesitz, Nationalgalerie, *Verzeichnis der Gemälde und Skulpturen des 19. Jahrhunderts*, *1976*, p. 268. Oil on canvas, 142 × 205 cm.

21. Franz Kugler, in *Kunstblatt*, no. 45 (1848): 177. Reprinted in *Kleine Schriften zur Kunstgeschichte* (Stuttgart, 1854), III, 664. In a description of Menzel's illustrations he wrote: ". . . es ist eine daguerreothypartige Realität in seinen Anschauungen, eine historische Tüchtigkeit in seinen Kompositionen, . . . die in solcher Art fast nicht ihres Gleichen findet."

22. The only one of the Frederick paintings that was in the possession of the Hohenzollern family; after 1918 it was in the collection of the Nationalgalerie, Berlin. The painting, measuring 295 × 378 cm, was destroyed in 1945.

23. Julius Grosse, *Die deutsche allgemeine und historische Kunst-Ausstellung zu München im Jahre 1858*, Studien zur Kunstgeschichte des 19. Jahrhunderts, München, 1859, pp. 124–25; about Menzel's painting, cf. 134–36.

24. The landscape painter Albert Hertel related that Menzel thought it quite humiliating to have his painting relegated to the "blue navy room situated toward the courtyard where the lackeys washed the teacups during balls at court." Menzel, who was very bitter about the rejection he had experienced during his early years, was well aware that the subject of the scene, the defeat of the Prussians, was an unacceptable theme for a history painting at that time. Cf. Gustav Kirstein, *Das Leben Adolph Menzels* (Leipzig, 1919), pp. 60–64.

25. Berlin, GDR, Staatliche Museen, Nationalgalerie. The painting, measuring 254 × 325 cm, was given to the Nationalgalerie by the Polish government in 1954. Cf. Werner Schmidt, *Adolph Menzel. Zeichnungen*, exh. cat., Berlin, Nationalgalerie, 1955, pp. 20–21.

26. *Geschichte Friedrichs des Grossen. Geschrieben von Franz Kugler. Gezeichnet von Adolph Menzel* (Leipzig, 1840), p. 544.

27. Quoted from Kirstein, *Menzel*, p. 103.

28. The total lack of understanding is responsible for the painting's own history: in 1859 it was exhibited in the town hall of Weimar, where it did not please the Archduke. Ironically, he won the painting a year later through the lottery of the "Association for Historical Art." In 1863 Menzel requested the loan of the canvas for an exhibition of all his historical works in Berlin. He received the painting rolled up and in the very same packing materials it had arrived in four years earlier at Weimar. Cf. Werner Deetjen, "Adolf Menzel und Adolf Schöll. Ungedruckte Briefe Menzels," *Jahrbuch der Preussischen Kunstdammlungen* 55 (Berlin, 1934) (Beiheft): 36–39.

29. Menzel in a letter to the critic Friedrich Pecht, dated 25 October 1859. Reprinted in Kirstein, *Menzel*, p. 103.

30. Berlin, GDR, Staatliche Museen, Nationalgalerie. The canvas measures 315 × 442 cm.

31. *The Coronation of King William I. at Königsberg 1861,* 1861–65, oil on canvas, 345 × 445 cm, Staatliche Schlösser und Gärten Potsdam-Sanssouci. GK No. 899. This large canvas was restored in 1978–79 and was exhibited (no. XXV) at the recent retrospective, *Adolph Menzel. Paintings, Drawings,* Berlin, GDR, Staatliche Museen, Nationalgalerie, 1980. Cf. Gerd Bartoschek, "Zur Entstehung des Krönungsbildes," ibid., pp. 49–60.

32. Berlin, GDR, Staatliche Museen, Nationalgalerie. Oil on canvas, 249 × 374 cm. Cf. Ludwig Justi, *Franz Krüger. Parade Unter den Linden,* Amtliche Veröffentlichung der National-Galerie, Berlin, n. d.

33. West Berlin, Nationalgalerie, *Verzeichnis,* 1976, pp. 140–42. Oil on canvas, 32 × 44 cm.

34. Ibid., p. 184. Oil on canvas, 66 × 89 cm.

35. Ibid., p. 144. Oil on canvas, 75 × 155 cm.

36. Ibid., pp. 274–75. For Menzel's relationship to Paris and French art and criticism, cf. Forster-Hahn, "Menzels Realismus im Spiegel der *französischen Kritik,*" in *Menzel* (Berlin, GDR, Nationalgalerie, 1980), pp. 27–47.

37. Dresden, Gemäldegalerie Neue Meister. Oil on canvas, 49 × 70 cm. For an analysis of Menzel's creative method and its bearing upon the meaning of his art, cf. Forster-Hahn, "Authenticity into Ambivalence: the Evolution of Menzel's Drawings," *Master Drawings* 16, no. 3: 255–83.

38. Düsseldorf, Kunstmuseum. Oil on canvas, 48.4 × 69.5 cm. Cf. also Kunstmuseum Düsseldorf, *Die Gemälde des neunzehnten Jahrhunderts bearbeitet von Rolf Andree* (Düsseldorf, 1968), no. 4433.

39. Duranty, "Menzel," *Gazette des beaux-arts* (1880): 122.

40. West Berlin, Nationalgalerie, *Verzeichnis,* 1976, p. 281.

41. Ibid., pp. 56–58. For the preparatory works, cf. Berlin, GDR, Staatliche Museen, National-Galerie, *Karl Blechen 1798–1840,* cat. by Lothar Brauner, 1973, nos. 201–205.

42. West Berlin, Nationalgalerie, *Verzeichnis,* 1976, pp. 264–66.

43. DEMAG AG, Duisburg. Oil on canvas, 43.5 × 57.5 cm. Recently discussed in *Die Düsseldorfer Malerschule,* Kunstmuseum Düsseldorf, 1979, no. 190.

44. Fully quoted and discussed by Ursula Riemann-Reyher, *Moderne Cyklopen. 100 Jahre "Eisenwalzwerk" von Adolph Menzel,* Staatliche Museen zu Berlin, Kupferstichkabinett und Sammlung der Handzeichnungen, Berlin, GDR, 1976.

45. Berlin, GDR, Staatliche Museen, Nationalgalerie. Oil on canvas,

158 × 254 cm. A condensed version of my research on this painting, "Adolph Menzels 'Eisenwalzwerk': Kunst im Konflikt zwischen Tradition und sozialer Wirklichkeit," appeared in *Die nützlichen Künste*, spring 1981, published by the Verein deutscher Ingenieure for the exhibition of the same title.

46. Berlin, GDR, Staatliche Museen, Sammlung der Handzeichnungen no. 1777. Gouache, 52.4 × 62.9 cm.

47. Berlin, GDR, Staatliche Museen, Nationalgalerie, Archiv.

48. Berlin, *Vossische Zeitung*, 2 March 1875.

49. Berlin, GDR, Märkisches Museum. Oil on copper, 315 × 230 cm.

50. Berlin, GDR, Staatliche Museen, Nationalgalerie. Oil on canvas, 119.5 × 170.5 cm.

51. Private collection, Winterthur, Switzerland. Oil on panel, 45 × 60 cm. Cf. also *Max Liebermann in seiner Zeit*, Nationalgalerie Berlin, Staatliche Museen Preussischer Kulturbesitz, 1979, no. 9.

52. For a discussion of Liebermann's early paintings, especially *Women Plucking Geese*, cf. *Max Liebermann in seiner Zeit*, pp. 25–26. August Strindberg, "Realismus," *Freie Bühne für modernes Leben*, I (Berlin, 1890): 1243.

National and International Aspects of Realist Painting in Switzerland

Hans A. Lüthy 5

FOR A VERY LONG TIME THE HISTORY of art has been mainly concerned with what went on in the cultural centers of the past: even today, "provincialism" tends to be a derogatory comment upon the quality of a work of art. In the last few years, however, researchers have shown greater regard for peripheral aspects of artistic creativity. Particular importance has now been attached to the reciprocal relationship between metropolitan and outlying areas.

Throughout the nineteenth century, for example, the unique attraction of Paris meant that she was receiving continual infusions of new blood, as provincial Frenchmen and foreigners moved to the capital. While the artistic climate of Paris itself has by now been very thoroughly researched, we often know little about the backgrounds of newcomers and of those artists who worked temporarily in Paris, although they were precisely the ones who provided strong new impulses to the art world.

The development of certain trends in the nineteenth century may have something to do with this interaction between artistic metropolis and the provinces—a belief based upon the hypothesis that in the specific case of European realism, such peripheral scenes of artistic activity may have made an original and significant contribution to the movement. It may be that just such a locale as Switzerland, where a number of different cultures came face to face, may provide a suitable example upon which to base a new theory. Moreover, in Switzerland a striking confrontation can be observed between such traditionally minded towns as Geneva, Berne, Basel, and Zurich and a wild, untouched and, in the nineteenth century, still largely inaccessible world of nature, the awareness of which was therefore all the more intense than in the more distant European cities.

In this chapter we shall refer to three Swiss painters, of varying degrees of importance, in order to describe and illustrate the relationships and interactions between province and capital. Between 1850 and 1890 Swiss painters continued as before to regard Paris as the artistic metropolis, even though from about 1840 on a few German-speaking Swiss had trained in Germany, either in Munich or in Düsseldorf. A large number of young Swiss studied in Paris under Charles Gleyre, a native of the Canton of Vaud, at the studio he had taken over from Paul Delaroche in 1843. Even now, the Gleyre studio is given too little credit for its role as a training center and meeting place of significance, at least for the development of Swiss painting. Having already made a name for himself in Paris with his painting *Les Illusions Perdues* (*Lost Illusions*), which won great acclaim at the Salon in 1843, Gleyre achieved fame and respect at home, too, with his historical painting *L'exécution du Major Davel* (*The Execution of Major Davel*), completed in 1850, but recently destroyed. The influence of Gleyre is strikingly apparent in biographies of many Swiss artists, one of the earliest of whom was Friedrich Simon from Berne.[1]

Friedrich Simon (1828–62)

Practically unknown even in his native Switzerland, Friedrich Simon produced a mere thirty or so paintings during a career beset with pulmonary disease; a third of these are to be found in museums in Geneva, Berne, Neuchâtel, and Winterthur (O. Reinhart Foundation). Simon received his formal training under Gleyre around 1850; during this period he also paid an extended visit to the Netherlands to study the country's art collections. Simon is apparently the only one of Gleyre's pupils of this period who turned his attention quickly to everyday subjects.

In 1852 Simon produced his first realist pictures, such as *Der Wilddieb* (*The Poacher;* fig. 5.1) and *Der Hufschmied* (*The Farrier*), both now in the Geneva Museum. *The Poacher* is no longer portrayed as a romantic adventurer (as in roughly contemporary French examples), but is shown within his family circle; even in the nineteenth century this picture was compared to seventeenth-century Dutch paintings. The year 1852 also saw the production of *Der Schlosser* (*The Locksmith;* fig. 5.2), now owned by the Oskar Reinhart Foundation in Winterthur, a work that is the earliest example of a painting of a craftsman in nineteenth-century Swiss art. Dutch and contemporary French influences can be clearly seen in the interior setting, which represents a closed and harmonious whole. Although the artist allows us a view into a back room, so that the family is included, there is no trace of sentimentality. Simon's work already displays that complete naturalness of human relationships which Albert Anker later so splendidly mastered.

In 1857 Simon sent an interior of a butcher's shop to the Salon. The jury rejected this work, alleging it had been copied from Rembrandt's picture *Der Geschlachtete Ochse* (*The Slaughtered Ox*), which had been acquired by the Louvre shortly before. However, as we learn from Auguste Bachelin, a friend and fellow-pupil of Simon's under Gleyre, Simon had no knowledge of the Rembrandt original he was supposed to have copied. Such occurrences are quite characteristic of the 1850s and testify to the general interest in the stylistic features of Dutch painting.

Yet there was a further factor at play here: around the middle of the century we see a "revival" in the appreciation of the work of Théodore Géricault, though as yet this phenomenon has not been the subject of any detailed examination. One event in this revival was, for example, the erection of Antoine Etex's Géricault monument in 1842, which preceded Charles Clément's first published version of his great Géricault biography in the earliest issues of the *Gazette des Beaux-Arts*, founded in 1859. In Berne, Géricault's memory was also kept alive by his Swiss pupil and lithographer Joseph Volmar (1796–1865), who had held the post of Professor of Drawing and Painting in Berne since 1836, and whom Friedrich Simon undoubtedly knew.[2]

The iconographic parallels between a major part of Simon's limited output and Géricault are unmistakable: titles such as *Der Hufschmied* (*The Farrier*), *Der Postwagen* (*The Mail Coach*), and *Pferdewechsel auf der Poststation* (*Changing Horses at the Mail Station*) speak for themselves. To take a specific case, it is hard to imagine that Simon's work *Der Schiffszug an der Zihl* (*Hauling on the Zihl*), completed in 1855, could have been done except under the influence of Géricault's *Kohlewagenzug* (*The Coalwagon*)—a work well known through lithographic reproductions.[3]

Albert Anker (1831–1910)

The second painter to be considered is Albert Anker,[4] who was born in the Bernese village of Ins on the language frontier between the German- and French-speaking parts of Switzerland. He also attended Gleyre's studio a short time after his friend Simon. From 1859 on he regularly exhibited at the Paris Salon; in winter he used to work in Paris, spending his summers in his native village of Ins, where he preoccupied himself with studies for large-scale works.

In the past, researchers have tended to characterize Anker above

all as a portrayer of Swiss peasant and village culture. After the nineteenth century he practically ceased to enjoy any international fame,
even though his works are still to be found in a few museums outside
Switzerland. In many respects Anker symbolized the dualism between
town and country. On the one hand, he received first-rate training
in Paris, where he steadily developed a good reputation based upon
carefully composed genre paintings, which he exhibited at the Salon
and at Goupil's gallery. He did not hesitate to go back to Chardin
and the Dutch school, and the influence of Gleyre can also be seen
in his work over a long period. On the other hand, he drew decisive
inspiration from the village environment and the world of trivial events
as he saw and experienced them.

At the 1864 Salon Anker exhibited *Kinderbegräbnis* (*A Child's
Burial;* fig. 5.3), the theme of which has much in common with *Die
kleine Freundin* (*The Little Friend on Her Deathbed;* fig. 5.4). He
naturally took Courbet as a starting point (cf. Boime, fig. 3.7) but
changed the theme to place greater emphasis upon the quite personal
world of the mourners. While Courbet's work echoed the only form
of this subject hitherto accepted—the heroic burial—its air of detach-
ment is now completely absent from Anker's picture, where the drama
retains qualities of personal tragedy. Anker depicted such episodes in
village life without any sentimentality or narrative framework, an important characteristic of realist painting after 1850. If a comparison
is made with Carl Friedrich Schick's work *Das tote Kind* (*The Dead
Child;* fig. 5.5), which was produced at the same time as Anker's
Die kleine Freundin, and which is now in the Kunsthalle in Karlsruhe,
Germany, then it is apparent that the German artist took greater
pleasure in telling a story and cluttered his picture with every
imaginable prop. Anker, on the other hand, was satisfied with a much
simpler set and managed to concentrate attention directly upon the
tragedy of the scene.[5]

In 1869, tragedy struck Anker himself: his two-year-old son, Rudolf,
died. Anker painted his son on his deathbed in a work that is one of
the earliest instances of an artist painting a member of his immediate
family on his deathbed.[6] Again, mention must be made of Géricault,
who painted General le Tellier in the same circumstances around 1819
—after the general had committed suicide.

Anker also painted a village-life cycle in a series of large-scale
compositions and paintings of individual figures, which are, for the
most part, rather unexciting scenes from the daily lives of farmers
and craftsmen. A final example of Anker's subjects is *Die Armensuppe*
(*Soup for the Poor;* fig. 5.6), a theme that had already been taken up
by François Bonvin in the late 1840s, suggesting the universality of
realist themes at this time.[7]

5.1 FRIEDRICH SIMON, *The Poacher*

5.2 FRIEDRICH SIMON, *The Locksmith*

5.3 ALBERT ANKER, *A Child's Burial*

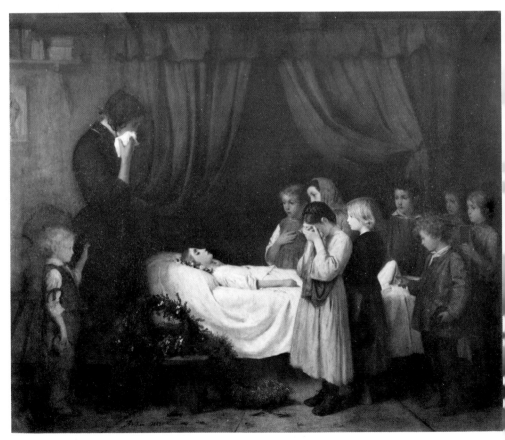

5.4 ALBERT ANKER, *The Little Friend on Her Deathbed*

5.5   KARL FRIEDRICH SCHICK, *The Dead Child*

5.6   ALBERT ANKER, *Soup for the Poor*

5.7 FERDINAND HODLER, *The Joiner*

5.8 FERDINAND HODLER, *The Washerwoman*

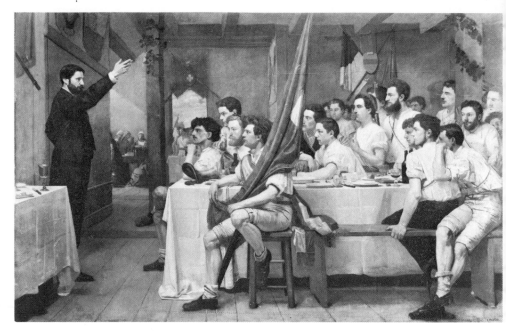

5.9   FERDINAND HODLER, *The Gymnastics Society Banquet*

5.10   FERDINAND HODLER, *Temperance Café*

5.11 FERDINAND HODLER, *Devotion*

6.1 VASILII PEROV, *Drowned Woman*

6.2 VASILII PEROV, *Last Tavern at the Edge of Town*

6.3   NIKOLAI GE, *The Last Supper*

6.4 ALEKSEI SAVRASOV, *The Rooks Have Arrived*

6.5   IVAN KRAMSKOI, *Mina Moiseev*

6.6   ILYA REPIN, *Tolstoi Plowing*

6.7 IAROSHENKO, *Woman Student*

6.8 ILYA REPIN, *Barge Haulers on the Volga*

6.9 VALERIAN IAKOBI, *Halt of the Convoy of Prisoners*

6.10 GRIGORII MIASOEDOV, *The Zemtsvo Dines*

6.11 KONSTANTIN SAVITSKII, *Repair Work on the Railroad*

6.12 KONSTANTIN SAVITSKII, *To War*

6.13 VLADIMIR MAKOVSKII, *Evening Meeting*

6.14 VLADIMIR MAKOVSKII, *On the Boulevard*

6.15 ILYA REPIN, *Religious Procession in Kursk Province*

6.16 IVAN KRAMSKOI, *Christ in the Wilderness*

6.17 ILYA REPIN, *Ivan the Terrible and His Son Ivan,
November 16, 1581*

6.18 ILYA REPIN, *Revolutionary Meeting*

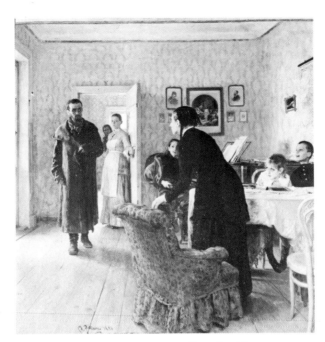

6.19 ILYA REPIN, *They Did Not Expect Him*

6.20 ILYA REPIN, *The Unexpected Return*

7.1   HENRY HERBERT LA THANGUE, *The Last Furrow*

7.2   HARRY FURNISS, *Drunk again!*
       The very last furrow.

7.3   HENRY HERBERT LA THANGUE, *The Man with the Scythe*

7.4   FREDERICK WALKER, *The Vagrants*

7.5   ALPHONSE LEGROS, *The Tired Wanderer*

7.6   GEORGE CLAUSEN, *High Mass at a Fishing Village on the Zuyder Zee*

7.7   ALEXANDER STANHOPE FORBES, *The Old Convent, Quimperlé*

7.8 Jules Bastien-Lepage, *Pas Mêche*

7.9 Alexander Stanhope Forbes, *Preparations for the Market, Quimperlé*

7.10 FRANK BRAMLEY, *Domino*

7.11 SIR JOHN LAVERY, *Under the Cherry Tree*

7.12 JULES BASTIEN-LEPAGE, *Les Foins*

7.13   GEORGE CLAUSEN, *Labourers after Dinner*

7.14 GEORGE CLAUSEN, *The Stone Pickers*

7.15 JULES BASTIEN-LEPAGE, *Pauvre Fauvette*

7.16 HERBERT DALZEIL, *The Cow Girl*

7.17 PETER HENRY EMERSON, *Coming Home from the Marshes*

7.18 HENRY HERBERT LA THANGUE, *The Return of the Reapers*

7.19   JEAN FRANÇOIS MILLET, *Going to Work*

7.20 JULES BASTIEN-LEPAGE, *Jeanne d'Arc écoutant Les Voix*

7.21 GEORGE CLAUSEN, *The Girl at the Gate*

II

One of the themes at the Fourteenth German Art Historians' Congress in Hamburg in 1974 was "Realism," and several speakers dealt with an essay by Georg Schmidt entitled "Naturalismus und Realismus: Ein Beitrag zur kunstgeschichtlichen Begriffbildung" ("Naturalism and Realism: A Contribution to the Definition of Concepts in the History of Art"), first published in the Festschrift for Martin Heidegger in 1959.[8] The most thorough such examination was by J. A. Schmoll gen. Eisenwerth in "Naturalismus und Realismus: Versuch zur Formulierung verbindlicher Begriffe" ("Naturalism and Realism: An Attempt to Formulate Categorical Concepts"), published in the 1975 Städel-Jahrbuch.[9] Above all, Georg Schmidt's essay made an appeal for a much sharper distinction between the concepts of naturalism and realism: he saw naturalism as an approach in which the world of visible phenomena is faithfully transposed into a picture or a sculpture, whereas realism is seen as a stylistic phenomenon of the nineteenth century.

Schmidt, a former director of the Basel Museum of Fine Arts, who died in 1965, had been concerned with the concept of realism long before 1959. He dealt with the subject at some length in a Hodler monograph published in 1942, but the work is practically unknown outside of Switzerland.[10] As he wrote in his foreword, Schmidt discovered Hodler in the 1920s and, as a devoted communist at the time, gave a social-critical interpretation to his work. In his monograph Schmidt revised his earlier views in favor of a closer analysis of what he called the realist-expressive style of the early Hodler, a term that he also applied to other European artists. Schmidt had had considerable influence upon the current debate among German art historians in particular and must be acknowledged as the true father of the modern concept of realism as it is found in the works of Hodler and others.

Ferdinand Hodler (1853–1918)

With this background, it is possible to examine the compositions of Hodler,[11] who was born in 1853—the same year as Vincent van Gogh. His father, a joiner, had a small business of his own but failed to make a success of it: Georg Schmidt described Hodler's home background as "petty-bourgeois proletariat." Both parents and almost all his brothers and sisters died as Hodler grew up, so that even as a child he was already familiar with the various faces of death. Left to provide for himself, he received his initial training as a painter from a manufacturer of landscape views for tourists. In 1871 he decided on his own initiative to go to Geneva, at that time the only Swiss town with a professionally run school of art, under Barthélemy Menn, a pupil of Ingres's and a friend of Corot's.

From 1874 on, Hodler already began to emerge as an artist of European stature. During this period he visited Paris to study, although no further details of this trip are known, and in 1878 he spent several months in Madrid. Apart from these two visits to foreign cities, Hodler hardly ventured away from Geneva except for short trips to the Canton of Berne during the summer. It was not until 1890 that Hodler first stayed in Paris for any length of time, when he went there for the exhibition of his first great symbolic composition, *Die Nacht* (*The Night*).[12] Nevertheless, in the 1870s and 1880s, information gleaned from newspapers and art magazines as well as from engravings and photographs allowed Hodler to keep abreast of developments in Paris. From 1879 on, Hodler also sent works to the Paris Salon.

From an iconographic standpoint, Hodler's early pictures emerged from a vacuum. His *Der Schreiner* (*The Joiner;* fig. 5.7), produced in 1875 and now in the Zurich Museum of Fine Arts, owes nothing to a Genevese or Bernese tradition—if we exclude Friedrich Simon, whom Hodler could hardly have known. The direct portrayal of a craftsman, almost aggressive in its impact, already reminded Georg Schmidt of the familiar pictures of mercenary soldiers, while contemporary critics in Geneva—displaying an accurate grasp of the new pictorial language being spoken by the young Hodler—characterized the picture as "brutally realistic." Compared to Anker and even to earlier French paintings on a similar theme, Hodler's *Joiner* heralds a new stage in the realist movement. One is reminded of the observation of Couture that there are just as many different personalities among craftsmen and manual workers as there are among the wealthy middle classes.[13]

A roughly contemporary painting of a *Washerwoman* (*Die Wäscherin;* fig. 5.8), now in a private collection, does not provide a direct interpretation of the subject's personality. The child at play draws attention away from the washerwoman, who, not very attractive by French standards, is firmly characterized by her head, arms, and clothing as a member of the lower class.[14]

A particular feature of artistic life in Geneva in the second half of the nineteenth century was the regular competitions held for young artists, each one with a set theme. The best known of these competitions were those for the Calame and Diday Prizes, held in alternate years; the Calame Prize was awarded for a landscape, the Diday for figure composition. In addition, competitions were held on special occasions: for example, a prize was offered in 1875 for "a Genevese genre or historical painting," roughly two-and-a-quarter by three-and-a-half meters in format, to commemorate the hundredth anniversary of the "Société des Arts." If only in the hope of earning some money, Hodler often took part in such competitions, and for the theme laid down by the "Société des Arts" he deliberately chose a topical subject: The Gymnastics Society Banquet. To everyone's surprise, Hodler won the competition, although he had to share the prize with an artist who had produced a conventional historical painting. While our only record of the cartoon for this picture is a photograph, the completed work has been preserved in the Zurich Museum of Fine Arts. Hodler's subject reflects that world of characteristically Swiss folk motifs which has remained viable to the present day in such typical and traditional popular events as gymnastics, shooting, and singing society festivals. It has often been said that the painting is based upon Anselm Feuerbach's *Das Gastmahl des Platon* (*Plato's Banquet*), a huge composition completed in 1869 for the Munich International Exhibition of Art, where it received great acclaim.[15] In fact, however, there is hardly any link between the two paintings. In complete contrast to Feuerbach's work, Hodler's *Turnerbankett* (*The Gymnastics Society Banquet;* fig. 5.9) must be seen as a typically realistic masterpiece, the main aspects of which almost exactly meet the criteria of realist art as formulated by J. A. Schmoll gen. Eisenwerth,[16] who noted that: (1) the choice of subject should be a topical event rather than an anecdote; (2) a part of contemporary reality with social relevance should be depicted; and (3) the composition should be subject to the law of truth, of "vérité," so that beauty and ugliness both have an equally rightful place in it.

In fact, Hodler's *Turnerbankett* breaks with a whole series of nineteenth-century conventions, the extent of which becomes especially clear when a comparison is made with the late classicism of Anselm Feuerbach, in which the traditional formal language predominates. Hodler's composition still displays some weaknesses in certain areas, but when viewed as a whole it is infused with an elementary force that finds vivid expression in the tightly packed group of listening gymnasts. Georg Schmidt's definition of Hodler's early style as "expressive realism" can also be understood in the light of *Der Schreiner* and *Das Turnerbankett*. In contrast to both a purely descriptive realism and one that tends toward genre painting, Hodler does not follow from existing traditions, but develops his own ideas, concepts that contain at least the promise of monumental significance.

We have already mentioned the fact that Hodler saw his entire family die within the space of a few years, and indeed in the 1870s he had already painted his first picture of a dead body, that of an unnamed farmhand from a village in the Canton of Berne, who had been laid out in a barn. The picture is now in the Museum of Fine Arts in Geneva and shows a pitiless portrayal of a corpse, without any symbolic overtones. A second, roughly contemporary painting of a woman on her deathbed shows that the subject was of more than passing interest to the young painter. The woman's body expresses the same implacable finality of death, intensified by the sparse and sketchily depicted interior, which at the same time suggests that the dead woman had led a hard life. The theme of illness and death recurs a number of times in Hodler's later work, the last example being the cycle he produced in 1913–14 portraying the illness and death of his mistress, Valentine Godé-Darel.[17]

A final emphatically realistic group in Hodler's early work comprises the interiors of simple taverns or even living rooms where he spent a large portion of his time. One of his cycles on Genevese history was painted for a restaurant as payment for unpaid-for meals in the Taverne du Crocodile as late as 1886–87. Here, too, the first pictures appeared between 1875 and 1877; one of the earliest instances of a complete series shows a craftsman type, reminiscent of the *Joiner* of 1875, pouring out a drink across a dinner plate, while a second man is sitting on a box, warming himself by the stove. The rough movement of the man who is drinking and the obviously secondhand furniture create the impression of disorderly circumstances, although the social-critical dimension, as is always the case with Hodler, is completely ignored. It is almost unthinkable that such pictures could have been produced without a knowledge of French realist painting, and in the almost total lack of communication between the figures it might be possible to detect the influence of François Bonvin. In *Le Café de la Tempérence* (*Temperance Café*; fig. 5.10), painted in 1879, this impression is stronger: the decor of the room, the view into a side room, and the anonymous-looking patrons, each preoccupied with himself, seem to be dominated by a similar subdued atmosphere.

In the early years of his artistic activity, from 1875 to 1880, the style and iconography of Hodler's painting may be termed absolutely realistic. From 1880 on, ever stronger idealistic elements are included in his work; yet up to 1889–90, when he produced *Die Nacht* (*The Night*), Hodler often painted both realistic and idealistic pictures at the same time. The smaller version of *Gebet im Kanton Bern* (*Prayers in the Canton of Berne*), entitled *Die Andacht* (*Devotion;* fig. 5.11), of 1880, now privately owned, certainly employs elements of realistic style, where a preacher's congregation is assembled, in a deliberately disharmonious juxtaposition, around those in prayer, and the main figures in the picture appear as true-to-life representatives of a lower-middle-class religious sect of which Hodler was, for a brief period, a member. Yet this produces a striking contrast with the theme itself, in that this is a group of people inspired by spiritual forces. Georg Schmidt explains this effect in terms of a desperate attempt to adapt to upper-middle-class society, by returning to the traditional motifs of nineteenth-century painting. In reality, however, it may be that the then twenty-seven-year-old Hodler was trying to break out of the almost total isolation into which he had maneuvered himself. In Hodler's

case there is no evidence at all of a political position opposed to bourgeois society. A number of unpublished letters to his painter-friend
Odier give us the impression that Hodler was a naïve youth, whose
joys and sorrows were in no way out of the ordinary. The main characteristic of realistic art is not in Hodler's view of the world but in his
radical rejection of the approach to painting that was current in
Geneva (and throughout Switzerland) at the time. The restrained
and dignified artistry taught by Barthélemy Menn's school had little
to offer Hodler beyond craftsmanship, though admittedly of an out-
standingly well-taught kind. It is therefore all the more surprising to
see Hodler emerge as a pure realist. Viewed in an international context, it might be reasonable to regard Hodler as belonging to the
second generation of realists, whose dates of birth roughly fall between
the years 1845 and 1865. These would be painters who went through
a markedly realistic phase in their early work, such as van Gogh, born
in the same year as Hodler, and Edvard Munch, born in 1863. It may
be mere coincidence that these artists also came from areas outside
the main centers of nineteenth-century art; on the other hand, they lend
themselves particularly well to fruitful comparisons. It is also most striking that it should have been painters whose early work was realistic in
style who became leading figures of European symbolism around 1890.
Thoughts such as these shall be the subject of another discussion, however, and will not be pursued here.

To return to my original point, we have so far left open the question of how far circumstances in general may favor realistic art in
Switzerland. Over and over again, regions without continuous artistic
tradition tend to produce markedly distinctive forms. In Switzerland,
on the one hand the countryside was portrayed in charming landscape views, while on the other, the country's heritage of folklore
was depicted, with figures in local costume, Alpine cowherds, and
Swiss-style wrestlers.[18] Such subjects were very popular with tourists
throughout the nineteenth century and have continued to dominate
the popular image of Switzerland abroad up to the present day. Artists
such as Simon, Anker, and Hodler worked in deliberate contrast
to these accepted norms or, when they took up the same motifs, gave
them a totally different treatment. The pictures of farmers and craftsmen produced between 1850 and 1880 may be an expression of the
fundamental wish to depict not only a charming façade but also the
realities of everyday life.

NOTES

1. On Simon, see Franz Zelger, *Katalog der Stiftung Oskar Reinhart
Winterthur, Band 1: Schweizer Maler des 18. und 19. Jahrhunderts* (Zurich,
1977), pp. 317–19, with older references. Still the best survey of Simon's

life is to be found in A. Bachelin, *Artistes Suisses, Frédéric Simon, Bibliothèque Universelle et Revue Suisse*, vol. XLIII, 1889, pp. 538–60, and vol. XLIV, 1889, pp. 84–122. Bachelin also gives a hitherto-unknown description of Gleyre's atelier.

2. Cf. Hans A. Lüthy, "Géricault und Joseph Volmar," in *Beiträge zur Kunst des 19. und 20. Jahrhunderts, Jahrbuch 1968/69 des Schweizerischen Institutes für Kunstwissenschaft* (Zurich, 1970), pp. 25–32.

3. Edgar Degas also took *The Coalwagon* as a model for a copy after Géricault (Zurich, Private Collection).

4. For a catalogue raisonné of Anker's paintings, see Kunstmuseum Bern, 1962. Also see Sandor Kuthy and Hans A. Lüthy, *Albert Anker* (Zurich, 1980).

5. For further reference, see Jan Bialostocki, "Vom heroischen Grabmal zum Bauernbegräbnis," in *Akademie der Wissenschaften und Literatur*, Wiesbaden, 1978, and also Anton Pigler, "Portraying the Dead," in *Acta Historiae Artium*, vol. IV (Budapest, 1956).

6. An early example is also found in a work by Jean Jacques Henner. See G. P. Weisberg, *The Realist Tradition: French Painting and Drawing 1830–1900* (Cleveland, 1980), fig. 65.

7. For further reference, see G. P. Weisberg, *François Bonvin, Sa Vie et l'Oeuvre*, Editions Geoffroy-Dechaume (Paris, 1980).

8. Reprinted in Georg Schmidt, *Umgang mit Kunst, Ausgewählte Schriften 1940–1963* (Basel, 1976), pp. 27 ff.

9. Neue Folge, Band 5 (Munich, 1975), pp. 247 ff.; cf. also Klaus Herding, ed., *Realismus als Widerspruch, Suhrkamp Taschenbuch 493* (Frankfurt, 1978).

10. Hans Mühlestein and Georg Schmidt, *Ferdinand Hodler* (Erlenbach-Zurich, 1942). All theoretical reflections are by G. Schmidt; H. Mühlestein furnished the biographical facts.

11. The literature on Hodler is quite extensive; there is an English Catalogue-Monograph, edited by Peter Selz (Berkeley, 1972). A complete bibliography on Hodler's work until 1890 will be given in Franz Zelger et al., *Der frühe Hodler*, ed. Swiss Institute for Art Research (Bern, 1981).

12. Hans Christoph von Tavel, *Ferdinand Hodler, Die Nacht, Werkmonographien zur Bildenden Kunst* Nr. 135 (Stuttgart, 1969).

13. See Linda Nochlin, *Realism and Tradition in Art 1848–1900* (Englewood Cliffs, N.J., 1966), p. 7.

14. See Eunice Lipton, "The Laundress in Late Nineteenth-Century French Culture: Imagery, Ideology and Edgar Degas," *Art History* 3, no. 3 (September 1980).

15. Anselm Feuerbach, *Gemälde und Zeichnungen aus der Staatlichen Kunsthalle Karlsruhe* (Karlsruhe, 1978), pp. 34 ff.

16. Schmoll, "Naturalismus und Realismus," p. 253.

17. Jura Brüschweiler, *Ein Maler vor Liebe und Tod/Ferd. Hodler und Valentine Godé-Darel* (Bern, 1976).

18. Cf. Hans Christoph von Tavel, ed., *Schweiz im Bild, Bild der Schweiz, Ausstellungskatalog* (Zurich, 1974).

Scenes from Life and Contemporary History

Russian Realism of the 1870s-1880s

Alison Hilton **6**

REALISM IN NINETEENTH-CENTURY Russian art was primarily a goal rather than a stylistic concept. In its most general sense, realism involved a commitment to truth, but the definition of truth appropriate to visual representation ranged, in Russian as in European art, from objective facts to moral concepts. In the 1870s, the chief issue for Russian artists was not style or even subject matter but the responsibility of the artist, as an independent, thinking person, to express his ideas about the conditions of contemporary Russian life. It is this conviction of the necessity of reflecting real life in art that characterizes the outstanding works of the realists and that is the focus of this essay.

The emergence of a realist movement is identified chiefly with the group of artists known as the Peredvizhniki, who established their independence from the official Academy of Arts and formed the Association of Traveling Art Exhibitions in 1870. The original leaders of the group, Ivan Kramskoi, Nikolai Ge, Vasilii Perov, Grigorii Miasoedov, and others, belonged to the generation born in the 1830s (they were contemporaries of Manet and Degas); a second cohort, born in the 1840s, including Ilya Repin, Vasilii Polenov, Konstantin Savitskii, and Nikolai Iaroshenko, joined the association between 1872 and 1878.[1] Their motives for exhibiting together varied, as did their individual styles. All agreed, however, on the importance of working and exhibiting outside of the bureaucratic control of the state. As Kramskoi later explained, "I sincerely wanted freedom, so sincerely that I was ready to use any means so that others could also be free."[2]

187

Origins of the Realist Movement: Philosophy and Criticism

The founding members of the Peredvizhniki were educated either at the St. Petersburg Academy of Arts or the Moscow School of Painting, Sculpture, and Architecture, where they received thorough grounding in technique and opportunities for individual specialization and study abroad.[3] Vasilii Perov studied at the Moscow School and received a scholarship to go to Paris in the early 1860s. Already inclined toward genre and satire, he concentrated not on the art in museums but on the scenes of daily life in poor neighborhoods. He grew discouraged by his ignorance of French customs and requested permission to return home early in order to "study and develop to the greatest extent possible the uncounted treasure of themes of city and village life of our own homeland."[4] Preference for Russian subjects was to become a credo for many of the realists. But aside from the Russian settings, the work of Perov and his colleagues shows the same general concern for rural and urban poverty, alcoholism, prostitution, and other mid-nineteenth-century problems that troubled many European artists and writers. The range of Perov's work of the 1860s—from the broadly anticlerical *Easter Procession in a Village* (1861) to the prosaic, monochromatic document of a prostitute's end, *Drowned Woman* (1867; fig. 6.1), and the poignant image of a peasant woman huddled in a sledge waiting for her drunken husband in *Last Tavern at the Edge of Town* (1868; fig. 6.2)—certainly reflects the scope of socially concerned artists elsewhere in Europe.

Unlike Perov, Nikolai Ge, educated at the academy and in Rome, found his main strength in interpreting historical subjects in the light of his social ideals. Better educated than most artists and attuned to the implications of the 1848 revolutions, Ge sought out Alexander Herzen, the founder of Russian liberal populism, and paid homage to the political philosopher in his first major work, *The Last Supper* (1863; fig. 6.3). He used a photograph of Herzen as a guide for painting Christ's head and thus quite explicitly drew a parallel between Christ's disciples and Herzen's liberal circle, and related the theme of betrayal to contemporary conflicts.[5] When Ge brought the painting back to St. Petersburg in 1863, he was welcomed as a leader and prophet by younger artists. In an unprecedented act, the Academic Council immediately granted him the title of professor. Ironically, this gesture and the implied promise of increased liberalization encouraged artists to seek still greater freedoms and led to the decisive rejection of the academy's authority later that year by a group of art students.

When Ivan Kramskoi and thirteen other senior students at the academy petitioned for the right to choose their own subjects for the Gold Medal competition of 1863, the Academic Council first showed signs of agreeing but then abruptly refused permission. Kramskoi protested, considering the matter to be one of principle, against arbitrary authority. The students withdrew from the competition and resigned from the academy, forfeiting their chances of obtaining further support for their studies, official commissions, recognition, and secure careers.[6] In order to provide a means of economic survival for the newly independent artists, Kramskoi organized a cooperative workshop, or *artel*, which solicited commissions and distributed them among the members, who then contributed a percentage of their earnings to a common fund. Basically, the *artel* was similar to the university student circles and workers' cooperatives that proliferated during the 1860s.[7] Economic independence as a key to social and moral independence was the goal of such groups; for Kramskoi, the goal was independence from "administrative guardianship" so that the artist could concentrate on "higher obligations."[8]

A large apartment, rented jointly by the *artel* members, was both an unofficial exhibition hall and a center for discussion of artistic and philosophical issues. Kramskoi introduced recently published works on aesthetics and social philosophy by such foreign writers as Pierre Joseph Proudhon (whose *Du principe de l'art et de sa destination sociale* appeared in Russian translation in 1865), Hippolyte Taine and Robert Owen,[9] as well as the Russian writers Dmitrii Pisarev and Nikolai Chernyshevskii, who dealt with social issues through the vehicle of literature. Pisarev, a pragmatist, declared the traditional arts, based on beliefs and superstitions rather than knowledge, to be useless for contemporary society.[10] Chernyshevskii's major thesis was that art must be true to reality and should serve chiefly as a "handmaiden of science" to "explain life" in a way that would be meaningful to ordinary people; above all, the artist should present the judgment of "a thinking man" on the events and issues of his time.[11]

Kramskoi evidently subscribed to these ideas. As early as 1858, he had written that the standards of ideal beauty worshipped by the ancients and promoted by the academy had no basis in real life.[12] During the early 1870s he wrote, "The heart of the matter lies not in paints and canvas . . . but in the worth of ideas and conceptions," and "Painting gives reality to thoughts. If this were not true, then painting would have no point."[13] He advised the young academy student Ilya Repin, "If you want to serve society, you should know and understand it in all its concerns, all its phenomena. . . . Indeed, an artist is a critic of social phenomena. [A painting] will be merely a photograph from nature, an étude, unless it is illuminated by the artist's philosophical outlook, and is the bearer of a profound idea of life."[14]

The dependence of the Russian realist artists on realist philosophy and criticism was considerable, especially in comparison with the relative independence and even vanguard position of the leading French realist painter, Gustave Courbet. However, only a few of the leaders were capable of understanding philosophical arguments, while some of the artists from the provinces were only minimally literate;[15] it is likely that many of them simply enjoyed the sense of participating in some way in the intellectual world of the capital. The *artel* and the longer lasting association of the Peredvizhniki brought young artists into contact with their peers and with more widely experienced members of the art community, writers, critics, and patrons. The most influential of these was the scholar and critic Vladimir Stasov.

Stasov viewed criticism as the act of interpretation that completed a work of art: "Every real work of art . . . bears within itself its *meaning* and its *allotted task;* to reveal both of these for the human race is the task of criticism."[16] Although he was familiar with European art and even recognized the innovations of Courbet, Manet, and the impressionists, Stasov believed that a national art was necessary to Russia's cultural development and insisted, as a matter of principle, that Russian artists respond to the particular requirements of Russian subject matter. In his enthusiastic promotion of Kramskoi, Perov, Repin, and other realists, Stasov sometimes emphasized as "national elements" motifs or details that may have been painted with no such intentions on the part of the artists. On the other hand, his writings also directed artists to particular subjects and may have warned them away from others. Historical painting, however accurately researched, was inconsistent with Stasov's realist principles. "Deeply realist artists," he wrote in 1879, "are unbreakably connected with just one period, that which they have seen with their own eyes, that which happened before their own inflamed senses. Their ability to comprehend and transmit belongs . . . exclusively to the present world, to present day life . . . and outside of this their work loses its strength, truth and fascination. The wave of inspiration is silenced and dissolved."[17] The relationship between Stasov's interpretation of realism and the actual content of realist art is complex; his writings are a valuable, though unreliable, guide to the artists' aims.

The formation of a joint association to exhibit works around the country was proposed in 1869 by a group of Moscow artists who had heard of the *artel* and its success and wrote to invite Kramskoi's participation. With the help of Stasov, Kramskoi gathered support among Petersburg artists; though only four other *artel* members agreed to the proposal, several independent genre painters and two students joined, bringing the total membership of the organization to seventeen. A definitive charter was prepared, which stated the goals of the association in their simplest form: "The Association has as its aim the establishment . . . of traveling artistic exhibitions with the prospect of: (a) creating the possibility for those who so desire to become acquainted with Russian art and follow its progress, (b) developing love of art in society, and (c) improving the market for artists' works."[18] Just over a year after its founding, on November 29, 1871, the association opened its first exhibition—on the premises of the Academy of Arts. Evidently neither the leaders of the Peredvizhniki nor the directors of the academy saw any danger in some cooperation. In St. Petersburg, sixteen artists showed forty-seven paintings, and in Moscow, twenty artists showed eighty-two works; the display was modest in comparison with the Academic Exhibition of 1870, where about two hundred works were shown. Altogether there were over 30,000 visitors, at least 8,500 in the provincial cities of Kiev and Kharkov.[19] Though buyers were to be found only in the capitals, the exhibitions traveled each year to about ten provincial towns in accordance with the group's program. For the first time conditions existed under which Russian art could be seen by a broad public.

Art of the Peredvizhniki: The Presence of Genre

Records and photographs of the exhibitions let us know what the paintings of the Peredvizhniki were like, but it is harder to pinpoint what distinguished them from the works of the academic artists. Important differences of both style and intention are expressed fully only in some of the outstanding works of Repin and other leading realists, but they can also be recognized in many less distinctive works by minor Peredvizhniki.

Landscape, genre, portraiture, and history painting were represented at the traveling exhibitions, as they were at the academic ones. Genre paintings, potentially the most explicitly Russian and social in content, seem in retrospect to characterize the Peredvizhniki best. However, genre works also appeared in academy exhibitions and even earned gold medals (though not the coveted large gold medals awarded for historical paintings).[20] Though given more attention by the Peredvizhniki, genre was still a minor category: out of forty-six paintings in the first exhibition, there were twenty-four landscapes and twelve portraits, but only ten "scenes from life."[21] Nonetheless, a pervasive genre character, what Stasov described as a "national" or popular element, could be found in a majority of works by the Peredvizhniki; landscapes, portraits, and historical paintings could convey a sense of the conditions of Russian life.

Of the landscapes at the first exhibition, Kramskoi felt that there was "soul" only in Savrasov's *The Rooks Have Arrived* (1871; fig. 6.4),[22] in which a close view of nature, of melting snow and birds nesting in quintessentially Russian birches, fills the foreground and sets off the church, bell tower, and village roofs in the middle distance and the broad muddy plain beyond. The human presence, a reminder that the landscape, village, and cycle of seasons were bound together in the eternal pattern of Russian life, relates this landscape to rural genre.

The relationship of portraiture to genre is best exemplified in the many paintings of peasants, like Perov's *Glum Fomushka* (1863) and Kramskoi's *Mina Moiseev* (1882; fig. 6.5), portrayed as a simple but wise man of the people. Nikolai Iaroshenko's *Stoker* (1878) is an especially powerful image of a laborer, with the monumentality of one of Velasquez's philosophers. An increasingly important type of genre portrait shows a well-known individual in a characteristic situation, as in Repin's portrait of Tolstoi in a peasant smock plowing a field (1887; fig. 6.6). The majority of the Peredvizhniki's portraits were of their fellow artists and other figures important in cultural life, such as Nekrasov, Dostoevskii, Turgenev, Tolstoi, and Stasov. These portraits bore the characteristics of realism: a physical likeness approaching photographic accuracy, often an expanded setting indicating the subjects' roles as thinkers or activists, and further, a sense of direct communication between subject and artist or subject and viewer.

A distinctive type of genre portraiture came into being in response to political events of the late 1870s and eighties: the composite image of the revolutionary. Iaroshenko was once placed under house arrest for including a recognizable likeness of a terrorist in a large painting,[23] so, instead of painting individuals, it became common for artists to combine features of actual political figures and other models who looked like revolutionary types. Far from being a contradiction of realism, such composite or universalized images fulfilled the main requirements of realist art. According to Chernyshevskii, in order to "represent life or remind one of life," art did not have to copy nature exactly but should "contain as little of the abstract as possible; everything in it must be . . . expressed concretely in living scenes and individual images."[24] The use of types based on judiciously combined individuals could avoid the abstraction or idealization of academic classicism. An example of a type portrayed as an individual is Iaroshenko's *Kursistka* (*Woman Student*) (1883; fig. 6.7), interpreted by the populist critic Gleb Uspenskii as the embodiment of a new ideal, the prototype of the "new people" who would bring about needed social changes.[25] A number of Repin's revolutionary subjects in *The Last Confession, Arrest of a Propagandist,* and other works of the 1880s belong to this category. The more complex concept of "contemporary history" and the relation of historical painting to genre will be discussed later in this essay.

Genre painting offered a broader range of subjects than did land-scape or portraiture, while it was also enriched by these traditions. Al-though Stasov and other critics did not designate separate categories of genre, there were clear differences on the basis of subject matter, format, and level of ambition. Three major types of genre were: (1) the genre portrait, (2) intimate scenes of peasant or urban life, such as Perov's *Last Tavern* and Vasilii Maksimov's *Sick Husband* (1881), and (3) multi-figured, broadly scaled scenes, such as Grigorii Miasoedov's *Reading the Emancipation Manifesto of February 19, 1861* (1873) and *The Zemstvo Dines* (1872), Konstantin Savitskii's *Repair Work on the Railroad* (1873) and *Meeting the Icon* (1878), and Repin's *Barge Haulers on the Volga* (1871–73) and *Religious Procession in Kursk Province* (1881–83). Not only artists but also critics and viewers were to become increasingly conscious of the range of meaning in genre painting in the 1870s and eighties.

The best known of all Russian genre paintings, Ilya Repin's *Barge Haulers on the Volga* (fig. 6.8), was shown not at the traveling exhibition but at the academy. The first independent piece by a young artist still finishing his training, the *Barge Haulers* was greeted as a key work that gave tremendous impetus to the development of Russian realism. The artist's approach to the subject and the reception of the work exemplify the situation of realism at the beginning of the seventies.

Repin first encountered barge haulers during an early summer excursion along the Neva River. In the midst of fine country houses and gardens, "a dark, greasy spot" seemed to be "creeping into the sunshine," a barge hauled against the current by a team of men so worn out and almost deformed that Repin called the scene "unbelievable, an incredible picture."[26] He later traveled to the upper Volga to get a closer view of the life of the barge haulers, and he got to know some of the men well. His early sketches emphasize the forward thrust of the group, by placing a boat to their left and a prominent hill to their right. The final version eliminates the hill and makes the boat a rather faint coda to the line of bargemen stretched out across a shallow, frieze-like space.

The new composition provided two important advantages: it allowed Repin to present the individual figures more clearly (ten are fully visible) and to set them off against the vastness of the Volga panorama. The line of figures runs parallel to the horizon and to the river itself, reinforcing the continuity of the human and landscape elements. At the same time, the predominantly vertical lines of the figures and the mast of the barge, all slightly varied in height and inclination, provide a contrasting rhythm. Significantly, the figures bend to the left, against the usual reading of a composition from left foreground back into the space of the right; this keeps the visual rhythm slow and emphasizes the physical effort of the men pulling the heavy barge.

Critics discussed both the social content of the work and the stylistic problems of balancing concrete observations with a more generalized interpretation of the theme as a whole, issues that continued to confront realist artists and critics throughout the next two decades. Stasov singled out Repin as the first who "dared to see and to put into his work that which is simple and true and which hundreds and thousands of people pass by without noticing."[27] He carefully described the various "types and characters" portrayed, and declared: "Repin is a realist, like Gogol, and like him is profoundly national. With an unprecedented boldness, he has cast off the last notion of any kind of idealism in art, and has plunged headlong into the depths of the national life, the interests of the people and the painful reality of the people."[28]

Fedor Dostoevskii, who opposed overt political messages in art, had gone to the exhibition with negative expectations. "But to my delight," he reported, "I had nothing to worry about. These are barge haulers, real barge haulers and nothing else. Not one shouts out from the painting to the viewer, 'See how pitiful I am and remember what you owe the people.' It is impossible not to love these defenseless folk. . . . Yet if they were not so natural, so innocent and simple, they could not have created such an impression and would not have made such a picture."[29]

It was no small matter that the work established Repin's reputation. The Grand Duke Vladimir, vice-president of the academy, saw a preliminary version and gave Repin an advance for the finished canvas. He planned to hang it in his billiard room. Repin, when he heard the news, remarked that it would be "quite a contrast" in that setting.[30] The work received international exposure when it was sent as part of the official Russian contribution to the Universal Exposition in Vienna in 1873. One critic called it the "most light-filled painting in the exhibition" and praised the "types, still-living Scyths."[31] When it was shown five years later at the Paris Universal Exposition, both Edmond Duranty and Paul Mantz commented favorably. The latter wrote: "Repin's brush has no pretentions to delicacy. He painted his Barge Haulers without flattering them, perhaps even exaggerating their lack of beauty. Proudhon, who was so affected by Courbet's Stone Breakers, would have found here a great occasion for inspiration."[32] Not only Stasov but also some foreign critics were most impressed by the sociological aspect of Repin's painting.

Others, especially artists, thought that Repin had achieved something that went beyond attention to a new subject. Ge, with characteristic generosity, told Repin, "It is remarkable. My *Last Supper* is nothing compared with this."[33] Kramskoi said that the work had made great strides for the realist movement: "Now, in the wake of Repin's *Barge Haulers* . . . it is no longer possible to stop."[34] These comments do not really specify what made *Barge Haulers* stand out, but it seems to have been Repin's success in combining specific detail with a general contour and emphasis that kept the work from being regarded merely as a genre picture and made its large size, its bareness, and its lack of beauty impressive. The character of Repin's contribution might best be seen in the context of other genre works painted around the same time.

Repin was certainly not the first, as Stasov claimed he was, to make the hardships of the poor the subject of a major painting. In the early 1860s, Stasov declared Vasilii Pukirev's *Unequal Marriage* (1862) worthy of the serious attention and large format "formerly the privilege of paintings on important subjects from political history."[35] Valerian Iakobi's *Halt of the Convoy of Prisoners* (1861; fig. 6.9) was one of the first large works to deal with contemporary political reality. The emotional effect is heightened by the death of a prisoner, close-up in the right foreground, and the visual echo of this motif in the pathetic group of women and children on the left. The foreground vignettes are set off against a mass of undifferentiated prisoners trudging into the distance. The composition follows a common formula of academic historical painting, in which the chief actors are highlighted against half-obscured crowds. But it was also a prototype for those genre works which engaged viewers in specific scenes while, through the presence of either large crowds or the vast Russian landscape, reminding them of the general truth of the situation depicted. Repin's *Barge Haulers* belongs to this type, though, as Dostoevskii noted, it avoids the obvious labels.

Genre works that attracted special attention at the exhibitions stood apart from traditional genre not only by virtue of their large scale, but also because of compositional devices that connoted dignity and monumentality and thus placed the paintings on a higher level than that of conventional genre. Both *Barge Haulers* and Miasoedov's *The Zemstvo Dines* (fig. 6.10) use horizontal compositions and frieze-like arrangements of solid, ponderous figures, familiar devices of academic painting. *The Zemstvo Dines* depicts a group of newly elected peasant members of the local *zemstvo* (a unit of government established through the reforms of the 1860s) waiting in a back courtyard, chewing on onions and crusts of bread, while their counterparts from the gentry enjoy a fine luncheon inside. Miasoedov's peasants are portrayed with the same care and respect as Repin's barge haulers. These figures are more massive and imposing than Repin's, but they are situated in a more restricted, less heroic setting. The message of this work is more specifically political (it criticizes ineffective reforms) and socially critical (it indicates class distinctions by the juxtaposition of the peasants with the elegant waiter glimpsed through a window), whereas Repin's painting offers a more generalized image of toiling human beings.

The most direct successor to the *Barge Haulers*, in both subject and composition, was *Repair Work on the Railroad* (1873; fig. 6.11) by Repin's friend Konstantin Savitskii. Here, as in Repin's painting, the chief impression is of repetitive toil and of the bending of many figures against an inert weight. Other echoes of Repin's barge haulers are the two strong men in the center foreground and the youth just behind them. The telegraph poles similarly recall the barge mast, and the small but significant figure of the overseer in the background has the same relative position as the members of the barge crew.[36] However, like Repin, Savitskii based his work on a specific observed scene, not on a general conception of labor.[37] In addition, by depicting the contemporary railroad workers rather than barge haulers, Savitskii drew attention to the changes that industrialization was beginning to bring to the countryside.

Like the liberal populists, some of the Peredvizhniki believed that the traditional peasant village was a remnant of proto-Russian society and should be preserved as the communal basis upon which to build a future society.[38] While many paintings of peasant life reflect the idea of the inherent worth of the peasantry, many show a more critical attitude. Miasoedov's *The Zemstvo Dines* pointed out the failure of reform from above. Repin's controversial *Arrest of a Propagandist* (1880–92) illustrated the ironic fact that the young populists who went out "to the people" to educate them and inform them of their rights did not always convince the peasants because of an ingrained hostility of the rural poor toward the urban intelligentsia. Savitskii commented on the fallacies of the liberal idealization of Russian religion and its role in conserving folk traditions in *Meeting the Icon*, which shows a large crowd of villagers from the poor huts in the background gathered to pray before the icon of the Madonna, which was brought from a town church on its annual round of the villages. The serious, pious peasants and their overawed children contrast with the indifferent guardians of the icon and the priest, whose heavy, vulgar face suggests a grotesquely sober parody of Perov's drunken clerics.

To War (1880–87; fig. 6.12) completes Savitskii's triad of major paintings that together show the disruption of the peasants' world. At a provincial station, a steam locomotive stands ready to be loaded with recruits (conscripts) for the Crimean War. This striking symbol of modernity is heightened by the deep perspective thrust of the platform, in contrast with the flat horizons behind the less agitated crowds of the previous two pictures. Most of the soldiers are peasant boys leaving home for the first time. One at the center strains for a last look at his family, and throughout the crowd are similar brief scenes, each suggesting a story. This type of painting has much in common with Victorian narratives like W. P. Frith's *The Railway Station* (1862). On the other hand, the intention of the artist here was to convey the sense of a much larger, unseen crowd in similar stations all over Russia.

Vladimir Makovskii also produced works featuring crowds as victims, particularly in urban settings, as in *Fall of a Bank* (1881) and *The Doss House* (1889), an enormous canvas in which the dozen figures spread across the foreground catalogue the varieties of poverty, while the background is half-filled with a mass of their companions huddled against the walls, waiting for the building to open. His more successful works have a smaller cast of characters and more specific focus, as in two similar paintings inspired by the mass arrests of populists toward the end of the 1870s, *The Condemned Man* (1879) and *The Acquitted Woman* (1882), or in *Evening Meeting* (1875–97; fig. 6.13), which depicts a group of radicals from all walks of life. Makovskii makes the conflict of old and new ways more intimate in *On the Boulevard* (1886–87; fig. 6.14), a quiet human drama set in a softly colorful cityscape. The two figures, a girl cradling a swaddled baby and a young fellow in large boots and carelessly open jacket, playing an accordion, do not communicate. There is complete separation and incomprehension between the peasant, who went to the city for work and forgot about his family back in the village, and his wife, who managed to find her way to him to show him their child and now has nothing to do but go back. It is another typical episode in the breakdown of traditional rural society.

Repin had won his reputation as a socially concerned and effective painter in 1873, but he needed experience and perspective before he was able to undertake subjects more complex and ambitious than the *Barge Haulers*. A three-year stay in Europe awarded by the academy provided this perspective. In Paris he found a much more varied and sophisticated art world than that of Petersburg. Although his letters concern generally approved art of the Salons (Regnault, Neuville, Carolus-Duran, and Gérôme figure frequently) and the old masters in the Louvre, he displayed some independence in judging new developments. He was certainly less biased than were most Frenchmen against the impressionists. When he visited the first exhibition of the independents, he compared it favorably with the Salon: "the remarkable thing here is the appearance of the realists," he reported home; "so far they are refused and are not to be found at the Salon but only in other small exhibitions. But they have a positive future, and now the best things can definitely be associated with this realist school."[39] Repin was acquainted with Louis Leroy, whose satirical article in

Charivari (April 25, 1874) set the tone for public reactions to the exhibition, but he seems not to have been cowed by what he called "the authority of the French."[40] He had opportunities to talk with Zola (whom he met through Turgenev) and he may have been aware of Zola's defense of Manet and the impressionists. In any case, he wrote specifically of his own admiration for Manet's spontaneity and "childlike truth," and he even imitated the sketchlike style when he painted his small daughter "à la Manet."[41] Repin spent a good deal of time sketching scenes of daily life on the boulevards, and he submitted to the Salon a distinctly French painting, *Parisian Café* (1874–75), which he described as "depicting the chief types of Paris in their most typical setting."[42] He spent a summer at Etretat and Veulles on the Normandy coast doing *plein-air* studies. Repin's letters from this period convey his pleasure in being temporarily free of the "demands and high ideals of Russian artists." Only a year after his arrival in Paris he wrote to Kramskoi: "I have now completely forgotten how to judge, and I do not regret the loss of this faculty, which was consuming me. On the contrary, I would prefer that it never returned, though I sense that back within the boundaries of our beloved homeland it will again exert its rights over me. . . . May God preserve Russian art from corrosive analysis! When will it push its way out of this fog?"[43]

This letter was taken by Kramskoi and Stasov as a sign of apostasy on Repin's part; they feared that their protégé was trying to become a fashionable, pseudo-French painter, that he had lost his "convictions regarding the main conditions of art, its means and especially its national strain."[44] Repin's reply affirms his growing experience of a variety of art. One cannot insist dogmatically on "the main conditions of art," he said, because "what for one century or even one generation is considered a fixed rule . . . for the next is . . . an absurd platitude. . . . The means of art change quickly and are dependent on the temperament of each artist." The national strain, which Stasov and Kramskoi considered so crucial, was for Repin simply an element of the artist's character or temperament.[45] He hotly disputed charges that he was imitating a foreign style and defended his interest in Parisian subjects and in Manet's "language" as part of his individual artistic exploration. Repin's stay in Paris did not produce a major painting, but it did give him confidence. On his return to Russia in 1876, he was able to look at familiar subjects with fresh eyes and to begin working out ways of presenting them in a fresh and original language.

Repin first spent several months in his native Chuguev, in the Ukraine, where he immersed himself in local impressions, made studies of landscapes and local people, and began to work out ideas for major paintings that he was to complete years later. Among the Chuguev studies are two small sketches of a religious procession similar to that in Savitskii's *Meeting the Icon*. Although he put off work on the painting because he did not want to compete with his friend, the theme continued to occupy Repin for years, and the resulting work (fig. 6.15) was a summation of and final word on religious traditions in times of change.

In order to refresh his old impressions and gather new material, Repin traveled to Kursk province (a region famous for its traditional processions) in the summer of 1881. His conception of the subject was changed by what he saw there. The district suffered from drought, which was aggravated by the irresponsible cutting of timber and left dusty, eroded hills pocked by stumps.[46] The processions of the icon that Repin witnessed were no longer just traditional ceremonies to bring good crops but the peasants' last hope for a miracle.

Repin's plan was to gather impressions and make a number of individual studies of figures and small groups; he would then bring together the most distinctive and appropriate types and compose a procession that would sum up the character of all he had seen. The new element in his conception of the subject was its contemporaneity. The new painting would indicate the specific conditions under which the people gathered in Kursk province in 1881.

Although the painting is very large and at first glance seems unorganized, Repin explained that every detail had a purpose and was subordinate to "the harmonious truth of the whole."[47] The landscape in all its ugliness is important both thematically and compositionally: the large, empty area of parched earth in the foreground echoes the bare hill and contrasts with the densely packed crowd, emphasizing the ironic connection between the landscape itself and the procession, between the real drought and the superstitious hope of relief. The participants represent all social classes. The central figure is a landowner's wife carrying an icon with a convoy of uniformed guards. Though placed well back, she is set off by the space in front, the banners behind, and the mounted gendarmes and the two masses of people at either side. On the extreme right, cut off by the frame as if they continue moving behind it, a dozen sturdy peasants carry the gilt and beribboned shrine; just behind them, two middle-class women hold the empty wood icon case, and a few paces after them, a priest in golden vestments swings a censer. The rest of the crowd, stretching out to the left, less closely packed and more individually described, consists of the poor and crippled, those who really believe in the icon. The hunchback with a crutch, hurrying to get closer to the center, was the subject of several studies; Repin regarded him as the most expressive character in the picture, embodying both suffering and faith.[48]

Some of Repin's friends were dismayed by the ugliness of some of the figures and the landscape. Polenov and Tretiakov went so far as to beg Repin to replace the commonplace women carrying the icon with a pretty girl that they remembered from an earlier version.[49] Repin chided his friends for their concern for superficial beauty and claimed, with some assurance, that he had arrived at a different and more truly artistic approach to reality.

> In a painting one may allow only such faces as the general intention of the work permits. Deliberate prettification would kill it. For the living and harmonious truth of the whole, one cannot avoid sacrificing details. . . . Above everything else stands truth to life. This always includes a profound idea, and to split it up into details, especially intentionally, is simply a profanation and a sacrilege.[50]

He reminded his friends that they could hardly expect to see beautiful faces in the forefront of a real crowd, "just there for your pleasure," nor would they find beautiful men and women in works by the great seventeenth-century realists Velasquez and Rembrandt.[51]

Repin's main point was that the complex whole of the picture was more important than its details and that any inappropriate emphasis would upset its balance. Whereas a beautiful girl would have been a vulgar addition, the earnest cripple, the complacent landowners, and the steward with his upraised stick were all essential to the situation depicted. Aside from the appropriateness of the types represented, the scale itself gave the picture unity and conviction. Repin's handling of figures and space—the repetition of characteristic shapes and gestures, the cutting of marginal figures by the frame to give the illusion that they surround and move past the viewer, the linear and aerial perspective—together produce a convincing effect of spatial and temporal continuity. This generalization both accentuates and works with the contrasting details that point to the particular time and place— the newly cut tree stumps, the cloud of dust, the position of the shadows —so that the picture achieves both the objective appearance of a real scene and an analysis of its component elements and their relationships. This combination of representation and analysis, of the concrete and the general,[52] marks a level of realist genre that was only latent in *Barge Haulers* and only hinted at in Stasov's earlier discussions of realism.

History and Contemporary Life

The ambivalence of the leading realists toward historical painting is attested in the hybrid character of some of the best known and most controversial works of the period, including Kramskoi's *Christ in the Wilderness* (1872), a composite of portraiture and history painting,

Repin's *Ivan the Terrible* (1883), a historical subject with an explicit connection to events of the 1880s, and Repin's *They Did Not Expect Him* (1884–88), described both as ideological genre and as contemporary history painting.

Kramskoi's *Christ in the Wilderness* (fig. 6.16) was not a traditional religious icon but almost a typological portrait. Kramskoi once explained to Repin that he saw Christ's ordeal in the desert as a symbol of the eternal human struggle against the "dark side of human nature,"[53] and in a sense the work is a spiritual self-portrait of the artist as a thinking, moral, and struggling human being. "I see clearly," Kramskoi wrote, "that there is one moment in the life of every man, when he hesitates . . . to turn to the right or the left, to take the ruble in place of God, or to refuse to yield a step to evil. . . . This is not Christ. This is the expression of my personal beliefs."[54] Kramskoi, who read Strauss and Renan, believed that Christ was not divine but human, and was also "the greatest of atheists, the man who destroyed the God of Heaven and placed him at the center of man's soul."[55] He seems to have felt that his more humble task as an artist was analogous: to destroy the conventionalized image of Christ, to remove it from the academic pedestal and instead bring a believable human Christ to life.

Kramskoi wished to personify his belief "in natural language . . . accessible to all."[56] But he could not reconcile the familiar and accessible traditional image of Christ with his profound desire to portray a human being. "I have a terrible need to tell others what I think. But how to tell them? How, in what way, can I be understood?"[57] The failure of this image as either art or communication underlines the difficulties realists faced in reconciling aims and methods.

Repin's *Ivan the Terrible and his Son Ivan, November 16, 1581* (1885; fig. 6.17) illustrates an incident symbolic of the violence and tragedy of Russian history. But it can also be related directly to contemporary events. According to notes Repin made later, he first visualized the scene of Ivan the Terrible killing his son under the impact of the assassination of Tsar Alexander II and the execution of the terrorists, "the bloody events of March 1, 1881," and he turned to the historical subject partly to gain some distance from the shocking events: "My feelings were overwhelmed by the horrors of the present. This was the general mood of life then. Such pictures stood before our eyes but no one dared to paint them. It was natural to seek an escape into the painful tragedy of history. . . ."[58]

While he was concerned with the historical parallels between Ivan's murder of his son and the recent regicide, Repin was above all sensitive to the personal agony caused by violence. Kramskoi admired the way in which the artist was able to communicate the "shock of the death" through the two figures alone. The "horror and helplessness" of both animal-like father and innocent son, he thought, so completely expressed the deepest human emotions that the painting could truly elevate the human spirit.[59] Repin evidently felt the emotional pressures of the human issues as well as the strain of the current political tension while he was at work on the painting. He wrote that he painted in a "frenzy,"[60] hardly able to get away from the canvas, but of course he devoted considerable study to the problem of expressing complex ideas in a concentrated and immediate way.

His first sketches give the basic composition of the two figures at the center of a large dark room and the color scheme of red and green. Though details were later altered, it is clear that he originally saw the scene much as he finally painted it. The expressions of the two closely juxtaposed faces were crucial to the emotional meaning of the painting. Repin made many studies of both, using as models the artist Miasoedov and the writer Vsevolod Garshin, among others. Garshin was especially valuable because his character, his "meekness, dovelike purity," was precisely what he imagined for the Tsarevich.[61] Besides the faces, the colors of the garments contributed to the contrast between the characters: the Tsarevich was painted in a delicate rose-pink caftan and the Tsar in a robe of dark, cold brown. The shocking red spurt of blood marks the dramatic and coloristic center of the canvas. The strong contrast of complementaries in the center—red and pink against the green boots of the Tsarevich—extends throughout the composition, through the rug, to the fallen bolster and chair, the greenish tile stove, and the red-and-green diamond pattern of the far wall. The color is not only intense and dramatic in itself, but it also reinforces the centrality of the composition. The details around the central figures, except for the murder weapon at the lower edge of the canvas, are minimal to the theme, but they are placed so that they can direct attention back to the center, to the dramatic focus of the painting.

Repin described his work on the painting as almost pathological in intensity. He hesitated to talk about it or show it to his friends, but finally he took Kramskoi, Iaroshenko, and a few others into his studio. "The painting was very effectively lit by lamps and the impression it made . . . went beyond all my expectations. The guests, stunned, were silent for some time. Then they spoke only in whispers. I covered the painting, but even then the mood did not dissolve."[62] Kramskoi's comments suggest that it was not the subject alone but also the emotional intensity that moved the audience. Repin himself stated that he hoped to convey the overwhelming power of Rimskii-Korsakov's music in his own work.[63]

When Repin turned to historical themes during the period in which he was also occupied with contemporary subjects, he chose ones that bore some relationship to the present. If he found relief from the "horrors of the present" in the "tragedy of history,"[64] he also found that an image from the past could be held up like a lens through which to see the present in a new perspective. Repin's aim was not to denature the contemporary tragedy but rather to find a vehicle for expressing its broader historical and psychological meaning. It was a difficult task, and one that Stasov believed was not possible for a realist artist, since "deeply realist artists are unbreakably connected with just one period."[65] It is no accident that Stasov's view of the limits of realism echoes Courbet's declaration of his principles in his "Realist Manifesto" of 1855.[66] In his most exhaustive article on realist art and theory, "Twenty-five Years of Russian Art," Stasov quotes Courbet's statement and applies it to contemporary Russian art:

> Courbet said that the task of today's artist is to "translate the truths, ideas and appearance of our times, each artist as an individual, and to feel and understand, to be not only an artist but a man; in a word to create *living art*." The artist does not have the right or the ability to represent centuries which he has not seen himself and has not studied from nature. The only possible history is the history of the artist's own time.[67]

In Stasov's opinion, Repin risked his artistic integrity when he painted scenes from the remote past, just as he did when he chose Parisian subjects.

Repin himself wrote of the artist's mission to confront issues of contemporary life and illuminate them in his work: "I try to embody my ideas in truth; surrounding life upsets me too much, it gives me no peace but demands the canvas. Reality is too shocking to allow one to embroider its patterns with an easy conscience."[68] In 1881 he wrote of his intention to move to Petersburg and "begin working on paintings which I have been thinking about for some time—paintings about the most stirring reality that surrounds us, that means something to us and that excites us more than all events of the past."[69] His treatment of the "stirring reality" of the present was based largely on his familiarity with events related to the populist movement of the 1870s and 1880s.

In his native Chuguev, Repin had encountered not only traditional religious processions but also some of the students who tried to arouse the peasants and who were arrested in large numbers in 1874 and 1878. Two works of this period show his impressions of these early contacts. *Convoy on a Muddy Road* (1876 or 1877) depicts an open wagon in which a prisoner is being conveyed on the first stage toward Siberia. It is just a small sketch; it vividly conveys the physical sensation of a cold drizzle and expresses sympathy for the prisoner, but it brings out no political questions. In *Arrest of a Propagandist* (1878–92) Repin began to explore the circumstances of the populist activists and the people they tried to change. The arrest in a peasant cottage—the protagonist tied up in the center of the room while police examine incriminating pamphlets and villagers look on with either regret or satisfaction—was a recognizable scene of frequent occurrence, particularly in the south of Russia. Similar scenes painted by Vladimir Makovskii and Nikolai Iaroshenko during the same period contributed, like Repin's work, to an increasingly familiar imagery of the populist movement.[70]

Repin was in Petersburg for the opening of the Ninth Traveling Exhibition on March 1, 1881, the day a group of terrorists assassinated the Tsar with homemade bombs, and he returned at the beginning of April, in time for the trial and execution of the regicides. "What a time of nightmare that was," he later recalled, "pure horror. . . . I remember the condemned with placards hung on their chests bearing the inscription 'regicide.'"[71] Repin was not in direct contact with any of the revolutionaries, but letters of the period express a relatively positive view of the revolutionary movement and its general aims.[72] During the decade of the 1880s, as he worked on images of contemporary and historical conflicts, his attitudes changed. His works showed the revolutionaries with sympathy but also with growing emphasis on their isolation and impotence.

Refusal of the Last Confession (1879–85) shows the confrontation of a prisoner about to be executed with a priest who offers him the last rites. While Repin did not actually enter "the darkness of the prisons to paint the proud and horrible last moments of the men and women condemned to death," as one author suggests,[73] he did devote some effort to learning the facts about the recent trials and to familiarizing himself with the literature of the revolutionary movement.[74] The subject of *Refusal of the Last Confession* was taken from a poem published in an illegal journal, in which the idealistic revolutionary is likened to "a hermit devoted only to God."[75] The religious fervor of the poem may have made Repin accentuate the spiritual abyss between the revolutionary and the representative of conventional religion, and to try to produce a visual equivalent of this condition rather than merely an anecdotal illustration of the text. The composition recalls Rembrandt's *Prodigal Son,* one of the paintings in the Hermitage that Repin most admired.[76] The essential difference is that here a thick darkness separates the figures instead of surrounding them and binding them together. The contrasting highlights on the prisoner's face and the priest's crucifix, a stylistic feature also associated with Rembrandt, reinforces the ideological barrier between revolutionary and priest and the impossibility of religious solace for the condemned man.

Two other paintings done soon after the execution of the regicides stress a heightened emotional effect without specific reference to persons or events. *Revolutionary Meeting* (1883; fig. 6.18) may be compared with Makovskii's painting of the same subject, *Evening Meeting* (1875–97; fig. 6.13). Whereas Makovskii's treatment is narrative and almost excessively descriptive, Repin's handling is unspecific and expressive. Repin stresses the coherence of the group and, instead of delineating its members, blurs the individualities by the intense contrast of bright highlights and the dark, hot colors, and by the extremely close focus. There is a strong hint of Rembrandt's style; Repin may have deliberately recalled the *Conspiracy of Claudius Civilis* in his effort to avoid Makovskii's prosaic approach and achieve an effect of urgency and involvement in the drama.[77] Related in style is *Solitary Confinement* (*Woman Revolutionary Awaiting Execution*) (undated), a laconic, monumental image on the scale of Kramskoi's *Christ in the Wilderness*. Although the figure was readily associated with various well-known revolutionaries, the painting is not a portrait; it focuses less on the specific situation than on the general hopelessness of a solitary human being.

Repin's most important painting on the theme of revolutionaries, *They Did Not Expect Him* (or *The Unexpected Return*) (1884–88; fig. 6.19), represents a more complex attitude toward a political subject than the psychological engagement shown in the preceding works. In visual and narrative terms this change can be seen as a change of focus. Attention is centered on the man just entering the room, but this attention is different from the unflinching concentration on the solitary prisoner. The concrete details and the daylight diffuse the drama and establish a convincing, everyday reality. The garden visible through the windows, the shadow of the footstool on the polished floor, the old armchair, the table covered with school books, the piano, map, and pictures all belong to a familiar environment, suddenly disrupted by the appearance of an alien figure, a political exile who had been absent so long that his schoolage daughter does not know him. Repin presents the situation through the responses and as if through the eyes of the family members.

Because of this diffusion of focus, the central figure had to fulfill special requirements.[78] The exile was intended to stand for all the revolutionaries and yet had to be depicted as a concrete personality. In the small first version of the painting, *The Unexpected Return* (1883; fig. 6.20), the exile is a young woman, and the impact of the painting depends on details that stress the tension between normally close family members and the estrangement forced on them by circumstances. The setting emphasizes this contrast. The impressionistic technique and light palette produce an atmosphere of peacefulness

and intimacy in the room and at the same time accentuate the fragility
of the illusion of peace. An engraving of Mount Vesuvius erupting,
the most prominent of the pictures on the far wall, is a symbol of the
catastrophic forces underlying the scene.

When he turned to a larger canvas, Repin not only gave the scene
more visual breadth, but he also enriched the iconographic sophistication by constructing a wider framework of associations within the
setting. He replaced the young woman with an older man, possibly
because he already identified the well-established, positive image of
the female revolutionary with a heroic stage of the movement that had
ended by 1884. The failure of an idealistic struggle, the sense of
defeat, frustration and estrangement, was a new theme that had meaning beyond the immediate events.[79]

Details of the setting are connected with Repin's attitude toward
the subject.[80] Aside from the furnishings appropriate to the modest
summer house, the decor consists of a map on the right-hand wall and
a group of framed photographs and engravings. A photograph of
Tsar Alexander II lying in state after his assassination places the
scene in time and establishes the loyalty of the family. The exile could
have been freed in the amnesty arranged for the coronation of Alexander III, so the presence of the photograph and its position nearly
opposite the exile's head underscore the irony of the revolutionary's
return to this home. The pictures on the far wall extend the suggestion
of time and history. The paired portraits of the populist writers of the
1860s, Nikolai Nekrasov and Taras Shevchenko, belong on the wall
as if they have been there for some time, whereas the photograph of
the dead Tsar belongs to the present and is causally related to the
presence of the exile. Dominating all these images, however, is a large
engraving after Karl Shteiben's well known *Christ on Golgotha* (1841).
This eminently accessible academic work serves to tie together all
the victims represented—the poets, the dead Tsar, and the exhausted
exile—within the universal and timeless theme of Christ's sacrifice.
Moreover, "golgotha" was a popular term for the prisoners' dock.[81]

The composition reinforces this iconography. The limited space of
the room is opened out in three directions, through the open door-
way, the window onto the garden, and the map of Russia on the wall.
But within the space of the picture, the exile is isolated, both from
his family and from his symbolic counterparts in the framed pictures,
by the firm dividing line of the door through which he arrived. He
is pinioned in a cell-like space by the converging lines of the floor-
boards and the frame of the door behind his head, which echoes the
shape of the cross of Golgotha. The cross and the portraits, which
reinforce the identification of the exile with the idealistic revolutionary
movement of the sixties, offer little comfort. The irony of the true

situation, the abandonment of earlier hopes of reform and reconciliation, certainly involved some feeling of disillusionment for the artist. Repin knew that his decision to portray contemporary life meant abandoning the more heroic images of earlier years for a depiction of confusion and failure.

Stasov praised Repin's paintings of revolutionaries for the immediacy and clarity with which they communicated ideas: "Besides the words 'They Did Not Expect Him,' there was no exegesis of the subject, but everyone understood it immediately. . . . Clearly there was really something important here that immediately touched everyone."[82] This statement summarizes Stasov's views of the essential values of realist art. It also implies that a painting must communicate ideas by its own appropriate means and not depend on literary explication. But Stasov did not describe the stylistic qualities that made a painting expressive and memorable.

The stylistic differences between *They Did Not Expect Him* and the other works on the revolutionary theme not only reveal Repin's varying attitudes toward the subject but also show his understanding of the effects of different styles on the interpretation of ideas. For distinct purposes Repin employed both the dramatic, emotional effects of warm, dark colors and intense highlights, in *Refusal of the Last Confession, Revolutionary Meeting,* and *Ivan the Terrible,* and the more objective impression created by the cool colors and even lighting in *They Did Not Expect Him.* In none of these works was he either wholly objective or wholly overwhelmed by his feelings about the subjects. On the contrary, he searched carefully for the best models and the best stylistic means through which to convey his ideas. Repin's goal of treating "surrounding life" with the kind of clarity and emphasis that would affirm the importance of both the subjects and the works of art was one that brought the question of realist style into focus for Repin himself as well as his supporters and critics.

Elements of Realist Style

Repin responded to Stasov's assertion that realist art must belong "exclusively to the present world" by taking it as a challenge: by painting works that in some way bridged the gap between past and present. Thematically, *Ivan the Terrible* carried associations with recent events, while portrayals of contemporary revolutionaries contained suggestions of a philosophical or historical framework broader than the specific events they depicted. Stylistically, Repin tried to avoid the limitations of both conventional academic historical painting and the overly prosaic, documentary approach to genre, historical, and contemporary subjects for which the Peredvizhniki were criticized.[83]

Repin's interest in older art played a role in his search for styles appropriate to his subjects. The artists he most admired, the seventeenth-century "realists," gave him needed confirmation for his own efforts to achieve realism, "truth to the whole," and vitality of expression. In 1883, Repin traveled through Europe with Stasov, in order to study European art, especially the work of Rembrandt and Velasquez, Rubens and Caravaggio. In Velasquez above all he identified the qualities that he considered most essential to genuine art:

> Such depth of understanding, originality, splendid talent and humble study, all this lies within him, in his profound passion for art, reaching ecstasy in each of his works. It is from this that what seems (to ignorant eyes) to be incompleteness arises. But in fact the tension of profound creativity did not allow him to finish details cooly. That would have destroyed a gift of God.[84]

Repin's trip sharpened his awareness of a gulf between the great art of the past and ephemeral modes in contemporary art. He became impatient and critical of "the endless garbage of imitations" that he saw not only in the Salons but even in the Louvre.[85] What is more important is that he continually related his observations of other art to his own goals. His refusal to pursue superficial beauty in *Religious Procession* was justified by the examples of Rembrandt and Velasquez. His emphasis on the lack of finish in Velasquez suggests that he looked to the latter for the very qualities that were becoming characteristic of his own style. Repin's search for confirmation in the great seventeenth-century realists seems to reflect a lingering uncertainty about the nature of modern art that some of his contemporaries in Europe shared.[86]

Nevertheless, the style of *They Did Not Expect Him* clearly owes something to French impressionism. The effects of natural light, so important in conveying both the mood and the meaning of the scene, were perhaps equally important as stylistic indications of contemporaneity. Repin's return to Paris in 1883 revived his interest in impressionism, and he used a modified impressionist technique in the only painting he did during his stay there, *The Annual Memorial Meeting at the Wall of the Communards, Père Lachaise Cemetery in Paris* (1883). The quick, broad brush-strokes and the bright, contrasting colors reflect the excitement of activity and participation conveyed in Repin's letters about the events.[87] Repin's treatment of a specific, limited subject related to his political interests in the modern, timely style of the French impressionists may have suggested a means of reinforcing the contemporary character of his more complex and ambitious painting as well.

They Did Not Expect Him and other major paintings of the period contain a variety of qualities that Repin identified with realism: subjects from real life, details that contribute to the verisimilitude of the situation and also introduce broader ideas, characterizations of the protagonists that convey both individual psychology and a sense of deeper conflicts, and a technique that combines both conscientious observation and a recognizable artistic temperament. The artist's feeling for his subject—whether in portraiture, historical painting, genre, or landscape, or whether profound ideas or merely visual impressions were to be conveyed—is central to an understanding of the realism in the art of Repin and his contemporaries. Two basic conceptions of realism in Europe, that it should be strictly objective and thus inherently unselective, were alien to the Russian's concept of realism.

A truthful portrayal of contemporary life in Russia implied at least some attention to exposure of injustice, suffering, and strife; although only a small proportion of pictures exhibited by the Peredvizhniki dealt with serfdom, poverty, antigovernment activities, or other controversial issues, the presence of a few such works at the exhibitions, always noted by Stasov, gave a measure of seriousness and significance to the art of the Peredvizhniki in general. A preference for humble subjects, simple, lowly genre, landscapes, still-life details of crude, ordinary objects rather than rare, elegant ones, was shared by realists in other countries, and this preference often had political implications: the choice meant a rejection of the ruling values of both society in general and the artistic establishment in particular. Similarly, subjects lacking conventional beauty were thought to be inherently more honest and truthful than the artificially picturesque or rhetorically elevated subjects of academic art. Ugliness could be a guarantee of authenticity. Repin added a new dimension to his defense of ugliness when he reminded Tretiakov that beautiful men and women did not appear in the foregrounds of paintings by Velasquez and Rembrandt. In a sense, Repin was authenticating his treatment of his own subject by citing the great realists of the past as his models.

"Truth to the whole," in Repin's terms, required not only a sincere regard for the subject but also the development of a stylistic language that would illuminate and not distort the content of a work, but certainly the language of an artist and not a pedant. Repin made this distinction and applied it to his current goals in 1883: "I am not a *feuilletonist*, but I cannot occupy myself with pure art alone. . . . With all my meager strength, I strive to embody my ideas in truth."[88] However, Repin added that he was not so naïve as to rely only on the truth of ideas to carry the weight of the work; like the great masters, he would "always strive for truth and innovation, in a word, go forward" as an artist.[89] Repin was not a typical realist or a typical member of the Peredvizhniki; Kramskoi and other friends recognized the individuality of his art. It was partly because of their ambitious goals and distinctive styles that Repin's mature works came to represent the culmination of the most productive stage of Russian realism.

NOTES

1. For a history of the Peredvizhniki, see Elizabeth K. Valkenier, *Russian Realist Art. The State and Society: The Peredvizhniki and their Tradition* (Ann Arbor, 1977).

2. I. Kramskoi, letter to V. Stasov, July 21, 1886, in S. N. Gol'dshtein, ed., *I. N. Kramskoi. Pis'ma, stat'i* (Moscow, 1966), II, 418.

3. N. Moleva and E. Beliutin, *Russkaia khudozhestvennaia shkola vtoroi poloviny XIX–nachala XX veka* (Moscow, 1967), pp. 10–25, and passim, gives a thorough account of the academic system and curriculum.

4. V. Perov, letter to the Council of the Academy of Art, June 4, 1864, in A. A. Guber et al., eds., *Mastera iskusstva ob iskusstve* (Moscow, 1969), VI, 393.

5. V. I. Porudominskii, *Nikolai Ge* (Moscow, 1970), pp. 28–29.

6. Kramskoi's account of the event is in his article "Sud'by russkogo iskusstva" (1880), in *Kramskoi. Pis'ma*, II, 304–42. V. Porudominskii, *I. N. Kramskoi* (Moscow, 1974), pp. 43–45, provides documentation. Valkenier, *Russian Realist Art*, pp. 34–36, summarizes the issues.

7. I. N. Punina, *Peterburgskaia artel' khudozhnikov* (Leningrad, 1966).

8. Kramskoi, letter to Stasov, July 21, 1886, in *Kramskoi. Pis'ma*, II, 418–19.

9. I. Repin, "Ivan Nikolaevich Kramskoi. Pamiati uchitelia" (1888), in Repin, *Dalekoe blizkoe* (Moscow, 1953), p. 175. Proudhon's book was translated and published in St. Petersburg within months of its publication in Paris; Owen's *Essays on the Formation of Human Character* appeared in Russian the same year. Taine's *Philosophie de l'art* (1865) was not yet published in translation, but a member of Kramskoi's circle, art critic V. Chuiko, had heard Taine's lectures in Paris, and he read his notes of them to the *artel* group.

10. D. Pisarev, "The Destruction of Aesthetics" ("Razrushenie estetiki," 1865), in Pisarev, *Sochineniia* (Moscow, 1956), III, 418–35.

11. N. G. Chernyshevskii, "The Aesthetic Relation of Art to Reality," in *Selected Philosophical Essays* (Moscow, 1953), pp. 287–312. This essay was Chernyshevskii's master's thesis, and an abstract was published in *Sovremennik* in 1855.

12. Kramskoi, "Vzgliad na istoricheskuiu zhivopis'" (1858), in *Kramskoi. Pis'ma*, II, 271–73.

13. Kramskoi, letters to F. Vasiliev, August 20, 1872, and February 13, 1875, in *Kramskoi. Pis'ma*, I, 126, 158.

14. Repin, *Dalekoe blizkoe*, 165–66.

15. Cf. Elizabeth Valkenier, "The Peredvizhniki and the Spirit of the 1860s," *The Russian Review* 34, no. 3 (July 1975): 250–53.

16. V. V. Stasov, letter to V. P. Stasov, January 1, 1844, in Stasov, *Pis'ma k rodnym* (Moscow, 1953), I, 33.

17. Stasov, "Khudozhestvennye vystavki 1879 goda," in V. Stasov, *Izbrannoe. Russkoe iskusstvo* (Moscow, Leningrad, 1950), I, 122.

18. *Ustav Tovarishchestva Peredvizhnykh Vystavok.* St. Petersburg, November 2, 1870. Quoted in E. Gomberg-Verzhbinskaia, *Peredvizhniki* (Leningrad, 1970), p. 42. The signers were: Kramskoi, Ge, Dmitriev-Orenburgskii, Zhuravlev, Lemokh, Korzukhin, Iakobi, Perov, Popov, Sverchkov, Trutovskii, Volkov, Grigoriev, Shishkin, Repin, and Vasiliev (in St. Petersburg) and Kamenev, M. K. Klodt, M. P. Klodt, K. Makovskii, V. Makovskii, Miasoedov, Perov, Prianishnikov, and Savrasov (in Moscow).

19. The figures are given by Stasov, "Peredvizhnaia Vystavka 1878," *Izbrannoe*, I, 102. Cf. Academy of Arts, U.S.S.R., *Pervaia Vystavka Tovarishchestva Peredvizhnykh Khudozhestvennykh Vystavok: Rekonstruktsiia* (Moscow, Leningrad, 1971), exhibition catalogue, a reconstruction of the first traveling exhibition on its centenary.

20. Cf. Moleva and Beliutin, *Russkaia khudozhestvennaia shkola*, pp. 45, 57–58. Genre had been introduced at the academy in the 1840s, under the designation "work from nature" or "composition study," and was first admitted for exhibition in 1859. The academy awarded small gold medals "for expressiveness" to V. Maksimov, V. Makovskii, and to Repin for *Barge Haulers*.

21. Stasov, "Peredvizhnaia Vystavka 1871 goda," *Izbrannoe*, I, 54.

22. Kramskoi, letter to F. Vasiliev, December 6, 1871, in *Perepiska I. N. Kramskogo* (Moscow, 1954), II, 13, describing the opening of the exhibition.

23. M. V. Nesterov, *Davnie dni. Vstrechi i vospominaniia* (Moscow, 1959), p. 67.

24. Chernyshevskii, "Aesthetic Relation of Art to Reality," p. 371.

25. G. Uspenskii, "Po povodu odnoi malen'koi kartinki," *Iz razgovorov s priiateliami*, in *Otechestvennye Zapiski*, no. 2 (1883): 557–58. For further discussion of such images, see A. Hilton, "The Revolutionary Theme in Russian Realism," in H. Millon and L. Nochlin, eds., *Art and Architecture in the Service of Politics* (Cambridge, Mass., 1978).

26. Repin, *Dalekoe blizkoe*, pp. 217–18. These memoirs, written around 1914, supplement the very meagre references to the painting in letters; they are, however, occasionally lyrical and imprecise.

27. Stasov, "Kartina Repina Burlaki na Volge," *S.-Peterburgskie Vedomosti* (1873), *Izbrannoe*, I, 67.

28. Ibid., pp. 67–69.

29. F. Dostoevskii, "Vystavka v Akademii Khudozhestv," *Grazhdanin*, no. 13 (1873).

30. Repin, letter to Tret'iakov, January 17, 1873, in I. Brodskii, ed., *Repin. Pis'ma, 1867–1930*, I, 54.

31. Friedrich Pecht, quoted by Repin, *Dalekoe blizkoe*, p. 283.

32. P. Mantz, "Exposition Universelle," *Gazette des Beaux-Arts*, XVIII (1878): 417; cf. E. Duranty, "Les écoles étrangères," *Gazette des Beaux-Arts* XVIII (1878): 164, where some reservations are expressed.

33. Repin, *Dalekoe blizkoe*, p. 311.

34. Kramskoi, letter to V. Polenov, April 5, 1875, in E. Sakharova, ed., *Vasilii Dmitrevich Polenov, Elena Dmitrievna Polenova, Khronika sem'i khudozhnikov* (Moscow, 1964), p. 174.

35. Stasov, "Akademicheskaia Vystavka 1863 goda," *Izbrannoe*, I, 42–43.

36. Savitskii's painting, shown at the 1874 exhibition, was criticized for its resemblance to *Barge Haulers;* Repin wrote to Kramskoi, February 17,

1874, *Pis'ma*, I, 110, expressing annoyance with the critic and noting that Savitskii had first encouraged his own interest in barge haulers.

37. Savitskii spent the summer of 1873 at a small railroad-side village near Tula and recorded the daily labor of the peasants drafted to work on the tracks. Cf. Z. Zonova, "Istoriia sozdaniia kartiny K. A. Savitskogo . . . ," *Gos. Tretiakovskaia Gallereia. Materialy i issledovaniia* (Moscow, 1958), II, 115.

38. Cf. Alexander Herzen, "The Russian People and Socialism: An Open Letter to Jules Michelet" (1851), in Herzen, *From the Other Shore and The Russian People and Socialism* (New York, 1956), pp. 163 ff. Influenced by Fourier and Saint-Simon, Russian populists believed that an egalitarian, peasant society in Russia would play a part in the renewal of Europe.

39. Repin, letter to Tret'iakov, May 23, 1874, *Pis'ma*, I, 132. Similar comments appear in a letter to Kramskoi, May 10, 1875, *Pis'ma*, I, 155.

40. Repin, letter to Stasov, March 20, 1875, *Pis'ma*, I, 150.

41. Repin, letter to Kramskoi, May 10, 1875, *Pis'ma*, I, 154. Cf. I. S. Zil'bershtein, "Repin v Parizhe . . . (1873–76)," in E. Grabar and I. Zil'bershtein, eds. *Repin. Khudozhestvennoe nasledstvo* (Moscow, 1947–48), I, 147, citing a similar letter to Stasov, September 30, 1875. Repin wrote to the critic N. Aleksandrov, March 16, 1876, *Pis'ma*, I, 175: "I admire this [direct painting] as I admire all the expressionalists, who are winning more and more recognition here."

42. Repin, letter to Tret'iakov, May 22, 1875, *Pis'ma*, I, 119. He also made several studies of street scenes, featuring newspaper sellers, street musicians, and other such types.

43. Repin, letter to Kramskoi, October 16, 1874, *Pis'ma*, I, 143.

44. Kramskoi, letter to Repin, August 20, 1875, in I. Grabar', *Ilia Efimovich Repin* (Moscow, 1938–39), I, 145.

45. Repin, letter to Kramskoi, August 29, 1875, *Pis'ma*, I, 163–64.

46. Repin, letters to Stasov, October 10, 1876, May 30, 1881, *Pis'ma*, I, 180, 254.

47. Repin, letter to Tret'iakov, March 8, 1883, *Pis'ma*, I, 275,

48. V. S. Mamontov, "Repin i Sem'ia Mamontovykh," *Repin. Khudozhestvennoe nasledstvo*, II, 48, identifies several figures, including the hunchback, who actually came from a small village near Moscow, not the Ukraine.

49. Tret'iakov, letter to Repin, March 6, 1883, *Pis'ma*, I, 274–75.

50. Repin, letter to Tret'iakov, March 8, 1883, *Pis'ma*, I, 275.

51. Ibid.

52. Stasov, "Zametki," *Izbrannoe*, I, 182–83, stresses both the concrete description of all the figures in the crowd and the "thematic principle"— the shared religious faith—that holds the image together. D. V. Sarab'ianov, "Russkaia realisticheskaia zhivopis' vtoroi poloviny XIX veka sredi evropeiskikh shkol," *Vestnik Moskovskogo Universiteta*, no. 1 (1974): 54–92, esp. 66–67, compares the idea of generalization and concreteness in Repin's work and in those of Courbet and Menzel.

53. Repin, *Dalekoe blizkoe*, pp. 146–48.

54. Kramskoi, letter to V. Garshin, February 16, 1878, *Kramskoi. Pis'ma*, II, 140–41.

55. Porudominskii, *Kramskoi*, p. 78.

56. Kramskoi, letter to V. Garshin, February 16, 1878, *Kramskoi*, Pis'ma, II, 140.

57. Ibid., p. 141.

58. Repin, "Zametki I. E. Repina o sozdanii im kartiny (Ivan Groznyi i syn ego Ivan)," n.d., Archive, Academy of Arts, Leningrad, fond A-3, K4, Op. 54, II, 4.

59. Kramskoi, letter to A. Suvorin, January 21, 1885, *Kramskoi. Pis'ma*, II, 167–68.

60. Repin, interview with I. Grabar', January 17, 1913, in Grabar', *Repin*, I, 258.

61. Repin, letter to Tret'iakov, August 10, 1884, *Pis'ma*, I, 298.

62. Repin, "Zametki."

63. Ibid.; cf. also Grabar', *Repin*, I, 258.

64. Ibid.

65. Stasov, "Khudozhestvennye vystavki 1879 goda," *Izbrannoe*, I, 122.

66. Gustave Courbet, "Exhibition et vente de 40 tableaux . . . ," Paris, 1855, trans. Linda Nochlin, *Realism and Tradition in Art 1848–1900* (Englewood Cliffs, N.J., 1966), pp. 33–34.

67. Stasov, "Dvadtsat piat' let russkogo iskusstva," *Vestnik Evropy* (4 issues, November 1882–October 1883), *Izbrannoe*, I, 419–530, 447.

68. Repin, letter to N. Murashko, November 30, 1883, *Pis'ma*, I, 292.

69. Repin, letter to Stasov, January 2, 1881, V. Lebedev, ed., *I. E. Repin i V. V. Stasov. Perepiska* (Moscow, Leningrad, 1948–50), II, 58–59.

70. E.g., Makovskii, *Condemned Man* (1879), Iaroshenko, *Arrest of a Woman Propagandist* (1887).

71. Repin, interview, 1914, in V. Kamsnskii, "Sredy v Penatakh," *Iskusstvo*, September 29, 1940, 14.

72. Cf. Repin, letters to Tret'iakov, April 8, 1881, to Stasov, February 16, 1881, January 20, 1882, *Pis'ma*, I, 250, 243–44, 265.

73. G. H. Hamilton, *Art and Architecture in Russia*, rev. ed. (Harmondsworth, 1975), p. 267.

74. Stasov and his brothers possessed copies of some of the illegal journals, and Repin would have had ready access to them. Cf. G. Pribul'skaia, "Peterburgskii period v zhizni i tvorchestve I. E. Repina," candidate's dissertation, Academy of Arts, U.S.S.R., Leningrad, 1975, pp. 84–91.

75. N. Minskii, "Posledniaia ispoved'," ("The Last Confession") was printed in *Narodnaia Volia*, October 1879, the organ of the terrorist movement. Repin and Stasov discussed the poem, but Repin apparently did not show Stasov the painting, and he does not mention it in any of his letters of the time. When he was forbidden to exhibit it at the 1884 traveling exhibition, he gave the painting to Minskii and inscribed it on the reverse with a dedication to him. Cf. I. Zil'bershtein, "Rabota Repina nad kartinoi 'Otkaz ot ispovedi pered kazn'iu'," in *I. E. Repin. Sbornik dokladov i materialov* (Academy of Arts, Moscow, 1952), pp. 55–56.

76. Repin, letter to Tret'iakov, July 10, 1883, *Pis'ma*, I, 282–83; cf. *Dalekoe blizkoe*, pp. 256, 291.

77. Cf. Repin, *Dalekoe blizkoe*, p. 360. Although his letters of 1883 do not mention individual works, and though he would not have known the original of *Claudius Civilis*, he could have been familiar with reproductions.

78. Details on the preparatory studies and revisions of this figure are given in: N. Zograf, "Novye podgotovitel'nye raboty k kartine I. E. Repina 'Ne zhdali'," in *Ocherki po russkomu i sovetskomu iskusstvu* (Leningrad, 1974), pp. 155–68; S. Korolkevich, "Rabota I. E. Repina nad kartinoi 'Ne zhdali'," Archive, Academy of Arts, Leningrad, fond 11, op. 1, no. 409.

79. He broadened the work compositionally by changing the proportions of the canvas. Recent discussions emphasize the evolution from a positive portrayal to a negative one. Cf. Zograf, "K voprosu ob evoliutsiia iskusstva peredvizhnikov v 1880–1890–e gody," in P. Lebedev and I. Gofman, eds., *Peredvizhniki* (Moscow, 1977), p. 100; Valkenier, *Russian Realist Art*, p. 91, stresses increasing guilt and confusion.

80. The function of details is similar to that in Victorian narrative painting; the affinity (noted also by Christopher Wood, *Victorian Panorama* [London, 1976], 246) suggests common precedents in Dutch seventeenth-century genre rather than direct reference to English models. On his trip to London in 1875, Repin admired works by Wilkie and Herkommer but scarcely mentioned other English artists.

The iconography of *They Did Not Expect Him* and its relation to other contemporary works is discussed more fully in Hilton, "The Revolutionary Theme in Russian Realism," pp. 115–21.

81. J. Billington, *The Icon and the Axe* (London, 1966), p. 435.

82. Stasov, letter to Repin, December 2, 1889, quoted in I. Zil'bershtein, "K istorii sozdanii kartiny 'Arest Propagandista'," *Repin. Khudozhestvennoe nasledstvo*, II, 342.

83. E.g., the critic P. Boborykin, "Kramskoi i Repin," *Novosti i birzhevaia gazeta*, March 24, 1883, identified the documentary aspects of realist genre and the emphasis on exposé as the cause of the decline of Russian painting. Kramskoi admitted, "Everyone says that Russian artists paint dryly, with too much detail," in a letter to the critic A. Suvorin, who urged the Peredvizhniki to find a middle path between ultra-realism and idealism. Cf. *Kramskoi, Pis'ma*, II, 124; further discussion in A. Sautin, "Repin i kritika," *Akademiia khudozhestv. Problemy razvitiia russkogo iskusstva* (Leningrad, 1974), VI, 50–54. Repin himself was criticized by artists of the younger generation for his "eternal over-emphasis" on ideas; cf. Elena Polenova, letter to N. Polenova, March 4, 1884, in Sakharova, ed., *Polenov-Polenova*, p. 340.

84. Repin, letter to Tret'iakov, May 29, 1883, *Pis'ma*, I, 281.

85. Repin, letter to Tret'iakov, July 10, 1881, letter to Polenov, July 17, 1883, *Pis'ma*, I, 283, 286. A detailed account of this trip, based on Stasov's diaries, is in I. Zil'bershtein, "Puteshestvie I. E. Repina i V. V. Stasova po zapadnoi Evrope v 1883 godu," *Repin. Khudozhestvennoe nasledstvo*, I, 429–524.

86. Cf. Albert Boime, *The Academy and French Painting in the Nineteenth Century* (New York, 1971), p. 132.

87. Cf. Repin, letter to Polenov, July 17, 1883, *Pis'ma*, I, 289; *Dalekoe blizkoe*, p. 297, and Stasov's much more detailed notes of the ceremony and concurrent meetings by the socialist women of Paris, in Zil'bershtein, "Puteshestvie," pp. 463–66.

88. Repin, letter to Murashko, November 30, 1883, *Pis'ma*, I, 292.

89. Ibid.

Rustic Naturalism in Britain

Kenneth McConkey 7

WE WOULD LIKE TO DESCRIBE A TYPE OF late nineteenth-century painting
that can be called rustic naturalist. We say "type" of painting rather
than "style" or "genre" because the works produced by some of the
young British artists of the 1880s and 1890s share common characteristics of technique and iconography. They are naturalistic representations of rustic subjects, which display a degree of sophistication that
derives directly from the naturalism of the Salon and from the work
of an earlier generation of French realist painters. However, images
precede art-historical labels, and before charting the history of rustic
naturalism in Britain, we must first consider one or two pictures.

In 1895 Henry Herbert La Thangue sent *The Last Furrow* (fig. 7.1)
to the Royal Academy Summer Exhibition.[1] The painting is about
six feet high and is not quite square. It shows an aged ploughman
slumped over the handles of the plough, his arms stretched and stiff,
in a kind of rigor mortis. The central white horse looks around with
what George Moore described as "mute sympathy," in "a very quiet
animal-like way; the movement is full of that dim perception of things
which pierces the gloom of the animal world."[2] In the background,
beyond the horses, the regular lines of the ploughed field blur at the
horizon and a grim sky. The picture's sobriety depends upon a carefully controlled composition, in which the dramatic curves of plough
and furrow take the eye in a diagonal sweep across the foreground
and off up the field.

When it was exhibited, much of the critical debate around the

painting centered upon its "French" handling and scale. Even though
pictures of ploughmen were common enough in the eighties and nine-
ties, the critics reflected a great deal upon the picture, particularly
speculating upon the condition of the man. The *Graphic* and the *Illustrated London News* were sure that he was dead; the *Times* felt
that he had simply "swooned"; while the *Athenaeum* suggested that he
had "stumbled in a furrow or dropped down in a fit."[3] The picture
even came in for its share of the coarse humor of Harry Furniss
(fig. 7.2).[4]

La Thangue's painting is, however, not so easy to dismiss. It serves
to focus our attention upon the fact that in the final quarter of the
Victorian age, many young artists—La Thangue was in his mid-thirties
—had turned their minds to problems associated with the realistic
representation of farm workers and fisherfolk, the British equivalents
of Millet's peasants. In works of this type, the figure is often seen
against a barren, featureless landscape, which sets the light and,
perhaps, the time of year. By the turn of the century, the whole range
of subjects—reaping, gleaning, tending the flocks, etc.—that had been
established in the mid-century by Millet and Breton had been extended and enriched and was of such universal appeal that it could
sustain a larger scale. Subjects and themes had often been overlaid
to the extent that in individual works, one finds oneself commenting
upon the quality of synthesis. The art of this period, therefore, demands
manifold criteria of judgment, inevitably richer than our narrow, hind-
sight-oriented, essentially abstract patterns of evaluation have permitted. In this age when literal representation achieves its apex, when
the term "photo-realism" is coined,[5] when artists have a whole range
of sophisticated techniques at their disposal, we find ourselves un-
ravelling a tangled skein that includes subconscious suggestion, conscious quotation, what was "in the air," and what was actually seen
and studied. We must realize that working upon a well-rooted tradition of rustic naturalism, the painter's task was not simply to reiterate
but to reinterpret, and in this context, originality has more to do
with eclecticism than with novelty.

The network of cross-reference can well be appreciated in La
Thangue's *The Man with the Scythe* (fig. 7.3), which was shown at
the Royal Academy in 1896.[6] Here the artist fused in an arresting way
the familiar Victorian "convalescent," found in the work of Myles
Birket Foster, with the theme of Death the Reaper, which is frequently
found in late nineteenth-century art. His closest point of reference
would have been John Everett Millais's *Time the Reaper,* which had
appeared at the New Gallery in 1895, but he would also have been
familiar with the earlier French and British treatments.[7] We should
also set *The Man with the Scythe* into the visual ambiance of Luke

Fildes's *The Doctor* (1891) and George Clausen's *The Girl at the Gate* (1889).[8] The quality of synthesis in style and subject matter was obvious to more discerning critics. The *Saturday Review*, for instance, found in the painting an "ingenious combination of symbolic purpose and realistic truth."[9] In the description of rustic naturalist painting in Britain, these are significant phrases.

At this point, other great themes could be looked at—themes such as maternity or youth and age, conveyed through subjects like cutting bracken, sowing, and gleaning—and studies within these subgenres remain to be carried out. For the historian, however, such groupings cannot simply remain on the level of the visual. He must know about rural activities and their social significance; he must understand the accumulated meaning of the work and establish its appropriate visual context. He should realize, for instance, that Courbet's *The Stonebreakers* was reshown at the Exposition Universelle in 1889 and compared with works by Bastien-Lepage.[10] He should also know that Birket Foster's *The Convalescent* was a popular print published by Agnews in 1893 and reproduced on at least two occasions in the *Art Journal*.[11]

However, before embarking upon this kind of study, the more basic question of why so many young painters in Britain turned their attention to such scenes remains to be tackled. The answer is complicated and rather prosaic and takes us back to La Thangue's student years in the 1870s. In those days, it seems that more consideration was given to the teaching of the useful arts, i.e., design and craft, than to the teaching of painting and sculpture. At the South Kensington Schools of Design, instruction was, as George Clausen recalled, perfunctory, to say the least: "Collinson the painting master—an amiable man—after posing a fat (draped) young woman, said to us, 'think of Rubens' and walked out! We were never taught the real principles either of drawing or of representation, and had to find out things for ourselves."[12] At the Royal Academy Schools, things were not much better. A critic in the *Magazine of Art* in 1885 summed up the situation that had prevailed there for at least ten years: ". . . as an educational institution . . . it has little or nothing to teach; and its students, as soon as they have passed the curriculum it imposes upon them make haste to betake themselves to France, to learn, not only how to paint and draw, but to forget as much as they can of the practice and theory acquired in its schools."[13]

When he looked into the public arena, the student can hardly have been encouraged. The *cause célèbre* of 1878, the Whistler/Ruskin trial, must have bewildered many young artists for whom the "coxcomb," as Ruskin called him, was a hero. Though Whistler won the case, his farthing damages signified merely a Pyrrhic victory and an object lesson to all would-be followers. Frederick Leighton, who had become president of the Royal Academy in 1878, was too worldly, too cosmopolitan a leader, to become embroiled in the internal politics of the Royal Academy Schools. His well-crafted orations on classical art must have seemed more suited to the ringing plains of windy Troy than the confines of Burlington House. Even as he airily pronounced the couplet from Goethe, "The chord that wakes in kindred hearts a tone, / Must first be tuned and vibrate in your own,"[14] in concluding his first address to the students, his school's gold medalist, Henry Herbert La Thangue, was about to take the channel packet boat and join the other English students who were already congregating in Paris.

Exposure to French teaching methods also meant exposure to the Salon, and this experience of French art confirmed the interest in realism that had been growing since the 1860s. The exchanges between British and French artists via Whistler, Fantin, and Legros in the early sixties are fairly easy to cite, but perhaps the most significant opportunity to make an appraisal of the French school was to be found in the Great Exhibition of 1862.[15] The masters of realism at this exhibition would have been Jules Breton, Gustave Brion, and Rosa Bonheur as much as Courbet.[16] Indeed, Courbet's *Fighting Stags* would, in English eyes, have prompted comparison with Landseer.[17] In the following year, one English critic, P. G. Hamerton, stressed the point that although "Courbet is looked upon as the representative of realism in France, the truth is that Troyon, Edouard Frère, the Bonheurs and many others, are to the full as realistic as Courbet. . . ."[18] In 1864, in the pages of the same journal, the *Fine Arts Quarterly*, the realist camp was expanded to include Millet, Breton, and Jacque,[19] and while the English market for small-scale and therefore collectable French pictures continued to grow, the "beautiful rustic caryatides" of Breton drew the attention of at least one English painter.[20] In 1863 P. H. Calderon recorded in his diary a visit to the Luxembourg with the young Fred Walker, who "passed rapidly over the usual lions there—the big Couture, the big Muller, even the Delacroix, but fastened upon the Jules Breton *La Fin de la Journée*, this he looked at intently, evidently the picture went home to him."[21] The effects of this encounter are evident in Walker's later work, particularly in the figure on the right of *The Vagrants* (fig. 7.4).[22] The general note of approval of Breton by the British art establishment was struck in 1870, when *The Art Journal* spoke of him as "one of the few artists we can never see too much of, and that by reason of the life and truth he is ever gaining afresh from nature."[23]

At the same time as we explore these contacts with French realism, we must, however, be mindful of the continuing tradition of English landscape, stretching back through John Linnell to Constable, and while artists like Linnell retained their public, the more robust vagrants and sense of social purpose in French art were seen and appreciated. Linnell's beautiful sunlit England, his rosy peasant girls and bonny babies were gradually rejected by the artistic community in favor of the more rugged world of Legros, Lhermitte, and Millet (fig. 7.5). This preference on the part of the art student clique was encouraged by the activities of enterprising dealers like Durand Ruel and Deschamps. We know that in 1872 a little delegation of art students, George Clausen, Frederick Brown, Havard Thomas, and others went down in a group to see Millet's *The Sower* and *The Angelus* at Durand Ruel's premises at 168 New Bond Street.[24]

At this point there was a vital contact with French art and training methods in the person of Alphonse Legros, who was teaching at the Lambeth School of Art. Reputedly the most gifted pupil of Lecoq de Boisbaudran, Legros promoted the interests of his compatriots and fellow pupils Cazin and Lhermitte.[25] Incredibly for Victorian England, this friend of Manet's was appointed Slade Professor of Fine Art in the year in which Degas wrote to invite him to exhibit at the Second Impressionist Exhibition. The combined effect of the enthusiasm for the type of realism represented by Legros and Lhermitte is to be found in George Clausen's first Royal Academy exhibit, *High Mass at a Fishing Village on the Zuyder Zee*, 1876 (fig. 7.6).[26] While in one sense this picture refers to the charming studies of children by artists like Jacob Maris, in a more important way it reflects the interest in Legros and Lhermitte and in their somewhat archaic realism, which, in the 1870s, owes as much to Leys as it does to Courbet. The tentative naturalism of the *High Mass* positively flourished in the work of Clausen's generation during these years of feverish activity. Encouraged by their French mentors and by the example of Walker, Pinwell, and North, they took a serious interest in the graphic arts.[27] There were regular *Black and White* Exhibitions at the Dudley Gallery, and Lhermitte acted as a juror on more than one occasion.[28] Journals such as the *Graphic* and the *Illustrated London News* provided an outlet for young artists and encouraged a reporting attitude.[29] The Royal Academy itself admitted the social subjects of Fildes, Holl, Herkomer, Macbeth, Morris, and J. R. Reid, as well as works by Legros and Lhermitte.[30]

This development was greatly accelerated by the London showing of pictures by Jules Bastien-Lepage.[31] More than any other artist of the period, Bastien-Lepage caught the imagination of the young painters of Clausen and La Thangue's generation. After his important retrospective exhibition at the Grosvenor Gallery in 1880, all of his major Salon paintings were displayed in London, along with works specifically created for the London market. And though he himself was fascinated by the light and atmosphere of the London streets, it was his pictures from his native village of Damvillers that drew the attention of young Englishmen.[32] Bastien's work was the center of furious debate, as the *Spectator* noted in 1880: ". . . round his pictures there gathers constantly a little knot of worshippers or scoffers, admiring and condemning in the most vehement manner. . . ."[33] From this heated discussion arose a form of naturalism that stressed the individual rather than the type, the particular setting rather than the generalized one. Within these areas of agreement, British artists responded to the naturalism of the Salon on a number of different levels and accepted that whole group of painters who seemed to be striving for the same goals as Bastien-Lepage himself.

Accordingly, Alexander Stanhope Forbes, to whom Bastien was "the greatest artist of our age,"[34] might on the one hand quote a figure pose from the French painter, but he was also capable of constructing a setting that recalled an important work by Lhermitte. His *The Old Convent, Quimperlé* (fig. 7.7) contains a boy similar to the subject of *Pas Mêche* (fig. 7.8), while the spatial arrangement of *Preparations for the Market, Quimperlé* (fig. 7.9), with its gable wall on the left and farmyard on the right, recalls Lhermitte's *La Paye des Moissonneurs* (cf. Lacambre, fig. 8.8). All these early pictures, which date from Forbes's summer expeditions to Cancale and Quimperlé with La Thangue in the summers of 1881, 1882, and 1883, were painted in an opaque impastose manner with square-stroke brushes.[35]

When he returned to England in 1884, Forbes went to Newlyn to assume leadership of the artists' colony there, and he abandoned the Brittany peasant for the Cornish fisherman. All the Newlyn artists shared his sympathy for "French" handling. The rather choppy strokes, painted across the form to suggest its breadth and solidity rather than its direction, were notably particularly in the work of Frank Bramley. Only one reviewer championed his method. Describing Bramley's *Domino* (fig. 7.10) in 1886, the writer in the *Magazine of Art* declared,

> . . . it is singularly broad and startlingly simple. . . . The square, massive brushwork of the painter imparts peculiar individualism to the intrepid handling; the rendering of cool, grey light that suffuses the room—broad and beamless where it floods the entrance—is admirably gradated throughout. It is not surprising that this picture, with its extraordinary force of effect and realistic fidelity, should confound the jaded and uninstructed observer, or that it should be pronounced by the distressed visitor . . . quite 'unfinished'. No record of impressions could be completer, or more convincingly thorough; yet the popular verdict appears less absurdly inept when we consider that the popular standard of 'finish' comprehends the feeble hesitation that spends itself in flimsy handling and a niggled and unintelligent touch.[36]

However, in a very short time, guttering candles in Bramley's work came to signify *A Hopeless Dawn,* and modern French naturalism was subverted by Victorian narrative, by a form of storytelling that imposed priorities that distorted the naturalists' neutrality.[37]

But was naturalism simply a matter of handling and finish? If one looks at the work of other British painters, it is possible to discern more complex responses. They extracted from Bastien-Lepage's work a distinctive attitude toward spatial rendering, a naturalist mise-en-scène, or a specific figure and field pattern. To locate some of these other examples, we leave Forbes and La Thangue roughing it in Brittany, and make our way to the Hôtel Chevillon at Grez sur Loing, south of the forest of Fontainebleau.

The group of British and American art students at Grez had originally been pupils of Carolus Duran.[38] One of the prominent members of the group, an artist who seems to have remained at Grez for nearly ten years, was the Irishman Frank O'Meara.[39] In his work there is an admiration for Corot and for the more poetic strands in Bastien-Lepage.[40] O'Meara must have set the pace for William Stott of Oldham, John Lavery, and the other painters of Grez, for they all seem to express a preference for a restricted palette, from which is created a moody twilight landscape that contrasts with the bright sunlight of Forbes's Brittany.[41] These poetic naturalists, whose peasants sometimes have a distinctly languorous look, had, as we might expect, only a temporary allegiance to such subjects. John Lavery, for instance, quickly abandoned the peasant in favor of society portraits, but this was not before he had executed a number of important pieces of rustic naturalism. The most significant of these was *Under the Cherry Tree* (fig. 7.11). The salient feature of this picture is its thickly impasted foreground of weeds and wild flowers, which have been viewed almost as if the painter had actually been standing upon them at the bottom edge of the picture plane. As the eye proceeds into the space, it encounters the familiar square strokes that describe the forms of the watering can, the barrow and the figures before passing to the smooth, thin layers of the river in the background. The effect of these alterations in handling is to heighten the sense of three-dimensional space, a feature that had often been observed in Bastien-Lepage's work. Writing in the *Magazine of Art* in 1883, W. C. Brownell had observed the "felicity" with which Bastien "reproduces the general effect, the landscape essence of the scene; . . . the way in which the foreground details are caressed and the distance softened and subdued, endues the whole with an infinite individuality as well."[42]

Lavery applied Bastien's pictorial strategies in more than one way. He claimed that his pictures *A Rally* and *A Tennis Party* were the result of following Bastien's advice to always carry a sketchbook and to commit to memory figures in motion.[43] But such pictures also led

Lavery away from rustic subjects into the charmed world of society portraiture.

For a deeper understanding of naturalistic representation, it is worth returning to the work of George Clausen. After painting Dutch genre scenes and a few sub-Whistler portraits, Clausen moved from London and went to live in the country near St. Albans.[44] For him the months spent in Brittany and Paris in 1882 and 1883 were merely a finishing school for the process that had already begun in 1880, when he stood as one of "the little knot of worshippers" in front of Bastien's work at the Grosvenor Gallery.[45] Not only had he acquired the broad handling of the *plein-airiste*, but having studied *Les Foins* (fig. 7.12) in detail, he was fascinated by its technique and subject matter.[46] In 1883 and 1884 he was to be found at work on paintings of resting farm workers, such as *Day Dreams* and *Labourers after Dinner* (fig. 7.13). However, Clausen and some of his associates in the New English Art Club began to see even more in naturalism. They began to acquire a sense of mise-en-scène, to employ a deliberate strategy in order to convey an individual's presence within a specific spatial context. This becomes apparent when we compare Clausen's *The Stone Pickers* (fig. 7.14) with Bastien-Lepage's *Pauvre Fauvette* (fig. 7.15).[47] To a certain extent Clausen has even surpassed his master in the confidence with which he "maps" the foreground. The eye zigzags across the picture's surface from the stones to the lunch basket, to the tree and the stooping figure at the horizon. Apart from reductions in scale and alterations in handling, there are no obvious perspectives. Essentially similar points about the rendering of a terrain might be made about Herbert Dalzeil's *The Cow Girl* (fig. 7.16). Such a work owes much to *Pauvre Fauvette*, but the choice of a wide-angle format and the more natural detail in the dead autumn leaves help to establish the receding plane.

During these years, perhaps in his desire for Beaux Arts thoroughness, Clausen experimented with photography.[48] He purchased the small portable Marion Miniature "Academy" camera, which had just come out on the market. Some of the one-and-a-quarter-inch plates from this period have survived, and it is possible to compare his photographs of Hertfordshire peasants with those who appear in the paintings. These make it clear that, far from literally transcribing the photographic image, he used it to support on-the-spot sketchbook notes. It seems likely that Clausen would have discussed this new medium and how best it could be used by artists. Through La Thangue and T. F. Goodall he got to know the East Anglian photographer Peter Henry Emerson, and he and his painter colleagues must have contributed a great deal to Emerson's ideas on naturalistic photography.[49] In his treatise Emerson declared, "By Naturalism it will be seen that we mean a very different thing from realism . . . the work of the realist would do well for a botany class, there is no scope for fine art in realism, realism belongs to the province of science."[50] It was, therefore, clear that Emerson identified the Pre-Raphaelites' indiscriminate "truth to nature" as a form of realism, and that naturalists, while incorporating some detail, should seek for the truth of the ensemble.[51] In a crudely simplified way, Emerson's photographic naturalism came to be associated with foreground focus and blurred distances. Yet the authors of the modern monographs on Emerson have not examined in detail his relationships with T. F. Goodall, Havard Thomas, and Henry Herbert La Thangue and the degree to which these painters and sculptors encouraged him to think along the lines formed by Corot, Millet, and Bastien-Lepage, "the pioneers who established the naturalistic trend which is now in the van of this nineteenth century."[52] The high viewpoints and processional character of the subjects suggest more than coincidence in the comparison of Emerson's 1886 photograph *Coming Home from the Marshes* (fig. 7.17) and La Thangue's *The Return of the Reapers* (fig. 7.18) of the same year.

At the same time as he depicted the contemporary peasant in his natural habitat, the painter or photographer could not help being conscious, in an age that highly valued the work of Millet, of the symbolic nature of the peasant's toil. The artist was working upon an accepted heritage of peasant painting, and it is unlikely that in such circumstances he gave much thought to the social or ideological significance of the work, beyond some general belief in the rightness of what he was doing. When there was such a strong tradition of painting field laborers, the artist thought more about how they should be shown than why they ought to be. He involved himself with problems of metier rather than with moralizing. Compared to the immediate encounter with La Thangue's *Reapers*, Millet's work looks like that of an Old Master, and his peasants *Going to Work* (fig. 7.19) appear as remote, emblematic beings, set against the sky, in the context of eternity.

Thus, the young artist of the 1880s, in his anxiety to demonstrate his understanding of the current language of naturalistic representation, provides textbook illustrations of its precepts. In his search for better forms of mimesis, he demanded a kind of discourse that was lacking in British art schools. He had become conscious of the limitations of Ruskin's Gothic eclecticism on the one hand and Courbet and Millet's realist types on the other.[53] As a result the naturalist painters rejected these approaches in favor of the greater truths of Man—the individual—and Nature—his native heath. In this respect Clausen realized that Bastien-Lepage had achieved a kind of ultimate. In 1888 he wrote:

Of the many characteristics of Lepage's work, perhaps the most remarkable is his sympathetic intimacy with his subject. Although the human interest is always dominant, nothing escapes him—nothing is trivial or unimportant. One reads in his works the life-history of the workaday human beings he painted— . . . all his personages are placed before us in the most satisfying completeness, without the appearance of artifice, but as they live; and *without comment, as far as is possible, on the author's part.*[54]

Four years later he was still prepared to concede that "[Bastien] has carried literal representation to its extreme limit. . . . he paints a man and the man stands before you and you ask yourself, 'What is he going to say?' "[55]

Therefore, when Clausen tackled a canvas nearly six feet high in a cottage garden at Cookham Dean in the autumn of 1889, he must have wondered how much more could be done. Having just returned from the Exposition Universelle, where he had spent a week in the painting galleries and found *Jeanne d'Arc écoutant Les Voix* (fig. 7.20) "magnificent," he must have felt that the final step in realistic representation had been taken. There was, however, a small advance in the progress of the work, later known as *The Girl at the Gate* (fig. 7.21), which may be of significance. When he saw the picture before it was completed, George Moore recounted that Clausen was painting a picture of Marguerite, the rustic maid from *Faust*.[56] Along the way that led to the completion of the work and its purchase by the Chantrey Bequest in 1890, the literary subject matter got lost, and the model, Polly Baldwin, Clausen's children's nursemaid, became simply *The Girl at the Gate*. Recalling the theoretical debate that raged at the original showing of *Jeanne d'Arc écoutant Les Voix*,[57] one could read this in either of two ways. One could claim that naturalism was so accepted by 1890 that the idea of addressing such a literary theme was already redundant. Alternatively, one could hold the view that the nerve of the naturalist was no longer strong enough to transcend nature and create a naturalistic subject picture.

NOTES

This chapter is a résumé of investigations begun seven or eight years ago. It is based partly upon an article, published in 1978, on the influence of Bastien-Lepage in Britain. This has been augmented recently by a number of exhibitions that I have been asked to organize or contribute to. I am grateful to all those who have extended such invitations to me, not least to Gabriel P. Weisberg, who has encouraged this chapter into print. As these researches have proceeded, the character of this chapter has altered, and seeing it in its present form, I now have a clearer idea of what I do not know. When this state of affairs has been remedied, it may be possible to foresee rustic naturalism in the expanded format of a book.

1. *The Last Furrow*, oil on canvas, 179×164 cms, R.A. 1895, no. 98. For a discussion of this work, see Kenneth McConkey, *A Painter's Harvest: H. H. La Thangue 1859–1929* (catalogue of exhibition at Oldham Art Gallery, 1978), pp. 12, 30–31.

2. Ibid.

3. Ibid.

4. Harry Furniss's illustration originally appeared in George Moore and Harry Furniss, *Criticisms and Caricatures* (1895), p. 31.

5. The term "photo-realism" was used by Walter Sickert in his essay "Modern Realism in Painting," in A. Theuriet, ed., *Jules Bastien-Lepage and His Art* (London: Fisher Unwin, 1892), p. 141.

6. McConkey, *La Thangue*, pp. 32–33.

7. See, for instance, works by Lhermitte (*Death and the Woodcutter*, 1893), Puvis de Chavannes (*The Young Maidens and Death*, 1872), and Millet (*Death and the Woodcutter*, 1859). As an assiduous student, La Thangue would also have been familiar with the etching *Death and the Woodcutter* by Legros and the illustrations of La Fontaine by Doré.

8. Both of these popular pictures were acquired for the English nation. The Clausen was purchased by the Chantrey Trustees and housed eventually in the Tate Gallery. Fildes's picture was commissioned directly by Henry Tate. In its turn, La Thangue's *The Man with the Scythe* was also a Chantrey purchase.

9. McConkey, *La Thangue*, p. 31.

10. See George Clausen, "Jules Bastien-Lepage as Artist," in Theuriet, *Jules Bastien-Lepage*, pp. 125–26.

11. See *Art Journal*, 1873, p. 268, and 1893, p. 63.

12. Sir George Clausen, R. A., "Autobiographical Notes," *Artwork*, no. 25 (Spring 1931): 17; quoted in Kenneth McConkey, *Sir George Clausen, R.A.* (catalogue of exhibition held at Bradford, Bristol, and Newcastle and at the Royal Academy of Arts, 1980), p. 15.

13. *Magazine of Art* 10 (1885): 346.

14. Frederick Leighton, *Lord Leighton's Addresses* (London, 1897), p. 33.

15. See C. P. Barbier, "The Société des Trois," in Frederick A. Sweet, ed., *James McNeill Whistler* (catalogue of exhibition at Chicago and Utica, 1968).

16. Rosa Bonheur showed *Ploughing in the Neighborhood of Nevers* (no. 129); Breton was represented by two works, *La Bénédiction des Blés* in Artois (no. 59) and *The Weeders* (no. 60); and Brion showed *The Blessing* (no. 76), *A Wedding Entertainment in Alsace* (no. 77), and *The Burial* (no. 77a). Other realist artists represented in the exhibition were Antigna, Pils, Troyon, and other Barbizon artists. Millet was represented by a rustic *Scene* (no. 159). So notable were the rustic subjects that the *Times* (14 July 1862, p. 7), noted that "pictures of rustic life at home or abroad . . . fill even a larger space in the French School than in our own. . . ." Its critic explored the comparison of British and French rustic pictures by declaring, "there is more truth and less trickery; more trust in the effect of the real thing, and less effort after attractiveness; more of the field or the cottage and less of the studio." The writer went on to single out particularly the work of Breton.

17. See R. Fernier, *Courbet, Catalogue raissonné*, no. 279. The *Times* noted the presence of this large work in a glancing comment: "Courbet, 'the

prince of realists' as he delights to call himself, but who here figures only as the painter of a vigorous combat of stags in a wood."

18. *Fine Arts Quarterly*, 1863, p. 243.

19. *Fine Arts Quarterly*, 1864, p. 236.

20. Maxime du Camp, *Le Salon de 1859*, p. 37. Breton's work had been known in England since 1856, when he had shown *Fire in a Haystack* at an exhibition at Mr. Griffith's Gallery in Pall Mall. See Gabriel P. Weisberg, *The Realist Tradition* (catalogue of an exhibition at Cleveland, Brooklyn, St. Louis, and Glasgow Art Galleries, 1980), pp. 129–31. The first of these annual exhibitions had been held in 1854; see *Art Journal*, 1854, pp. 90, 123, and 187. Criticism of French art in these years concentrated upon its relative suggestiveness, by comparison to the hard edges of Pre-Raphaelite painting. This general point was made by the *Times* critic (13 May 1856, p. 11) when faced with a display of pictures that included works by Troyon, Breton, Antigna, and Meissonier. "It is a great relief to pass from the exhibition of English pictures to the little gallery in Pall Mall which contains the French ones. In a moment the visitor finds himself in a new world, in another atmosphere amid different beings; and he who has been exhausted with the obtrusive surfaces and sharp outlines in which our national artists indulge will gaze with interest upon the veiled colours and impalpable contours in which the French School delights."

21. Quoted in H. S. Marks, *Frederick Walker, A.R.A.* (London, 1896), p. 37.

22. The comparison between Walker's *The Vagrants* and Breton's *The Recall of the Gleaners* was first made by Rosemary Treble in an unpublished paper entitled "Frederick Walker: A Hard-edged Idyll" delivered at the Association of Art Historians Conference at Glasgow University in 1976.

23. *Art Journal*, 1870, p. 149. This statement was made in a review of the seventeenth exhibition of works at the French Gallery, when Breton's *Going to Mass* was shown (no. 82). The critic commented in particular on Breton's "vigor" and "naturalism."

24. *Black and White*, 8 July 1905, p. 45, quoted in McConkey, *Clausen*, p. 56.

25. See Mary Michele Hamel, "A French Artist: Léon Lhermitte," Ph.D. diss., Washington University, 1974, p. 21. Also Dennis Farr, *English Art 1870–1940* (Oxford, 1978), pp. 23–24, and Anna Gruetzner, "Two Reactions to French Painting in Britain," in *Post-Impressionism* (Royal Academy of Arts, 1979), p. 178.

26. McConkey, *Clausen*, p. 18.

27. The standard work on this generation of English illustrators remains Forrest Reid, *Illustrators of the Eighteen Sixties* (London, 1928; Dover Reprint, 1975). See also Ronald Pickvance, *English Influences on Vincent van Gogh*, catalogue of exhibition at Nottingham, Newcastle, London, etc., 1974.

28. See Mary Michele Hamel, *Léon Lhermitte*, catalogue of an exhibition at the Paine Art Center, Oshkosh, Wisconsin, 1974, p. 27.

29. Clausen, for instance, placed illustrations in both periodicals.

30. The change in the character of British art that takes place in the later 1870s has not seriously concerned the authors of the standard works on Victorian painting, who tend to assume that all the pictures produced during this period (1873–1901) form a coherent category.

31. See Kenneth McConkey, "The Bouguereau of the Naturalists: Bastien-Lepage and British Art," *Art History* 1, no. 3 (September 1978): 371–82.

32. McConkey, "Bastien-Lepage and British Art," pp. 377–79.

33. *The Spectator,* 12 June 1880, p. 751; quoted by McConkey, "Bastien-Lepage and British Art," p. 374.

34. Francis Greenacre and Caroline Fox, *Artists of the Newlyn School,* catalogue of an exhibition held in Newlyn, Plymouth, and Bristol Art Galleries, 1979, p. 16.

35. See Greenacre and Fox, *Newlyn School,* pp. 20–21, and McConkey, *La Thangue,* pp. 8, 10.

36. *Magazine of Art* 9 (1886): 443–44.

37. *A Hopeless Dawn* (coll. Tate Gallery), a canvas that depicts a young, distressed fisherman's wife and her aged mother, who have been waiting all night for the return of the fishing fleet, was Bramley's Chantrey purchase of 1888.

38. See W. H. Low, *A Chronicle of Friendships, 1873–1900* (New York, 1908), and R. L. Stevenson, "Forest Notes," *Cornhill Magazine,* 1876, pp. 545–61; quoted by McConkey, "Bastien-Lepage and British Art," pp. 375–76.

39. See Anne Crookshank and the Knight of Glin, *The Painters of Ireland, c. 1660–1920* (London 1978), pp. 253–54, and Julian Campbell, "Irish Artists in France and Belgium, 1850–1914," Ph.D. diss., Trinity College, Dublin, 1980.

40. Frank O'Meara (1853–88) was gifted with an exquisite sense of tone, as works like *Towards the Night and Winter* (1885) and *October* (1888) reveal. His sensitive and poetic nature was apparent to all the artists working in Grez. See Walter Shaw Sparrow, *John Lavery and His Work* (London, 1911), p. 44.

41. See Peyton Skipwith, *William Scott of Oldham and Edward Stott, A.R.A.,* catalogue of an exhibition held at Rochdale and Oldham Art Galleries and at the Fine Art Society, London, 1976, nos. 3, 4, and 5. Stott of Oldham was also a friend and rival of the expatriate American painter Thomas Alexander Harrison. See McConkey, "Bastien-Lepage and British Art," p. 381, note 27, and The Royal Academy of Arts, *Post-Impressionism,* no. 305 (entry by Anna Gruetzner).

42. W. C. Brownell, "Bastien-Lepage: Painter and Psychologist," *Magazine of Art* 6 (1883): 267.

43. John Lavery, *The Life of a Painter* (London 1940), p. 57.

44. See McConkey, *Clausen,* p. 29.

45. We learn something about Clausen's months at the Académie Julian from the unpublished letters of the Canadian painter William Brymner. Clausen was apparently admired by the other British and American students for his opinions on color, which Brymner considered "better than old Bouguereau's" (letter dated 12 November 1883). His daring in this respect may not have impressed his mentor. When a three-day sketch competition on the theme of *Noah's Sacrifice* was held, Clausen came in twenty-fourth in a class of sixty-five. I am grateful to Charles C. Hill of the National Gallery of Canada for bringing these letters to my attention.

46. Clausen had been invited to contribute a picture to the Grosvenor Gallery summer exhibition of 1880 and chose to exhibit *La Pensée* (coll. Glasgow Art Gallery), a picture of a young lady dressed in outdoor clothes, seated in a drawing room. The mode of conception in this instance recalls Gervex and Duez, see McConkey, *Clausen,* pp. 26–27.

47. For a discussion of the spatial context of Bastien-Lepage's picture, see Kenneth McConkey, "*Pauvre Fauvette* or 'petite folle': a study of Bastien-Lepage's *Pauvre Fauvette,*" *Arts Magazine,* January 1981, pp. 140–43. See also McConkey, *Clausen,* pp. 44–46.

48. McConkey, *Clausen*, pp. 29, 38–39, 112.

49. P. H. Emerson's main theses are contained in *Naturalistic Photography for Students of the Art* (London, 1889; Arno Reprint, 1973).

50. Ibid., p. 24, quoted by Peter Turner and Richard Wood, *P. H. Emerson: Photographer of Norfolk* (London, 1974), p. 18.

51. Emerson, *Naturalistic Photography*, pp. 24–25.

52. From an address entitled "Photography: A Pictorial Art," given to the Camera Club on 11 March 1886, quoted by Nancy Newhall, *P. H. Emerson, The Fight for Photography as a Fine Art* (New York, 1978), p. 39.

53. Ruskin actually used the term "Naturalism" to describe "the third constituent element of the Gothic mind"—"that is to say the love of natural objects for their own sake, and the effort to represent them frankly, unconstrained by artistical laws." Reading Ruskin's chapter on "The Nature of Gothic" in *The Stones of Venice*, vol. 2, 1853 (Library Edition, vol. X, London, 1904), pp. 215–39, it becomes clear that Ruskin applied the term to the Gothic cathedral sculptors' apparent love of natural forms. The meaning with which he invested the term was therefore different from Castagnary's more social definition. See John Rewald, *The History of Impressionism* (New York, 1961), pp. 148–50; Weisberg, *The Realist Tradition*, pp. 188–89; and Geneviève Lacambre's "Toward an Emerging Definition of Naturalism," chapter 8 of the present volume.

54. George Clausen, "Bastien-Lepage and Modern Realism," *Scottish Art Review* 1 (1888): 114.

55. Clausen, "Bastien-Lepage as Artist," p. 115. Without wishing to violate history, one might respond to Clausen's question "What is he going to say?" with the words *"Pas Mêche!"* (see Weisberg, *The Realist Tradition*, pp. 208-10).

56. McConkey, *Clausen*, pp. 52–54.

57. A separate study of artistic responses to *Jeanne d'Arc écoutant les Voix* is in progress.

Toward an Emerging Definition of Naturalism in French Nineteenth-Century Painting

Geneviève Lacambre **8**

THE AMBIVALENT RELATIONSHIP between realism and naturalism has troubled artists and critics since the middle of the nineteenth century.[1] Often these concepts were used interchangeably, since distinctions between the two tendencies were not always apparent to those who were committed to nineteenth-century realism.[2] By the end of the century, when naturalism, with its emphasis on scientific exactitude, psychological examination, and a large-scale format, had triumphed at public exhibitions, naturalist canvases, whether French or foreign, sold very well to official and private patrons. At the same time, however, naturalism was being violently disparaged by some critics and artists who advocated more imaginative modern trends under the auspices of an elitist avant-garde. This contradictory response is all the more reason that the origins of the naturalist movement should be clarified.

Realism and Naturalism in Context

In a famous manifesto published in the newspaper *Le Figaro* on September 18, 1886, the critic Jean Moreas pointed to the "infantile method" of naturalism.[3] Albert Aurier, then a young defender of Paul Gauguin and the symbolists, concurred with Moreas's characterization: "For eighty years, the nineteenth century, in its childish enthusiasm, has proclaimed the omnipresence of observation and scientific inquiry; for eighty years it has maintained that no mysteries could withstand lenses and scalpels. But now at last, our century seems to realize the futility of such efforts and the childishness of such bragging."[4]

If the era of positivism seemed over, some critics mourned the passing of all it had encompassed. While there were those who believed that "no longer will any artist . . . content himself with the myopic copying of social anecdotes, . . . foolish imitation of nature's warts, shallow observation, trompe-l'oeil or the glorious banality of being as accurate as the daguerreotype,"[5] others thought differently, pinning their continued hope for the future of naturalism on the theories and opinions of earlier writers.

Another point is certain: those who vitriolically attacked naturalism in the 1880s managed to give the movement the attention and publicity Jules-Antoine Castagnary (writing in the 1860s) hoped it would attain. Unusual insights into the reception of naturalism can be gleaned from the critics of the time who noted that great confrontations had brought forth romanticism and naturalism; others, like Jean Moreas, in a letter of 1889, underscored the significance of the tendency when he identified only three schools of art in the century: romanticism, naturalism, and symbolism.[6] Among critics who soundly attacked the naturalism of the 1880s was Josephin Peladan, who observed that "nothing remains of the Romantic cathedral." In condemning naturalism, Peladan predicted the death of art for those who stubbornly persisted in following the tenets of physical reality. He declared prophetically that "the color photography of tomorrow will be able to accomplish—and better—what 2300 of the 2488 exhibited paintings are trying to do."[7] For him, naturalism resulted in works that "look like what they are, compared to art—that is: *Nothing*."[8] The fact that all of this happened at a time when naturalist canvases were actually in demand makes it imperative to reconstruct the evolution of the critical response to realism as early as 1859. In this way a perspective on the movement will emerge, making it possible to see how different aspects of reality were construed by the critics.

In his appraisal of the 1859 Salon, Castagnary—a young, energetic art critic who sided with the more progressive tendencies in painting—favorably commented on about 100 of 3,045 paintings, noting that there were "some admirable landscapes, remarkable genre scenes, several fine portraits."[9] These were canvases where naturalist traits emerged as well, works that departed from the banal religious and historical themes of the day. Their artists were Millet, Théodore Rousseau, Daubigny, Corot, Troyon.

In reviewing the Salon, Castagnary recognized and defined naturalism; in fact it was he who imposed the term. The concept was not altogether new, for it was Géricault (who died in 1824) whom Castagnary identified as "the vigorous initiator of Naturalism."[10] However, he tried to distinguish between the naturalist instinct of the new generation and their forerunners' archaic tendencies toward the picturesque.[11] This style, which was so prevalent in nineteenth-century genre painting, did not apply in defining naturalism. Naturalism and the picturesque were seen as mutually exclusive.

In 1861, Castagnary denounced the presence of the picturesque in the work of Evariste Luminais, who had exhibited a Brittany *Fairground* at the Salon.[12] To Castagnary, the painting was merely an anecdotal response to one of Baron Taylor's or Charles Nodier's journeys through the French provinces. Such reservations can also be expressed about such paintings as *The Ex-Voto* by Ulysse Butin in *The Realist Tradition* exhibition. In both instances the selection of theme was not enough to convey a naturalistic impression.

With this criticism in mind, it is easy to see why Castagnary also expressed reservations about Alexandre Antigna's *The Fire*. But in basing his negative interpretation on the fact that the canvas earned a medal and was acquired by the state, Castagnary probably failed to take into account the special circumstances of the short-lived Second Republic. For the Second Republic had a sharp eye for quality in works of art inspired by the revolutionary movement of 1848. The state, for instance, bought works by Courbet, Rosa Bonheur, and others. "Monsieur Antigna," noted Castagnary, "is not a Realist at all. He is a Romantic, slightly dipped into Naturalism."[13] What seems to constitute the slight naturalist coating is the rather dramatic suggestion of a lived experience that imbues this imposing painting, just as it did the large, lost compositions by Jules Breton entitled *Misery and Despair* and *Hunger*.

In 1866, Emile Zola likewise warned against classification by subject matter: Bonvin, in Zola's view, had put too many minute details into his *La Grand-maman*, thus robbing the painting of its life.[14] Vollon's *Kitchen* also lacked atmosphere. In both these works, and in others, technique did not necessarily match intention. A popular theme might well be but a pretext for expressing a poetic sentiment, as Castagnary observed with regard to the *Recall of the Gleaners* by Jules Breton, who, in Castagnary's opinion, "sees nature through his imagination, thereby embellishing and belittling it."[15] He also found Breton closely related to the peasant scenes of Léopold Robert and commented on the picturesqueness of both painters' imagery.

But the most imposing task for the naturalists was to convey a lifelike impression, to record all aspects of modernity wherever it could be detected. In his *Philosophie du Salon de 1857*, Castagnary already indicated the naturalists' preferences: "Nature in landscape painting, character in portraiture, humanity in genre painting—these are the proper concerns of art. Life everywhere: scattered all over the canvas in landscape painting, concentrated in portraiture."[16] A genre painting will successfully avoid being literary only if it represents a specific moment, an instant. If it shows continuous duration, it becomes picturesque and sentimental. The last point is illustrated by a work by Mme. Chaudet entitled *Child with a Dog*, which depicted, in anecdotal fashion, a story in which a family dog was killed in error.[17]

At the beginning of the Second Empire, sentimental and picturesque genre painting, especially of Germanic and Scandinavian origin, experienced a tremendous vogue, particularly after Knaus, Achenbach, and others were represented at the 1855 exhibition and their works were reproduced in the popular *Le Magasin pittoresque*—a journal that had an exceptionally wide distribution among members of the middle class. However, romanticism excluded neither nature nor contemporary life. In 1863, Castagnary observed that the "Naturalists attacked from all sides," asserting themselves against the dominance of the classical and romantic schools. He formulated a lengthy definition of naturalism:

> The Naturalist school affirms that art is the expression of life in all its modes and varying degrees; its only object is to reproduce nature and lead it to its greatest power and intensity. Art is the equilibrium of truth and science . . . the Naturalist school reestablishes the severed relationship between man and nature. By its double focus on country life . . . and city life . . . it attempts to embrace all forms of the visible world. It already has restored line and color to their proper function, never again to go their separate ways.[18]

This defense of naturalism, coming at an early moment in its development, was understood; Castagnary became a key spokesman for this burgeoning new tendency.

Included in the naturalist school are not only the landscape painters, but also Millet, Bonvin, and Fromentin, whose *Arab Falconer* on his proud horse revealed his as a naturalist, even if the gallant stance of the horse may yet be a little too lopsidedly picturesque.[19]

Fromentin's paintings are often as difficult to classify as his novel *Dominique* is hard to place in literature. But Castagnary emphasized correctly that the representation of exotic subjects can—just like themes from country life—progress from romanticism to naturalism. Zola observed that, in 1866, Fromentin painted an Orient that, despite a prodigious handling of color, lacked light.[20]

Knowing how to evoke the light of the Middle East was, in itself, a naturalist characteristic. Painters like Belly and, above all, Guillaumet were soon to develop in this direction. There is probably a whole group of fin-de-siècle paintings that we will have to include someday in the naturalist category. The Goncourt brothers seem to concur. In their novel *Manette Salomon*, published in 1865, they had the Orientalist painter Tournemine in mind when they created the personage of Coriolis, whose luminous views of Asia Minor drew attention at the Salon. The Goncourts noted that Coriolis painted a different Orient from that of Decamps, whom they accused of being encumbered by "memories, old habits and ways of painting" and of not catching "the emotion of nature."[21]

This means that the naturalist painter largely rejected the tradition and models of the past; it is one fundamental way in which their works can be differentiated from the earlier realist generation. Indeed, in 1866, Zola criticized Ribot and the Hispanic bent of his works, saying: "The trouble is that he didn't create anything—his world existed for a long time."[22] Of course, this was only Zola's opinion. Another figure in the Goncourt novel, the art critic Chassagnol, proposed that in order to "capture" nature, an artist had to abandon the northern light of his studio, this "cadavre de lumière," an abstract light.[23] In The June 1880 issue of the review *Le Voltaire*, Zola wrote an article entitled "Naturalism at the Salon," where he, too, concluded that naturalism had to denounce "the false light of the studio."[24]

This fundamental change in the painter's working method was of great concern to Manet and his friends. We recall his statement that "A great painter who would paint in living daylight, under a real sun . . . who would paint in NORMAL light to say it simply, would surely see and paint other things."[25] Of course, the landscapists, Daubigny and the Barbizon painters, had already experienced this fundamental truth.

The character of the painter Crescent in the Goncourts' *Manette Salomon*, who resembles Millet, is sensitive to the changing times of day. "His palette is that of twilight, when the church bells ring the Angelus."[26] The recording of a specific moment is charged with significance, as it is in the works of Zola, or of Huysmans, whose novel *Les Soeurs Vatard* begins, "deux heures du matin sonnèrent"[27] ("the stroke of two o'clock in the morning").

In stressing the rejection of traditional training and of the timeless light in the studio in order to investigate the effects of true light on nature, the Goncourt brothers accurately identified the new attitudes so essential to the development of naturalism. To them, naturalism alone was modern art—a modern art that could only evolve by avoiding the realism of an artificial court style, which Chassagnol derided heatedly as a "caricature of contemporary truth" and an "*épatement de bourgeois*."[28]

Castagnary, in his assessment of the changes from realism to naturalism, was subtler in his judgments than many other writers or critics. He had met Courbet only once, around 1860, and even though in 1866 he welcomed the arrival of a new generation of painters such as Claude Monet, he still gave the leading role to Courbet as the promoter of a new style. He wrote:

> In 1855, it was possible to believe that the international exhibition
> would turn into a wholesale liquidation of the past. . . . It came
> differently. . . . Still young and hampered by its unfortunate limi-
> tation to landscape painting, the Naturalist school, represented by
> the likes of Dupré, Rousseau, and Corot, could not stand up to the
> achievements of artists of Ingres's and Delacroix's stature, whose
> works, though purely imaginative, are nonetheless very remarkable.
> . . . Today, the tables are being turned—there are as many genre
> scenes as there are landscapes, and Courbet spearheads the move-
> ment. . . .[29]

There were also Millet, François Bonvin, and a whole army of
young painters. Defending Courbet's *Woman with a Parrot*, Castagnary
felt called upon to act as spokesman for those who surrounded Courbet—for "all the young idealists and realists (for Naturalism comprises
both) who follow him: Millet, Bonvin, Ribot, Vollon, Roybet, Duran,
Legros, Fantin, Monet, Manet and Brigot. . . ."[30]

Thus understood, naturalism, rather than being seen as a development within realism, would appear to be more than realism, or an
"objective naturalism," as earlier expressed by Joseph Sloane in his
pioneering volume *French Painting Between the Past and the Present*.
Its aim would be not simply to render reality but, far beyond, to express Life itself. It purported to "write history"[31] by recording the life
of the moment. Naturalism was a style that gradually superseded
realism through its advocacy of scientific accuracy, photographic verisimilitude, and largeness of scale. It became the most visible art
form by 1880.

Castagnary, in 1867, took great care to reject what the symbolists
would support at the end of the century. The following quotation
sounds like a reverse echo of Peladan's vehement remonstrations noted
earlier: "There is no need to return to history, to take refuge in
legends, to summon powers of imagination. Beauty is before the eyes,
not in the brain; in the present, not in the past; in truth, not in dreams;
in life, not in death. . . ."[32]

At the close of the Second Empire, Castagnary's optimism seemed
attributable to the "ascent of free art"[33] he found at the 1868 Salon.
Despite Nieuwerkerke, who tried to dampen it, Castagnary's optimism
spread—largely because of Daubigny, whose presence on the Salon
jury was instrumental in admitting yesterday's "refusés" to the Salon.
But this success was short-lived. Castagnary had every reason to
rebel against the jury's refusal to admit Manet to the Salon of 1876—
Manet, who had decided to exhibit the *Bon bock* in his own studio
rather than join the impressionist artists, who, as of 1874, had been
forced to organize their independent shows. In 1874, Manet had still
succeeded in exhibiting his *Gare St. Lazare* at the Salon, where the

painting was praised for its "powerful light" and "distinguished tonality."[34] It was indeed Manet who appeared as the champion of the emergent naturalist movement, a movement that, before 1870, found its spokesman in Zola rather than in Castagnary, who hardly appreciated its beginnings.

Zola rejected realism and, in a letter of 1864 to Antony Valabregue, confessed to prefer "the canvas which, in scrutinizing Reality closely, consents to lie just enough to make me sense the human being in an image of creation." For Zola, Manet was "above all a naturalist"; his works were the best example of "nature seen through a temperament." Manet did indeed reject tradition. During a sitting for his *Portrait of Zola*, he declared: "I don't know how to invent. No matter how hard I tried to paint according to the lessons I have learned, I have not produced anything of value."[35]

This need to "abandon old routines"[36] in order to be a true naturalist also appears in Huysmans's judgment, in 1879, of Renoir's *Portrait of Madame Charpentier*. The portrait introduces us to the inner circle of the naturalist movement in literature, as Charpentier was the publisher of this group. Huysmans was obsessed with the natural, the spontaneous. His favorite artists were Degas, Manet, and Eva Gonzalez, whose painting *Une Loge aux Italiens* (fig. 8.1) he particularly appreciated, praising "la pose si naturelle." He also found Caillebotte excellent. But those who turned out clever stereotypes or skilled handiwork merely exasperated him—for instance, Jeannin or Bergeret, with their still lifes and flower pieces. In the *Episode de la Bataille de Champigny* by Detaille, he saw only the wretchedness of a cattle train. To him, there was an abyss between the modernism of Degas and Caillebotte—a modernism also championed by Duranty in 1876—and the contrived modernism of Bastien-Lepage or Cervex.[37] *Really* naturalist art that would unite all the required qualities seemed difficult to come by. It is true, however, that by the time Huysmans was writing, many essential features of naturalism were already so widely acquired and well assimilated that they were taken for granted by many painters. In particular the conquest of painting in the open, of *plein air*, as a direct consequence of moving away from the study of light in the studio, was recognized as a major naturalist trait.

The impression of circulating air in a painting, so much admired by Emile Zola in Manet's *Luncheon on the Grass*[38] and by Huysmans in his *Chez le père Lathuile*,[39] was the result of slow conquest, thanks to landscapists and painters of country life.

Nor can we forget the first successes of artists such as Rosa Bonheur —for instance, her *Labourage nivernais* (cf. Boime, fig. 3.22)—or Charles Jacque and Troyon—successes that attest to the beginning development of a naturalism unafraid of completing large formats.

They fall into the period around 1850, the heyday of the Second Republic. But the development was soon obscured by the politics of aesthetics pursued during the Second Empire, with its bourgeois taste for historical and picturesque genre scenes.

In this regard, the role played by Daubigny seems particularly significant. Daubigny was always present at the Salons of the Second Empire, where he held a semiofficial position and where his paintings met with considerable success. Many were bought by the emperor and his administration. During this period, Daubigny quietly continued to set an example, which was not lost on most of the landscape and country-life painters at the beginning of the Third Republic. Daubigny's floating studio, le Botin, drifting along on the rivers of the Île de France, foreshadowed Monet's work habits by affording close communion with nature.

A relationship with the natural elements was also what artists were after who moved around the outskirts of Paris, who installed themselves at Barbizon and in the villages of Normandy and Brittany, or in the valley of the Creuse and elsewhere, either on a permanent basis or for summer visits.

While this return to nature was, of course, important to the practitioners of naturalism, it did not in itself insure the creation of naturalist works of art. The "return to nature" came in all possible variations, from realist to picturesque—even symbolist, as Le Sidaner and Carrière were able to prove. We must realize that naturalism is not only a question of iconography or of theme but goes beyond that: it is a pictorial technique, a style. There is no doubt that it underwent the treatment of Manet and the impressionists, who can rightfully claim the naturalist label, but we must still examine just how far the definition can be expanded. Around 1880, when literary naturalism took organized shape with the *Soirées de Médan,* a network of affinities existed between visual artists who were friends of this literary group. We are all aware, for instance, of relationships between Degas and Raffaëlli or Lhermitte. The naturalists also did not hesitate to overstep the rules of their own movement, if only in part, or only in appearance.

We therefore might do well to dwell on certain works of art that by title or theme seem to belong to the category of history painting, but that Zola and Huysmans classified as naturalist art in 1880, namely *Tobias* (cf. Chu, fig. 9.17)[40] and *Ismael* by Jean Charles Cazin (fig. 8.2) and Jules Bastien-Lepage's *Jeanne d'Arc.* Zola did not particularly support the mystical naturalism of Cazin, but he did find Bastien-Lepage's naturalist attempts quite arresting.[41] Huysmans, on the other hand, objected: "Just like the other pictures by Bastien-Lepage, his *Jeanne d'Arc* is the work of a sly schemer who tries his hand at faking naturalism in order to please."[42]

But the question still remains: is it only because of the native costumes that the naturalist label applies? Surely this is partially the case, for it is in keeping with a new movement that derived from naturalism and tried to "actualize" religious painting. This trend, which also fueled certain pursuits of the Pre-Raphaelites in England, affected James Jacques Tissot when he undertook the representation of New Testament figures in Palestinian peasant garb, or Fritz von Uhde when he painted *Christ among the Villagers*,[43] gathered in a contemporary peasant house, and the *Disciples at Emmaus* in a similar setting. In this, Uhde followed the example of Munkaczy, who, precisely in 1880, turned from contemporary subjects to religious themes with his famous *Christ before Pilate*[44] without any change in technique.

Thus, the painting technique that began to take hold at this time is no doubt partly responsible for this development: large formats, vigorously executed in bold, quick brushstrokes as opposed to the sweetness and careful finish of most academic canvases. Bastien-Lepage, Roll, and Julien Dupré provide good examples of this tendency. The color scheme was now brighter, but it created an effect of softly diffused light rather than that of sunny atmosphere poking holes through trees, as in Renoir's canvases of 1876, where a dappled light effect colored the ground. This, no doubt, constituted a major technical difference from impressionism. But could this reflect the tendencies and discoveries of previous years? Could it be that experimentation, which had been hindered by the spread of new academic studio "recipes" solely designed for the tastes of the Third Republic, could not reveal itself in the open?

The Triumph of a Naturalist Style

One of the exterior signs of the "officialization" of the naturalist aesthetic by government and public officials during the Third Republic was the movement away from modest scale (which had originally been supported by Castagnary) in favor of formats worthy of museums and other public buildings. Large canvases were advocated; the central administration was quick to acquire many of these for the museum in Paris as well as for provincial centers.

No sooner did the new museum of modern art in Paris (the Luxembourg) acquire such paintings as Bastien-Lepage's *Les Foins* (cf. McConkey, fig. 7.12), Friant's *Toussaint* (fig. 8.3), Marie Bashkirtseff's *Meeting* (fig. 8.4), Roll's *Manda Lamétrie fermière* (fig. 8.5), or Dagnan-Bouveret's *Horses at the Watering Trough*, than the notoriously brown canvases of the academic history painter, Ferdinand Cormon, began to brighten with vast blue skies, and the prehistoric hordes in his *Cain* (fig. 8.6) had chariots filled with blood-dripping chunks of meat more richly painted than Victor Gabriel Gilbert's *Meat Haulers.* Suddenly, Edouard Manet was no longer taboo: the Salon, now in the hands of the artists themselves, gave him a medal for his *Portrait of Pertuiset*[45] in 1881, and in 1882 he exhibited his *Bar at the Folies Bergère;* it was not necessary for him to submit it to the jury. On January 1 of the same year, Antonin Proust gave him the *Légion d'honneur.*

This did not mean that the battle was over—even if the naturalist aesthetic touched many artists. Academic reticence remained strong, forcing the naturalists into secession in 1890, along with the symbolists, who, though in the opposite camp, were also modern. Together, they created the Salon de la Société Nationale des Beaux-Arts on the Champs de Mars, where naturalist-inspired paintings, whether in theme or execution, were in the majority, indicating rather clearly that Bastien-Lepage's technique had spread throughout Europe, as evidenced by paintings from abroad.

Purchases by the Luxembourg Museum around 1900, at the time of the Paris Fair, confirm that the government held great enthusiasm for naturalist painting, French or foreign. Was this due to the fact that the favored artists proposed a meaningful portrayal of urban and country life? The number of works utilizing industrial themes was striking, in an otherwise rather limited selection: Cormon's *Forge* (Musée de Tourcoing) and Constantin Meunier's *Au Pays Noir* (Musée de Saint Etienne) were of modest format; the American painter Lionel Walden contributed the *Docks at Cardiff* (fig. 8.7), a somewhat more imposing work, with skillful light reflections on railroad tracks on a humid night. All the works share a somber, brownish—perhaps symbolic—tonality deemed appropriate for the theme. And yet, weren't painters such as Maximilian Luce soon to paint these same factories with a profusion of reds, blues, and yellows inspired by neoimpressionism? The subject of contemporary life—advanced by the naturalists—could obviously be painted using different pictorial techniques.

In the collection of the Luxembourg Museum at the end of the nineteenth century, the naturalist label can be reserved for certain works—some that were acquired through the famous Caillebotte bequest, or Manet's *Olympia,* given in 1890 by a group of artists who were mostly naturalists. Among the works designated as naturalist are large-scale compositions by Rosa Bonheur, Bastien-Lepage, Lhermitte (fig. 8.8), Roll, Friant, Belly, or Guillaumet; even the landscapes by Daubigny, Chintreuil, or Léon Pelouse—monumental images that offer a partial, rustic, almost idyllic vision of contemporary life, like a late Jules Breton or certain examples by Jean François Millet—must be included.

What finally distinguishes these naturalist works is that they show their subjects as if caught—frozen—in a specific, characteristic instant, akin to the photography of the period in their attitude, though not in their scale. Thus they bear witness to a way of life in haunting images that remain engraved in a viewer's mind. They are also the equivalent in the visual arts of such verbal descriptions as those of a strike, from Zola's *Germinal* (represented both by Roll and Munkaczy), the wash-house of Gervaise, the café in Zola's *L'Assomoir*, or farm life, from Huysmans's novel *En rade*.

A painting of 1878 by Gervex, *Rolla* (fig. 8.9), was sent to the provinces as soon as it was bequeathed to the Luxembourg Museum in 1926 and then was sent to Bordeaux in 1933, as a painting of no importance. Daubigny and Millet's paintings were then in the Louvre, but the naturalist paintings of the 1880s were not, and if they entered the Louvre they stayed in storage for years and years or were sent to provincial sites. A first step in the reappraisal of naturalist art occurred in the 1930s, and later, after the Second World War, the exhibition of a collection of impressionist paintings continued this tendency. The next step is to consider some of the works shown in Cleveland—especially in the second half of the Realist Tradition exhibition—and others. They must be given their rightful place in nineteenth-century art as examples of a specific way of painting—in what we should begin to see as a firmly developed naturalist style.

Translated by Ursula Korneitchouk

NOTES

1. A discussion of the relationship between these terms was first initiated at a symposium held May 16–18, 1938, at the Baltimore Museum of Art. The outcome was a book edited by George Boas, *Courbet and the Naturalistic Movement* (reissued New York: Russell and Russell, 1967). Later, Joseph C. Sloane, in *French Painting Between the Past and the Present*, Princeton, 1951, proposed the equation that objective naturalists equal realists. In selecting the title *The Realist Tradition: French Painting and Drawing, 1830–1900*, the recent exhibition that opened at the Cleveland Museum of Art in November 1980 rightly restored the term "realism" to its proper place. It also divided the exhibition into two segments, grouping the second section under the heading "the emergence of naturalism." For further reference, see Gabriel P. Weisberg, *The Realist Tradition*, pp. 188–264.

2. This was quite different in the field of literature. French literary historians have always had a very clear idea of what they meant by "naturalism," as documented by the publication of *Les Cahiers Naturalistes*, a journal dedicated to the dean of naturalism, Emile Zola, since 1955. Other discus-

sions of naturalism were similarly quite clear from a colloquium held at Cerisy (1976) and in a special issue of the *Revue des Sciences Humaines* published by the University of Lille. For further reference, see Philippe Bonnefis, Introduction to the special number "Naturalisme," *La Revue des Sciences Humaines* 160 (1975): 471–72.

3. Republished in *Les premières armes du symbolisme* (Paris: Léon Vanier, edit., 1889), p. 39.

4. Albert Aurier, *Oeuvres posthumes* (Paris, 1893), p. 293.

5. Ibid., p. 293.

6. Cf. *Les premières armes du Symbolisme*, p. 7.

7. Josephin Peladan, *La Décadence esthétique. L'Art ochlocratique* (Paris, 1888), pp. 54, 156.

8. Ibid., p. 186; he wrote "Nulles."

9. Jules-Antoine Castagnary, *Salons (1857–1870)* (Paris, 1892), I: 72.

10. Jules-Antoine Castagnary, *Les libres propos* (Paris, 1864), p. 244.

11. Ibid., p. 248. See also Castagnary, "Salon de 1866," in *Salons*, p. 232, and Edmond and Jules de Goncourt, *Manette Salomon* (Paris, n.d.), p. 348.

12. Castagnary, *Les Artistes au XIXème siècle: Salon de 1861*. Engravings by H. Linton (Paris, 1861), p. 20.

13. Ibid., p. 27.

14. See Emile Zola, *Le Bon combat. De Courbet aux Impressionnistes.* Anthology of writings on art by Gaetan Picon and Jean-Paul Bouillon. (Paris, 1974), p. 68.

15. Castagnary, *Les Artistes au XIXème siècle*, p. 59.

16. Castagnary, *Salons*, p. 11.

17. *Child with a Dog* by Mme. Chaudet (1767–1832), was exhibited at the 1801 Salon under the title *Child asleep in his crib guarded by a courageous dog who has just killed, close to him, an enormous viper.* It was also exhibited in the Luxembourg Museum during the Restoration and became the property of the House of Lords. It was transferred to the Louvre in August 1871 (after it had come from the collection of M. Constant Dufeux, architect of the Luxembourg Palace, who had recently died). Later it was sent to the Legion of Honor at Saint Denis. It entered the Louvre in 1882 and was added to the inventory (RF 706) only a short time before it was sent to the Rochefort Museum (1892). It is characteristic that this genre scene was not acquired by the museum and entered, only by chance, the Louvre collections.

18. Castagnary, *Salons*, pp. 111, 104–105.

19. Ibid., p. 153.

20. Emile Zola, *Mon Salon, Manet, Ecrits sur l'art.* Chronology and preface by Antoinette Ehrard. (Paris, 1970), p. 86.

21. Goncourt, *Manette Salomon*, pp. 161–62.

22. Zola, *Le bon combat*, p. 67.

23. Zola, *Mon Salon*, pp. 228–29.

24. Ibid., p. 335.

25. Goncourt, *Manette Salomon*, p. 230.

26. Ibid., p. 230.

27. See Françoise Gaillard, "Deux heures du matin sonnèrent . . . quelques remarques sur la temporalité dans le roman naturaliste," *Revue des sciences humaines* 160 (1975): 553 ff.

28. Goncourt, *Manette Salomon*, p. 347.

29. Castagnary, *Salons*, p. 225.

30. Ibid., p. 240.

31. Ibid., p. 242.

32. Ibid., p. 241.

33. Ibid., p. 255.

34. Castagnary, *Salons* (Paris, 1892), II: 118.

35. Zola, *Le bon combat*, pp. 302, 142, 105.

36. J. K. Huysmans, *L'art moderne* (Paris, 1908 ed.), p. 70.

37. Ibid., pp. 65, 76, 135–37.

38. Zola, *Mon Salon*, p. 69. He says: "Dîner sur l'herbe."

39. Huysmans, *L'art moderne*, p. 714.

40. Now in the collection of the Musée des Beaux-Arts, Lille.

41. Zola, *Mon Salon*, p. 342.

42. Huysmans, *L'art moderne*, p. 150.

43. Now in the collection of the Musée d'Orsay, Paris.

44. Now in the National Gallery of Budapest; sketch in the Musée d'Orsay, Paris.

45. Among the prizes awarded by the jury, one notes that Baudry received the medal of honor in painting and that Manet shared with sixteen others the second-class medal. In the supplement to the illustrated Salon catalogue, published by F. G. Dumas, Librairie d'Art L. Baschet, 1881, a drawing by Manet is reproduced, p. 439, representing *Portrait de M. Pertuiset, le chasseur de lions.*

Lecoq de Boisbaudran
and Memory Drawing
A Teaching Course between Idealism and Naturalism

Petra ten-Doesschate Chu **9**

ONE OF THE MANY SIDE EFFECTS OF the romantic movement was a gradually increasing dissatisfaction with academic art education, in particular with its very foundation, the teaching of drawing. To the romantic mind, filled with notions about individualism and nature, the traditional way of training budding young artists by having them copy, slavishly and endlessly, engravings of facial features and limbs and bodies in various strained positions had deprived them of the ability to see and understand nature for themselves and had guaranteed that their future production would be cast in a predetermined, stereotyped mode.

As early as 1763, Jean-Jacques Rousseau criticized this type of drawing education and prescribed, for his fictitious pupil Emile, a revolutionary training:

> I will definitely not give him a drawing teacher, who would only let him imitate imitations and make him draw after other drawings. I want him to have no other master than nature, no other model than objects. I want him to look at the original and not at its representations on paper; let him draw a house after a house, a tree after a tree, a man after a man, so that he will get used to observing the appearance of the real body and will not mistake faulty and conventional imitations for real imitation.[1]

Rousseau's words did little to change drawing education, and almost a century later Delacroix wrote:

> Who does not remember those pages of noses, ears, and eyes that have distressed us in our youth? Those eyes, methodically subdi-

vided in three equal parts, the center one of which was occupied by the pupil represented by a circle; that inevitable oval that formed the starting point of the drawing of the head, which is neither oval nor round, as everybody knows; finally all those parts of the human body, copied endlessly and always separately, that one eventually, like a latter-day Prometheus, had to assemble to form a perfect man; —these are the notions received by beginners, which are a source of errors and confusion for one's entire life.[2]

Yet, as Delacroix well knew, by the middle of the nineteenth century, when he wrote these lines, several enlightened drawing teachers were already applying new teaching methods that often represented a decided departure from standard academic practices.[3] Though generally these teachers did not belong to the Ecole des Beaux-Arts or any part of the academic establishment, their impact was eventually felt and transmitted into academic circles.

Perhaps the most interesting of these educational reformers was the painter Horace Lecoq de Boisbaudran (1802–97; fig. 9.1), a man who in age belonged to the romantic period, but who influenced most strongly the realist and naturalist generations.

Born four years after Delacroix, Lecoq de Boisbaudran was admitted to the Ecole des Beaux-Arts in 1819 and studied successively under Jacques Peyron and Guillon Le Thierre.[4] He made his debut at the Salon of 1831 and regularly exhibited his paintings, mostly portraits and religious scenes, during that decade.[5] After 1844, however, he ceased showing his works at the Salon, as his interests had gradually shifted from the actual practice of art to the teaching of it.

In 1841 Lecoq had accepted a post as assistant professor at the Ecole Royale et Spéciale de Dessin et de Mathématique, ancestor of the present Ecole Nationale Supérieure des Arts Décoratifs. Often nicknamed the "Petite Ecole" (Little School), to distinguish it from the Ecole des Beaux-Arts, the "Grande Ecole," the Ecole Royale et Spéciale de Dessin was intended to "educate artisans and workers in the applied arts and industries," but it served at the same time as an unofficial prep school to the Ecole des Beaux-Arts.[6] It was at this school, where he was to teach for twenty-eight years, that Lecoq developed a teaching method that offered an alternative to standard academic practices. He first outlined this method in a pamphlet, published in 1848, entitled *L'Education de la mémoire pittoresque, or The Training of the Pictorial Memory*. In its original form it was limited to the teaching of drawing, but in a later edition, published in 1862, Lecoq added a chapter on the memorization of colors and another chapter with suggestions for the training of advanced art students.[7] The expanded version of *L'Education de la mémoire pittoresque* was followed by two more pamphlets, *Coup d'oeil sur l'enseignement des beaux-arts*

(*A Glance at Fine Arts Instruction*), published in 1872, and *Lettres
à un jeune professeur* (*Letters to a Young Professor*), published in
1876, an elaboration on *L'Education de la mémoire pittoresque*.[8]

In the meantime, Lecoq had in 1866 become director of the Petite
Ecole, which he gradually reformed to suit his own educational prin-
ciples. Heavily attacked by traditional-minded art educators, however,
he felt compelled to offer his resignation after three years, in 1869.
He subsequently taught at the Lycée Saint-Louis and the Ecole
Spéciale d'Architecture and gave private instruction in his home.
He died at the respectable age of ninety-five.

Little is known about Lecoq's own artistic production during the
period of his teaching. Although he is known to have painted and
drawn till the very end of his life, he never exhibited his work after
1844 and seems to have been reluctant to show it, notably to his
students, whom he did not wish to influence through the example of
his own style.

Lecoq was a teacher to the core and dedicated his life to the perfection and completion of his educational method. To this purpose, he
thoroughly studied the established teaching methods used in various
Parisian institutions, and he also took an active interest in any new,
alternative way of teaching art that presented itself. Thus, at the age
of sixty, he did not hesitate to enroll as a student in the short-lived
atelier of Gustave Courbet, eager to observe what promised to be a
revolutionary approach to teaching.[9] Unfortunately, nothing is known
of Lecoq's reaction to his experience in Courbet's atelier, but the
quiet, self-effacing Lecoq may well have been taken aback by the
boisterous egotism of his teacher. Though the two artists both felt
very strongly about the importance of preserving the individuality
of young aspiring artists, Courbet thought that this could best be
done by leaving them alone as much as possible to give them a chance
to teach themselves,[10] whereas Lecoq firmly believed that a good
teacher and a proper curriculum would not only preserve the individuality of the student but also develop and perfect it.[11]

Lecoq's teaching method was based on the principle that the visual
memory could and should be trained. In itself, this idea was, of course,
not new. Leonardo da Vinci had advised aspiring artists to train their
visual memory and had recommended, in the way of practical exercise, that at night, while lying in their beds, they should review in
their imagination the outlines of forms they had studied that day.[12]

Similarly, in the eighteenth century, Sir Joshua Reynolds, in his
Discourses on Art, had admonished young artists:

> I would particularly recommend, that after you return from the
> Academy (where I suppose your attendance to be constant) you

8.1 EVA GONZALEZ, *Une Loge aux Italiens*

8.2 JEAN CHARLES CAZIN,
Hagar and Ishmael

8.3 EMILE FRIANT, *La Toussaint*

8.4 MARIE BASHKIRTSEFF,
The Meeting

8.5 ALFRED ROLL, *Manda
Lamétrie fermière*

8.6   Fernand Cormon, *Cain*

8.7   Lionel Walden, *Docks at Cardiff*

8.8 Léon Lhermitte, *La Paye des Moissonneurs*

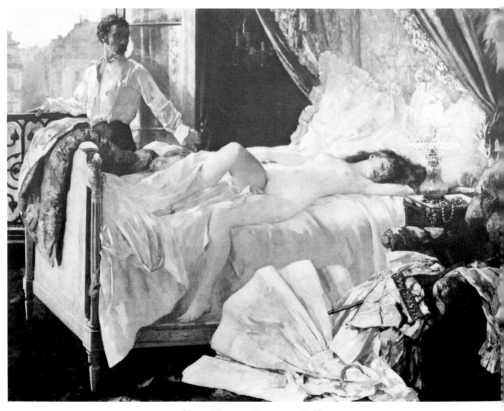

8.9 Henri Gervex, *Rolla*

9.1   HORACE LECOQ DE BOISBAUDRAN, *Self-Portrait*

9.2 REUTEMANN, *Memory drawing*

9.3 EMILE PIERRE METZMACHER, *Memory drawing*

9.4 ALPHONSE LEGROS, *Memory drawing after cast from the "Discobolos"*

9.5 LÉON LHERMITTE, *Memory drawing after detail of Poussin's "Time and Truth"*

9.6   NICHOLAS POUSSIN, *Time and Truth*

9.7 GEORGES BELLENGER,
*Compositional drawing made
from memory after
observation of life model*

9.8 GEORGES BELLENGER,
*Compositional drawing made
from memory after
observation of life model*

9.9 Léon Lhermitte, *Memory drawing: Choir Rehearsal*

9.10 Félix Régamey, *Memory drawing: Avenue de l'Observatoire*

9.11 JACQUES VALNAY-DESROLLES, *Memory drawing: Stone Quarry*

9.12 LÉON LHERMITTE, *Memory drawing: Nine Peasant Women in Interior*

9.13 GUILLAUME RÉGAMEY, *Memory drawing: Horse Stable*

9.14 JEAN CHARLES CAZIN,
Memory drawing: Landscape

9.15 LÉON LHERMITTE, *Memory
drawing: Landscape with Trees*

9.16 LÉON LHERMITTE, *Compositional drawing made from memory after observation of life model*

9.17 JEAN CHARLES CAZIN, *Tobias*

9.18 Henri Fantin-Latour, *Fairyland*

9.19 Léon Lhermitte, *The Quartet*

9.20 AUGUSTE RODIN, *The Walking Man*

9.21   EDOUARD MANET, *Le Déjeuner sur l'herbe*

9.22 Paul Gauguin, *Ia Orana Maria*

10.1 *Trompe-l'oeil*

10.2 DUANE HANSON, *Couple with Shopping Bags*

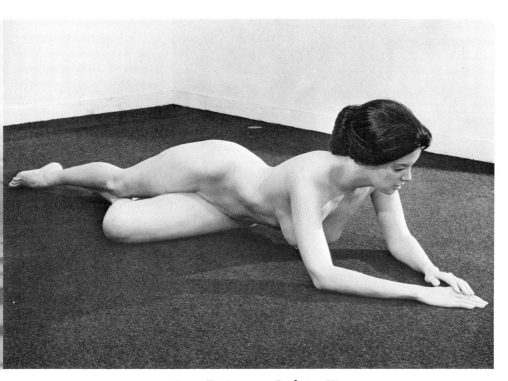

10.3 John DeAndrea, *Reclining Woman*

10.4 JACQUES TALRICH,
Jeremy Bentham

10.5 CATHERINE ANDRAS,
Horatio Nelson

10.6 MRS. GOLDSMITH,
William and Mary

10.7 *Votive Equestrian Statue of Philip the Fair*

10.8 *Equestrian Statue of Paolo Savelli*

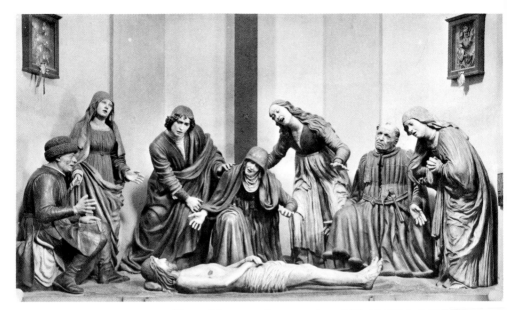

10.9   GUIDO MAZZONI, *Lamentation of Christ*

10.10   GAUDENZIO FERRARI, *Crucifixion*

10.11 EGYPTIAN, *Male Portrait Head*

10.12 DONATELLO, *Judith and Holofernes*

10.13 DONATELLO, Detail of fig. 10.12

10.14 ANTONIO CANOVA,
Domenico Cimarosa

10.15 EDOUARD DANTAN, *Making a
Life Cast*

10.16 Vincenzo Vela, *Death Mask*   **10.17** Vincenzo Vela, *Death Mask*

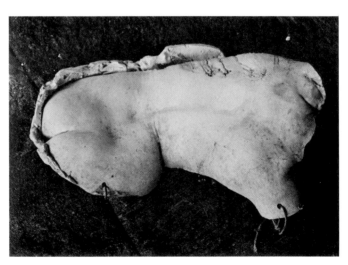

10.18 Vincenzo Vela, *Life Cast of
a Woman's Back*

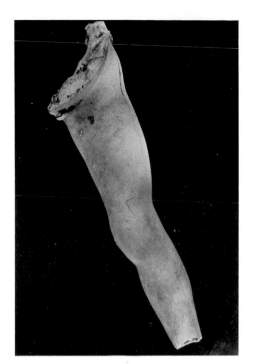

10.19 VINCENZO VELA, *Life Cast of a Child's Leg*

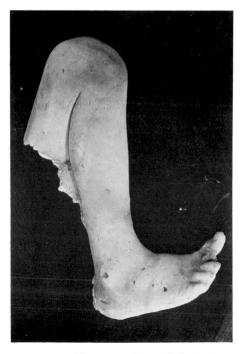

10.20 VINCENZO VELA, *Life Cast of a Child's Leg*

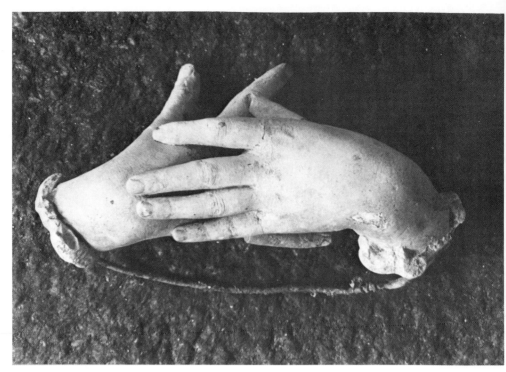

10.21 Vincenzo Vela, *Life Cast of Two Female Hands*

10.22 Vincenzo Vela, *Italy Thanking France*

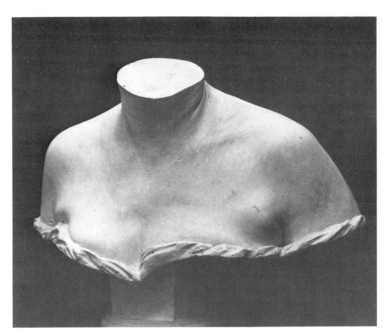

10.23 MARCELLO (ADELE D'AFFRY), *Life Cast of the Artist's Own Shoulders*

10.24 MARCELLO (ADELE D'AFFRY), *Study for Pythia*

10.25 A. RIVALTA, *Vincenzo Drago Monument*

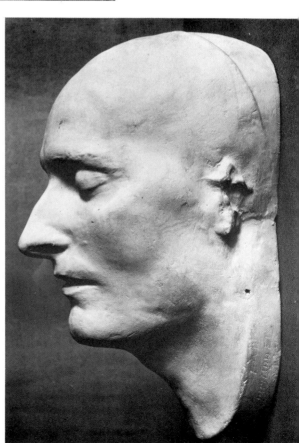

10.26 DR. FRANCESCO ANTOMMARCHI, *Death Mask of Napoleon*

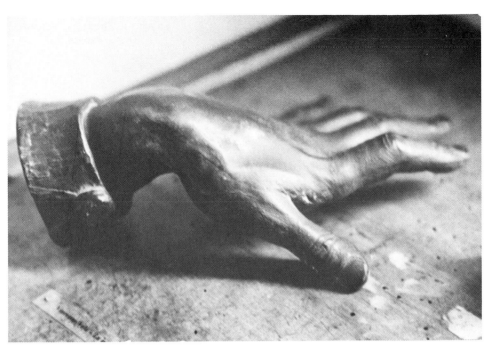

10.27   VINCENZO VELA, *Left Hand of the Artist's Wife*

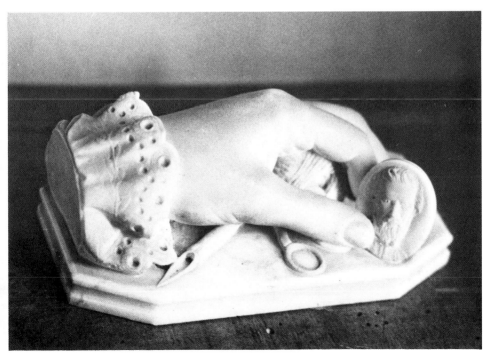

10.28   VINCENZO VELA, *Left Hand of the Artist's Wife*

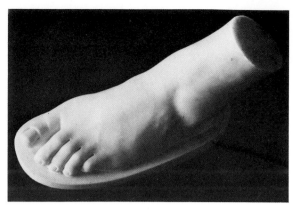

10.29 JOHN HOGAN, *The Left Foot of Lady Cloncurry*

10.30 ANONYMOUS SCULPTOR, *The Right Foot of Rachel*

10.31 *Life Cast of Rodin's Right Hand*

10.32 AUGUSTE RODIN, *The Hand of God*

would endeavour to draw the figure by memory, I will even ven-
ture to add that by the perseverance in this custom you will become
able to draw the human figure tolerably correct, with as little effort
of the mind as is required to trace with a pen the letters of the al-
phabet.[13]

With the onset of the romantic period, the interest in visual memory training seems to have increased. To romantic artists, memory was
an important means of enhancing subjectivity, a tool to be used in the
transformation of observed reality into personal vision. As early as
1834, Etienne Rey, a teacher at the Ecole des Beaux-Arts in Lyon,
published an "analytic, mnemonic, and synthetic method for the
teaching of drawing," in which, invoking the authority of Reynolds, he
emphasized the importance of memory exercises throughout the
student's training.[14] Both Ingres and Delacroix are known to have had
prodigious visual memories, and Ingres, especially, encouraged young
artists to cultivate their mnemonic faculty. Upon seeing Degas's drawings, for example, Ingres is quoted as having said: "That is good,
young man, never [draw] from nature. Always from memory and
from engravings after the masters."[15] When Lecoq published his
L'Education de la mémoire pittoresque, therefore, it was not the idea
of memory training in itself that was novel, but rather Lecoq's intentions and method.

Lecoq had devised a step-by-step curriculum that he believed would
prepare young artists to remember quite complicated prototypes in
the shortest possible time.[16] Students would start with the simplest
models, straight lines of various lengths, angles of different degrees,
and a series of simple curves, which were intended to develop the
faculty of estimation; next they would be presented with an outline
engraving of a simple anatomical detail, for example, a nose in profile.
After a brief lecture on the anatomical construction of the nose and
its most salient characteristics, they were asked to learn the model by
heart, either by copying it over and over again until they could repeat
it mechanically or, even better, by making careful mental notation of
the form in all its details. Though Lecoq did not require a particular
mnemonic technique and in fact was reluctant to prescribe one, he
did insist on absolute faithfulness to the model: only when their
memory drawings were flawless were students permitted to proceed
to the next model.

During the following weeks, students would be presented with a
series of engraved models, gradually increasing in difficulty, which they
had to memorize in a gradually decreasing period of time. After
three months they were expected to be able visually to retain entire
heads in all their details of hairdo and headgear; after four months,
complicated anatomical details. Next, students would be asked to

copy engravings after classical sculpture and after paintings and drawings by the masters (fig. 9.2). Subsequently, they would proceed to the copying of casts and of original paintings and sculptures in the Louvre (figs. 9.3–9.6). These exercises led to mnemonic life drawing, which was a crucial as well as an ambiguous part of the training. Since the life model is, in general, far from perfect in form, Lecoq considered it to be unwise to place too much emphasis on its exact memorization, as this would fill the students' memory with imperfect, even ugly forms and would thereby spoil their good taste. Hence, he asked students to make not exact memory drawings from the model, but idealized ones, though only after they had carefully studied and repeatedly drawn the model faithfully from life (figs. 9.7, 9.8).

All these exercises prepared the students for what Lecoq called the "true artistic application of memory," that is, for the mnemonic drawing of fugitive effects in nature and of the rapid and spontaneous movements of figures. To this purpose, the students were asked to walk through the city or the country and to observe with great attention the animated scenes that presented themselves. For their first exercises from freely encountered life, they were urged to choose very simple subjects, for example, a soldier marching, a beggar at the church door, or a peasant carrying a load. After that they were urged to reproduce more complex actions: a religious ceremony, a street incident, an interior, animals, or a landscape (see figs. 9.9–9.15). During this phase of the training, the students were increasingly free to follow their own inclinations and in so doing were expected to develop their own artistic personalities.

To the teacher, this last part of the curriculum had the disadvantage that it was hard to check the drawing against the original motif. But, in Lecoq's words, a drawing of real life done from memory must have "certain marks of artless truth that are unmistakable."[17]

In the second edition of his *L'Education de la mémoire pittoresque,* Lecoq indicated that his method could be expanded to the training of memory of color, but he warned that initially this part of the training should be kept absolutely separate from the training of the memory of forms. Therefore he advised that students be presented with color charts with increasing numbers of colors and an increasing variegation and subtlety of hues, which they, after careful study, would reproduce from memory. While experimenting with his color training method, Lecoq observed that innate abilities to memorize form and color were rarely equal in his students. That strengthened him in his opinion that it was important to train students in both areas so that their skills in handling color and form would balance each other.

It is important to realize that Lecoq always maintained emphatically that his method was in no way intended to replace traditional teaching methods, but that it should complement them. In his *Lettres à un jeune professeur,* he recommended that memory drawing not be taught until the students could draw reasonably well from engravings, and that throughout the training period, memory drawing and drawing directly from the engraved model, the cast, or the life model should be practiced simultaneously. His aim was not to turn out artists who could work largely or exclusively from memory. In fact, he may well have frowned upon the exclusive use of memory in drawing and painting because this was generally associated with the practices of cartoonists. Artists like Constantin Guys and Daumier, for example, always did their drawings, watercolors, and paintings from memory or "de chic," and admitted that they felt hindered by the presence of the model, with its multiplicity of detail.[18]

To Lecoq, memory drawing was not a working method to be used by itself but an exercise, which, combined with other exercises, made up the training of an artist. Through his mnemonic drawing exercises, he aimed to develop three faculties in his students: observation, the power of imagination, and the ability to record fugitive effects in nature.

Foremost to Lecoq was the faculty for observation. Like many others in his century, he believed that traditional academic methods taught artists to draw according to traditional formulae, or schemata as E. H. Gombrich calls them,[19] but did not teach them to look for themselves. Lecoq's method was intended to force young artists to use their eyes, because only through attentive observation and careful mental notation of all salient characteristics of their subject would they be able to retain it in their memory and to reproduce it subsequently in a faithful manner. Lecoq liked to define visual memory as *observation conservée,*[20] or "stored observation," and in judging the memory drawings of his students he looked not for technical perfection and sophistication but rather for "exact naïve resemblance" to the subject. He insisted on what he called the "naïveté of memory," and believed that the exercise of it was the only way to develop accuracy and precision in drawing.[21]

Through memory training Lecoq also hoped to develop the power of imagination. Though he realized that the question of the relation between imagination and memory was much debated by aestheticians and artists alike, he believed that the imagination would be served and enriched by a well-trained and well-stocked memory, which could provide the imagination with "more numerous, more varied, and more precise elements."[22] Lecoq was so convinced of the correctness of his view that he suggested that his students should, after completing their mnemonic training, participate in psychological experiments to resolve this age-old philosophical debate concerning the rapport between memory and imagination.

The third faculty that, in Lecoq's opinion, was fostered by a well-trained memory was the ability to record fugitive effects in nature. The emphasis he placed on this aspect of his students' training at times makes him seem an impressionist avant-la-lettre. Already in the first edition of his *L'Education de la mémoire pittoresque,* Lecoq stated that a trained memory is indispensable for the rendering of "animals, clouds, water, rapid movement, [facial] expressions, color, and fugitive effects,"[23] and in the second edition he pointed to the importance of color memory training for the rendering of solar, lunar, and atmospheric effects, and, in general, the "fugitive beauty" of nature.[24] It was in order to train his students' ability to capture movement and change that Lecoq added to his basic curriculum what we might call a graduate program. First outlined in the 1862 edition of his *L'Education de la mémoire pittoresque* and later expanded in his *Lettres à un jeune professeur,* this advanced course, or *enseignement supérieur,* was by far the most innovative of all Lecoq's teaching proposals.

The program consisted essentially of the study of the life model, moving outside in nature or against an architectural background. Sometime in the early 1850s, Lecoq began to invite selected groups of advanced students to a secluded spot in the countryside with large old trees and a pond. There several models, some nude, others dressed in draperies of different colors, were asked to move around freely and spontaneously, sometimes walking or running, sometimes sitting or lying down. The students were supposed to take rapid mental notes of the moving models and then to sketch them from memory, either as they had observed them or in idealized form (fig. 9.16). The emphasis in these exercises was clearly on the capture of transient effects, as is apparent from an account by one of Lecoq's students. He quotes his teacher as saying at one of these sessions, "My children, look carefully at that effect, never will you see it again," and then asking the students to draw the effect from memory.[25]

Similar exercises from the moving model were held in some rooms and halls of the Palais de Justice that were temporarily unused by officials. There models dressed in classical fashion walked beneath the porticoes, leaned over balustrades, or majestically descended the monumental stairs.

Though Lecoq and his students were very enthusiastic about these exercises, they were not continued for very long because of practical difficulties. Nevertheless, in his brochures, Lecoq strongly urged that this part of his program be taken over by the large art schools, which because of their size, prestige, and finances would have less difficulty in organizing outdoor sessions.

Lecoq believed that the benefits of his graduate program were many. Not only would the program enable students to perfect their rendering of the moving body, both nude and draped, but it would also give them an opportunity to study firsthand the varied play of light on a subject, as well as the effects of aerial and linear perspective. Moreover, by varying locales and costumes from classical to Gothic to Louis XIV, the students would be able, as it were, to transport themselves to different periods of history. Finally, but not least in importance, by their exposure to a careful choice of localities, models, and costumes, the students' taste for the beautiful, the grand, and the noble would be developed to the full. In Lecoq's own words: "They (will) have lived in poetical epochs and countries, where their spirit has been elevated and ennobled. They (will) carry in their memory, like precious materials, a store of nonedited pictorial data, which their imagination can idealize by combining them in thousands of ways, . . ."[26] One may have noted that in Lecoq's educational scheme these exercises from moving models were placed after the drawings done from memory of scenes of actual reality, of city life, landscapes, peasants, and the like. To Lecoq, this last part of his program was only needed by those students who aspired to the grand art of history painting. For all other students, whether they chose to become applied artists, sculptors, or landscape, portrait, or genre painters, the basic program would be sufficient.

The importance of Lecoq's teaching and his educational ideas has at least two aspects. First of all, Lecoq's teaching method offered a valid alternative to traditional academic methods. Rather than having his students slavishly copy worn-out schemata, Lecoq taught them by means of memory drawing to observe intelligently and to reproduce almost "artlessly"—without reliance on other works of art. He revolutionized the traditional life-drawing class, the *pièce de résistance* of the academic curriculum, by posing models more naturally, both inside and outside the studio, and by encouraging his students to use their trained memories to work from freely moving instead of stiffly posed models. Moreover, rather than casting his students in a common artistic mold, Lecoq encouraged their personal inclinations and tried to develop their innate talents.

Second, Lecoq's teaching method provided his students with a safe and satisfying middle course between the two major contrasting tendencies of the nineteenth century, idealism and naturalism, the first generally associated with the academic establishment, the second with a rebellious avant-garde. With his dual emphasis on a careful study of nature, on the one hand, and a thorough knowledge of past art and a sense of the *beau idéal,* on the other hand, Lecoq established a connecting link between two seemingly irreconcilable directions.

In the course of his lengthy teaching career, a very large number of students passed through Lecoq's classes. Many of them became well-known artists, such as the painters Henri Fantin-Latour, Alphonse

Legros, Léon Lhermitte, Georges Bellenger, Jean-Charles Cazin, and the brothers Félix, Fréderic, and Guillaume Régamey; the sculptors Jules Dalou and Auguste Rodin; and the medalist Oscar Roty. The considerable diversity in the work of these artists is a credit to Lecoq, whose primary educational principle was always to preserve and, if possible, to strengthen the natural inclinations of his students.

Few of his students could be said to have become what Lecoq seems to have considered the ideal final product of his training method, namely a history painter with a naturalist's attitude toward subject matter. The one who perhaps most completely achieved this ideal was Jean-Charles Cazin, who possessed all the qualities that Lecoq expected of a student who had successfully completed his entire program, namely the "faculties of observation and [visual] memory, the love of art and nature, and an understanding of the beautiful traditions of the past."[27] One of Lecoq's favorite students, and for some time the *massier*, or "student in charge," of his atelier, Cazin produced, after a hesitant beginning as an independent artist, a series of history paintings, from 1876 on, that created something of a stir in Paris upon their exhibition, among them *The Flight into Egypt* (1877), *Tobias* (1880; fig. 9.17), *Hagar and Ishmael* (1880; Tours, Musée des Beaux-Arts), and *Judith* (1883).[28] In these paintings, Cazin attempted to revive history painting by transporting biblical, mythological, and historical figures and scenes to the familiar surroundings of contemporary life. Though vague efforts in this direction had been made by earlier artists, such as the Pre-Raphaelites in England and Millet and Puvis de Chavannes in France, Cazin gave a clear focus to a tendency that was to continue in the works of several late nineteenth-century artists, such as Bastien-Lepage, Jules Breton, Maurice Denis, and Gauguin. The combination of observation and imagination and of realism and idealism that one finds in these works could be explained as a direct outcome of Lecoq's outdoor sessions, where students were asked to draw life models from memory in idealized form against backgrounds that had been carefully observed and memorized. Though there are no precise data on the working method that Cazin used in the execution of these paintings, we can assume that they were done largely from memory after careful study of the models and the natural landscape settings. This, at any rate, was the practice Cazin is known to have followed in other works, notably his landscapes, which were all executed in the studio, with a minimum of preparatory sketches, but after careful observation of the subject.[29]

Cazin was not the only student of Lecoq's who fulfilled his teacher's highest expectations by producing history paintings. Fantin-Latour also ventured into the same direction, particularly during the later part of his career. Rather than biblical, historical, or mythological scenes, however, Fantin's history paintings are poetical evocations, mostly based on musical themes. While Cazin's history paintings give evidence of the positive lesson that could be learned from Lecoq's method, Fantin's works show its pitfalls.

Paintings like *Fairyland* (1863; fig. 9.18) and the somewhat later *Tannhäuser on Venusberg* (1864; Los Angeles, County Museum of Art) are pastiches based on Fantin's extensive studies in the Louvre. These works seem to give strong support to the objections voiced by many opponents of Lecoq's teaching method, those who claimed that the excessive emphasis on memory training stocked the artist's brain with pictorial data and hampered the development of originality and imagination.[30]

Even in his realistic paintings, Fantin seems to have gained little from Lecoq's training. His portraits, genre scenes, and flower pieces were all done directly from the model without the exercise of memory. Typically, all these works represent relatively static subjects, for, despite Lecoq's training, Fantin had, to use his own words, "a horror of movement, (and) of animated scenes, . . ."[31]

Unlike Cazin and Fantin, the majority of Lecoq's students had no ambitions in the direction of history painting but preferred landscape or genre painting, or else sculpture, illustration, or the industrial arts. Nevertheless, the impact of Lecoq's teaching can be found in the works of several of them.

Among the landscape and genre painters, the one who perhaps benefited most from Lecoq's training was Léon Lhermitte. Though Lecoq has been accused of having wronged Lhermitte by keeping him on too prolonged a diet of drawing,[32] it could be argued that Lecoq, with his keen sense of his students' natural inclinations, realized that Lhermitte's potential lay in black-and-white media rather than in color. A drawing like *The Quartet* (1881; fig. 9.19) not only shows Lhermitte's tremendous power as a draftsman but also illustrates the prodigious effects that an artist with a well-trained memory could achieve. Though superior and technically more accomplished than the earlier drawing of *The Choir Rehearsal* (fig. 9.9) done during his training period with Lecoq, *The Quartet* displays a similar interest in capturing the actions of his human subjects, in the careful individualization of each figure, and in treating each part of the composition with equal care.

Lhermitte's memory also served him well in his paintings of outdoor scenes, which, like those of Cazin, were executed largely in the studio. Following is Lhermitte's own description of his working method, which clearly indicates how, during the creative process, he used his memory: "When a subject preoccupies me—we will say a painting of a harvester—I depart into a field and advise a man who harvests well, and then I slacken no longer: two hours, three hours later, with him, like him, I go, I come, I am with him step by step: I look at him from near and far away, I strive to grasp the rhythm of his movement, his cadence, . . ." Once Lhermitte had learned the figure by heart, so to speak, the composition slowly developed in his head. "I begin by developing my idea a long while in my head. Then, in the evening by lamplight, I shape and reshape it. Once my composition stops, the picture is made. There remains only to execute it. It is at this instance, at the end of the work, that my studies are useful to me, and that the model intervenes."[33] It is clear from this passage that although Lhermitte did not work from memory exclusively, memory played an important part in the genesis of his paintings, particularly during the conceptual stage.

A method similar to Lhermitte's was used by another student of Lecoq's, Auguste Rodin, who in an intereview of 1906 described his procedure:

> I am accustomed to having my models wander naked about the studio. They walk, or rest . . . I familiarize myself with all of their movements. I constantly note the association of the feelings and the line of their bodies, and by this observation I accustom myself to discover the expression of the soul, not only in the features of the face, but in the entire human form.[34]

Though Rodin does not seem to have been one of Lecoq's prize pupils, he himself claimed that he benefited from Lecoq's training throughout his career. Thus he wrote at the end of his life: "At the time Legros and I and the other young people did not understand, as I do now, how lucky we were to have fallen in with such a teacher. Most of what he has taught me is still with me today."[35]

The mark of Lecoq's training can perhaps best be seen in Rodin's early work, such as the *Age of Bronze* (1876) and *The Walking Man* (1877–78; fig. 9.20). The intense naturalism of these works, which in the case of the *Age of Bronze* even led to the accusation that Rodin had cast the figure from life, are concrete examples of what Lecoq meant by "observation conservée." Naturalistic as they are, however, both sculptures are in the tradition of the great masters of the past and are endowed with a nobility that elevates them above the commonplace. In these works, Rodin appears to come up to the highest expectations of Lecoq, who saw the ideal artist as one who is "animated with a passionate feeling of beauty; true lover of nature, he does not see its imperfections and discovers in her traits of beauty that escape the eye of the indifferent. He idealizes these and combines them in his works, giving them the stamp of his personality."[36]

The influence of Lecoq was not limited to his own students but extended to several artists of their generation. Some of them read Lecoq's pamphlets, others learned about Lecoq's ideas through conversations with his students. Thus, for example, James McNeill Whistler, though never a formal student of Lecoq's, became interested in memory drawing through his close friends Legros and Fantin-Latour. Whistler gradually developed his own mnemonic technique, whereby he made an exact verbal transcription of the subject. His friend Thomas Way described Whistler's technique in an account of an evening walk of the two friends along the road by the gardens of Chelsea Hospital.[37] According to Way, Whistler suddenly stood still, struck by a group of buildings with lighted windows that seemed golden in the misty twilight. Refusing a sketchbook that Way offered to him, he intensively observed the scene for some time and then said, "Now see if I have learned it," whereupon he recited a full description of the scene as one might recite a poem. Whistler seems to have relied strongly on memory during the later part of his career, particularly in the execution of his more evocative works, such as the Nocturnes, in which, much like the romantic artists, he seems to have exploited memory as a means toward selection and subjectivity.

Another artist who may have been influenced by Lecoq's teaching was Edouard Manet. Judith Wechsler has pointed out that he shared with Lecoq strong reservations about academic teaching practices, notably the traditional life-drawing class.[38] Antonin Proust quotes Manet as having said, with reference to the atelier of his teacher Couture:

> I do not know why I am here. All we look at is ridiculous. The light is false, the shadows are false. When I arrive in the studio, I seem to be entering a tomb. I realize that one cannot ask a model to undress in the street. But there are fields and, certainly in the summer, one could make studies after the nude in the countryside, since it seems that the nude is the first and last word in art.[39]

At least one of Manet's works may be seen as an attempt at a more natural rendering of the nude, the *Déjeuner sur l'herbe* (1865; fig. 9.21). According to Proust, the idea for this work came to Manet during a walk the two friends took along the Seine near Argenteuil. Several women were bathing in the river, which prompted Manet to say: "It seems that I must make a nude. All right, I will make one for them. When we were in the studio, I copied the women of Giorgione, the women with the musicians. That painting is dark. The background is too dense. I want to redo all that and paint it with a transparent atmosphere and with figures like the ones we see there."[40] Unfortunately, little is known about the procedure Manet followed in painting the *Déjeuner sur l'herbe,* and it is doubtful that he followed Lecoq's precepts for its execution. Nevertheless, the painting is in the spirit of Lecoq's teaching, not only in the revolutionary approach to the rendering of the nudes but also in its blend of actual observation and reliance on tradition.

Like Manet, Degas shared certain convictions with Lecoq, particularly with regard to the importance of memory training for the development of accurate observation. Thus Degas once said: "If I had to found an art school, I would rent a house with six floors; I would place the model and the beginners under the roof and as the student progressed, I would make him go down one floor and another, until he arrived on the first floor. Every time he would like to consult the model, he would have to climb to the sixth floor and to redescend."[41] It is clear that to Degas, with his preference for moving subjects, visual memory must have been of great importance. Yet Degas, particularly in his later works, seems to have been interested in memory drawing not only for its ability to record fleeting effects but also for its selective power. In that respect, his interest in visual memory was closer to that of Daumier and Guys than to that of Lecoq himself.

Aside from Manet and Degas, the impressionist painters in general seem to have had little interest in Lecoq's theories and method, although their posing of models in the open air, as Monet did, for example, for his *Women in the Garden* (1867; Paris, Musée du Jeu de Paume) or Renoir for his *Young Woman in the Sun* (1875–76; Paris, Musée du Jeu de Paume), may in part and indirectly have been influenced by Lecoq's ideas.

The lesson of Lecoq de Boisbaudran was handed to a younger generation by his two favorite students, Cazin and Legros. Both artists inherited from their teacher a strong interest in art education. Cazin, after having taught for three years at the École Spéciale d'Architecture in Paris, became director of the École de Dessin of the city of Tours in 1868. Lecoq's *Lettres à un jeune professeur* were written for that occasion, since the still rather inexperienced Cazin had asked his teacher for advice as to the establishment of a good art education program.

Alphonse Legros, after his move to England, became director of the Slade School of Art of the University of London, a post that he was to hold for seventeen years, from 1876 to 1893. Although he apparently put into practice some of Lecoq's educational ideas, Legros seems to have placed little emphasis on memory training.

Whereas nothing is known about the students that were trained by Cazin and Legros, we do know that an interest in the application of memory to art was transmitted to a number of artists of the younger, post-impressionist, generation. Among these special mention must be made of Gauguin, who throughout the greater part of his career seems to have advocated that artists work from memory. Thus he advised younger painters: "It is better to paint from memory. That way your work will be yours; your sensation, your intelligence, and your soul will outlast the scrutiny of the observer";[42] and to Emile Schuffenecker he wrote: "One advice, don't paint too much from nature. Art is an abstraction. It should be derived from nature by dreaming before it, while thinking more of the ultimate creation."[43]

Like Degas, Gauguin valued painting from memory as a natural selection process, an ideal means toward the synthesis that he tried to achieve in his work. As we have seen, this was not the role that Lecoq had assigned to mnemonics, for to him visual memory was a precision instrument rather than a "sieve that would select and retain from the object that which the artists thinks important," as H. R. Rookmaker characterized the concept of memory of Gauguin and the synthetists.[44]

What does relate Gauguin and Lecoq, however, is their common interest in combining the fruits of observation and imagination in their art. Gauguin's *Yellow Christ* (1889; Buffalo, Albright-Knox Art Gallery), and especially his *Ia Orana Maria* (1891; fig. 9.22), are akin to Cazin's *Tobias* in that they transport historical scenes to the artist's own environment, a device that, as we have seen, probably had its direct origins in Lecoq's teaching.

Gauguin's emphasis on memory painting had an important effect on the artists of the Pont-Aven group as well as the Nabis,[45] who transmitted his ideas of memory as an instrument to achieve synthesis and abstraction, to the twentieth century.

NOTES

1. "Je me garderai donc bien de lui donner un maître à dessiner, qui ne lui donnerait à imiter que des imitations, et ne le ferait dessiner que sur des dessins: je veux qu'il ait sous les yeux l'original même et non pas le papier qui le représente, qu'il crayonne une maison sur une maison, un arbre sur un arbre, un homme sur un homme, afin qu'il s'accoutume à bien observer les corps et leurs apparences, et non pas à prendre des imitations fausses et conventionnelles pour de véritables imitations." Author's trans., Jean-Jacques Rousseau, *Emile* (Paris: G. Havard, n.d.), p. 35.

2. "Qui ne se rappelle ces pages de nez, d'oreilles et d'yeux, qui ont affligé notre enfance? Ces yeux, partagés méthodiquement en trois parties parfaitement égales, dont le milieu était occupé par la prunelle figurée par un cercle; cet ovale inévitable, qui était le point de départ du dessin de la tête, laquelle est ni ovale ni ronde, comme chacun sait; enfin, toutes ces parties du corps humain, copiées sans fin et toujours séparément, dont il fallait à la fin, nouveau Prométhée, construire un homme parfait:—telles sont les notions qui accueillent les commencans [sic], et qui sont pour la vie entière une source d'erreurs et de confusion." Author's trans., Eugène Delacroix, "*Le Dessin sans maître*, par Mme Elisabeth Cavé," *Revue des deux mondes*, September 15, 1850, p. 1140.

3. See Albert Boime, "The Teaching Reforms of 1863 and the Origins of Modernism in France," *Art Quarterly* 1 (1977): 1–39, passim.

4. For Lecoq's biography, see esp. Félix Régamey, *Horace Lecoq de Boisbaudran et ses élèves* (Paris: Honoré Champion, 1903).

5. Few works by Lecoq de Boisbaudran can presently be traced. A painted self-portrait in the Louvre (fig. 9.1) and an unsigned drawing in the Cabinet des Dessins of the Louvre are all I have been able to find. According to Régamey, *Lecoq de Boisbaudran*, p. 7, most of Lecoq's paintings and drawings went, upon his death, to his cousin, Dr. Pierre Rondeau.

6. For a brief history of this school, see Mary Michele Hamel, "A French Artist: Léon Lhermitte," (Ph.D. diss., Washington University, 1974), p. 16.

7. The original edition as well as the expanded reprint of 1862 are hard to find. I have used the 1913 reprint edition published by Henri Laurens, Paris, with an introduction by L.-D. Luard, entitled *L'Education de la mémoire pittoresque et la formation de l'artiste* (hereafter Lecoq, *L'Education*). An English translation was published in 1911 by Macmillan & Co., London, under the title *The Training of the Memory in Art*.

8. Repr. in Lecoq, *L'Education*, pp. 65–102 and 103–107 respectively.

9. See Roger Bonniot, *Gustave Courbet et Saintonge* (Paris: H. Klincksieck), pp. 15–16.

10. See Courbet's letter in the *Courrier du dimanche* of December 25, 1861, repr. in Pierre Courthion, ed., *Courbet raconté par lui-même et par ses amis* (Geneva: Pierre Cailler, 1950), vol. 2, pp. 204–207.

11. Lecoq, *L'Education*, p. 83.

12. See André Chastel, ed., *The Genius of Leonardo da Vinci* (New York: Orion Press, 1961), p. 204.

13. Sir Joshua Reynolds, *Discourses on Art* (New York: Crowell-Collier, 1961), p. 36.

14. See Léon Rosenthal, *Du Romantisme au réalisme* (Paris: H. Laurens, 1914), p. 106.

15. "C'est bon! Jeune homme, jamais d'après la nature. Toujours d'après le souvenir et les gravures des maîtres." Author's trans., Paul Valéry, *Degas, danse, dessin* (Paris: Gallimard, 1938), p. 62.

16. In the description of Lecoq's method that follows, I have relied on the texts of both *L'Education de la mémoire pittoresque* and the *Lettres à un jeune professeur*, as reprinted in Lecoq, *L'Education*. References are provided only for direct quotes. All translations are the author's.

17. ". . . certains caractères de vérité ingénue, auxquels on ne saurait se tromper." Lecoq, *L'Education*, p. 135.

18. See Howard P. Vincent, *Daumier and his World* (Evanston: Northwestern University Press, 1968), p. 252, n. 4.

19. E. H. Gombrich, *Art and Illusion: A Study in the Psychology of Pictorial Representation* (Princeton University Press, 1972).

20. Lecoq, *L'Education*, p. 21.

21. Ibid., p. 29.

22. ". . . des éléments plus nombreux, plus variés, plus précis." Ibid., p. 36.

23. ". . . les animaux, les nuages, les eaux, les mouvements rapides, les expressions, la couleur, et les effets fugitifs." Ibid., p. 23.

24. Ibid., p. 42.

25. See Hamel, "A French Artist," p. 19.

26. "Ils ont, en quelque sorte, vécu dans les époques et les pays poétiques. Leur esprit s'y est élevé et ennobli, ils rapportent dans leur mémoire comme de précieux matériaux, une foule de faits pittoresques et inédits; leur imagination saura les idéaliser, en les combinant de mille manières, . . ." Lecoq, *L'Education*, pp. 151–52.

27. ". . . les facultés d'observation et de souvenir, l'amour de l'art et de la nature, l'esprit des belles traditions." Ibid., p. 152.

28. See Léonce Bénédite, *J. C. Cazin* (Paris: Librairie de l'art ancien et moderne, n.d.), p. 23.

29. Ibid., pp. 59–60.

30. Lecoq, *L'Education*, p. 30.

31. Quoted in Edward Lucie-Smith, *Fantin-Latour* (Rizzoli International Publications, Inc., 1977), p. 22.

32. Frédéric Henriet, *Les Eaux-fortes de Léon Lhermitte* (Paris: Alphonse Lemerre, 1905), p. 16.

33. Quoted in Hamel, "A French Artist," p. 25.

34. Quoted in Albert Elsen, *Rodin* (London: Secker and Warburg, 1974), p. 154, n. 3.

35. "A ce moment Legros et moi, et les autres jeunes gens ne comprenions pas, comme je le comprends maintenant, la chance que nous avions eue de tomber sous la main d'un tel professeur. La plus grande part de ce qu'il m'a appris, me reste encore." Lecoq, *L'Education*, p. 1.

36. ". . . animé du sentiment passionné du beau; véritable amant de la nature, il n'en voit pas les imperfections et découvre en elle des beautés qui échappent à l'oeil de l'indifférent. Il les idéalise et les combine dans ses oeuvres en leur donnant l'empreinte de sa personnalité." Ibid., p. 82.

37. *Memoirs of James McNeill Whistler, the Artist* (London, 1912), pp. 67–68.

38. "An Aperitif to Manet's *Déjeuner sur l'herbe*," *Gazette des Beaux-Arts*, 6ème pér., vol. 91 (1978), pp. 32–34.

39. "Je ne sais pas pourquoi je suis ici, . . . Tout ce que nous avons sous les yeux est ridicule. La lumière est fausse, les ombres sont fausses. Quand j'arrive à l'atelier, il me semble que j'entre dans une tombe. Je sais bien qu'on ne peut pas faire déshabiller un modèle dans la rue. Mais il y a les champs et tout au moins l'été, on pourrait faire des études de nu dans la campagne, puisque le nu est, parait-il, le premier et le dernier mot de l'art." Author's trans., Antonin Proust, *Edouard Manet: Souvenirs* (Paris: H. Laurens, 1913).

40. "Il parait . . . qu'il faut que je fasse un nu. Eh bien, je vais leur en faire un. Quand nous étions à l'atelier, j'ai copié les femmes de Giorgione, les femmes avec les musiciens. Il est noir, ce tableau. Les fonds ont repoussé. Je veux refaire cela et le faire dans la transparence de l'atmosphère, avec des personnes comme celles que nous voyons là-bas." Author's trans., Ibid., p. 43.

41. Lecoq, *L'Education*, p. 7.

42. "Mieux est de peindre de mémoire, ainsi votre oeuvre sera votre; votre sensation, votre intelligence, et votre âme survivront alors à l'oeil de l'amateur. . . ." Author's trans., C. Morice, *Paul Gauguin* (Paris, 1919), p. 213.

43. "Un conseil, ne peignez pas trop d'après nature. L'art est une abstraction, tirez-la de nature en rêvant devant et pensez plus à la création qui résultera." Author's trans., M. Malingue, *Gauguin* (London/Paris, 1948), p. LXVII.

44. H. R. Rookmaker, *Synthetist Art Theories* (Amsterdam: Swets & Zeitlinger, 1959), p. 129.

45. About the importance of memory painting for the Nabis, notably Vuillard, see Claude Roger-Marx, *Vuillard, His Life and Work* (New York: AMS Press, 1977), pp. 171–91.

Realism in Sculpture
Limits and Limitations

H. W. Janson **10**

For Fritz Landshoff at Eighty

WHEN THE HISTORY OF ART BECAME an independent intellectual discipline around 1900, our Founding Fathers—preeminently Riegl and Wölfflin—preached a doctrine that today strikes us as very strange but keeps reverberating in our own minds whether we are aware of it or not: the history of art, they claimed, is the history of style, of forms changing over time, or rather evolving like organisms in nature, responding only to their own built-in "laws," which could be altered neither by external circumstances nor by individual artists. Their ideal was an "art history without names," most clearly visible in the realm of ornament. Style, for Riegl, Wölfflin, and their countless followers, meant "period style," which governed all the visual arts equally: architecture, sculpture, painting, and the applied arts were assumed to march through history in a kind of lockstep.[1]

No one, I think, would be prepared to defend this proposition today. Yet we shy away from openly acknowledging that the various visual arts that, since the eighteenth century, we have been in the habit of calling the fine arts each have histories of their own significantly different from the rest. The purpose of this paper is to help clarify one of these differences, for realism in sculpture necessarily moves on a different plane from realism in painting.

Let me begin by citing an observation from the *Due Lezzioni* of Benedetto Varchi: "God, faced with the task of creating man, made him as a sculptor would rather than a painter."[2] It is perhaps the most striking formulation of a basic difference between the two arts that was acknowledged ever since classical antiquity and recurs throughout the *Paragone* literature of the Cinquecento: sculpture, simply by virtue of its three-dimensionality, is real, while painting can be no more than illusion or deception. Whatever virtues may be claimed for painting to prove its superiority—and there were many—this was an obstacle that even the most ardent partisan of the brush could not breach. Realism in sculpture thus has a meaning basically different from realism in painting, notwithstanding the fact that until the nineteenth century the criterion for realism was the same for both arts, i.e., deceiving the beholder. We all know the Greek anecdotes about birds pecking at painted grapes or the sculptured horses of Lysippus being mistaken for live animals by real horses.[3] Similar claims were made for Giotto; according to Boccaccio, "the human sense of sight was often deceived by his works and took for real what was only painted."[4]

Today, equipped with experimental knowledge and a more sophisticated understanding of the process of vision, we realize that none of these "deception stories" could possibly be true. Nobody, animal or human, is ever actually deceived by any painting, no matter how illusionistic. We do not even need binocular vision in order to recognize a flat surface when we see one, regardless of the painter's efforts to make us look *through* it rather than *at* it. Wiley Post, the one-eyed aviator, could land his plane as precisely as any other pilot, and the birds confronted with painted grapes would have been in the same position. Like Wiley Post, they were in motion with respect to a stationary field and would have realized that the grapes were flat rather than round.[5] The actual limits of deception in painting are extremely narrow: a successful *trompe-l'oeil* may consist of flat, overlapping objects attached to surfaces simulating bulletin boards or barn doors (fig. 10.1), or of a lifesize insect seemingly perched on the picture.[6] In either case, the deception works only if the depth of the illusionistic space does not exceed a quarter of an inch or so, at a viewing distance of two feet.

Now let us try to visualize the outer limits of illusion in sculpture. They have been very nearly reached by Duane Hanson in such works as *Couple with Shopping Bags* (fig. 10.2). Encountering these two in a museum, we might well wonder how they managed to get past the guards at the entrance. Why didn't they have to check their packages like the rest of us? It is only their lack of movement that gives them away. If we were dogs, we would know from their smell that they are not actual people, but an appropriate odor could be added. A blind man experiencing them by touch alone would be "disillusioned" as soon as his fingers reached the exposed skin surfaces. But with the array of plastics at our command nowadays, a convincingly resilient surrogate flesh could be contrived and might be heated to normal skin temperature. We are left, then, with motion as the one element that cannot be convincingly supplied; the figures might be constructed like automata, but I suspect that even the most sophisticated computer could not be programmed to govern their movements so they would look natural and spontaneous. Illusionistic sculpture of this single-minded sort, then, still has some way to go. John DeAndrea's *Reclining Woman* (fig. 10.3) offers even greater challenges regarding smell, feel, temperature, and motion; in her present state, she gives herself away immediately by displaying the age-old convention of "no pubic hair for female nudes."[7]

What differentiates such works from the contents of wax museums like Madame Tussaud's, apart from the use of more up-to-date materials, is essentially the anonymity of the subjects. The shock-of-recognition effect now rests on the type rather than on the famous individual. The wax image of *Jeremy Bentham* (fig. 10.4) by Jacques Talrich about 1830 rivals anything by Duane Hanson. The tradition of sculpture in wax utilizing real costumes, hair, and headgear is actually a very old one. Its status as an art was unquestioned until the idealist aesthetics of Neoclassicism, and the current revival of hyper-realistic sculpture has alerted historians to the antiquity and importance of these images. Their very location sometimes suggests how seriously they were taken: a number of them are in Westminster Abbey, such as *Horatio Nelson* (fig. 10.5) by Catherine Andras, of about 1805. They exemplify the notion of sculpted images as "stand-ins" for their subjects, with the clear purpose of perpetuating their bodily presence beyond the grave. Before 1800, wax effigies of this kind seem to have been limited to royalty. Conspicuous examples are Rastrelli's *Peter the Great*, now on display in the Hermitage Museum, probably dating from soon after the Czar's death in 1725, and *William and Mary* (fig. 10.6), a generation earlier, by Mrs. Goldsmith, in Westminster Abbey. Interestingly enough, the making of wax figures seems to have been a specialty of women artists. We have had occasion to mention three, and there are a good many more.[8] The reasons are not far to seek: tinting and handling wax demanded delicacy rather than physical strength, and wigs and clothing also called for traditional female skills. As a rule, the images had to be lifesize, although there are miniature wax figures as well, such as the mid-seventeenth-century one of Gustavus Adolphus of Sweden, by an anonymous artist, in the Museum für Kunst und Gewerbe, Hamburg.[9] The ancestors of these Baroque wax figures were ex-votos placed as thanks offerings for divine favor in certain churches, such as the Santissima Annunziata in Florence, which until the Counter-Reformation was so filled with these images, including equestrian ones, that there hardly was room for the congregation.[10] The same is true of S. Maria delle Grazie in

Mantua, where they were arrayed in niches along the nave walls. A number of them are still in place, such as a spectacular image of a criminal who had survived torture, a feat regarded as due to the miraculous intervention of the Virgin.[11] The earliest such ex-voto of which we have a visual record stood in Notre-Dame, Paris, until the French Revolution (fig. 10.7). It was put there as a thanks offering for a victory over the Flemish by Philip the Fair in the early fourteenth century. Apparently both rider and horse wore actual cloth and armor; the rest, we may assume, was made of wood and the exposed parts realistically painted.[12] The intention of all these ex-votos was very obviously to stand in for the donor, hence the desire to make the resemblance—or better perhaps, duplication—as complete as possible. Astonishingly, these free-standing lifesize statues were tolerated by the church at a time when any free-standing figure was suspect as conducive to idolatry. Perhaps it was their temporary character that made them acceptable. Their appearance—and their modest level of quality—may be judged from the wooden equestrian statue of the condottiero Paolo Savelli above his tomb in S. Maria dei Frari, Venice (fig. 10.8). Not an ex-voto in the strict sense, it was probably made for Savelli's funeral and subsequently "parked" atop his sarcophagus, which was certainly not intended as its base.[13]

In the Early Renaissance, the ex-voto tradition of sculptural realism seems to have generated another, related kind of sculpture that flourished especially in the Emilia: the vividly painted terracotta Lamentation groups, such as that by Guido Mazzoni in S. Giovanni, Modena (fig. 10.9). Their ancestors, iconographically, were Gothic Entombment groups, of painted stone, in niches. Now, with the disappearance of medieval idolophobia, they became free-standing, sometimes right in the middle of the nave. The link with the ex-voto tradition may be seen in the figure of Nicodemus, which often is the sculptor's self-portrait. These groups are intentionally "theatrical," extracting a maximum of emotional participation from the beholder not only through dramatic gestures and facial expressions but also by the meticulous imitation of the colors and textures of flesh and cloth. Since they were meant to last longer than ex-votos—whose function was limited to the lifetime of the donor—they avoided the use of actual hair and clothing.

Perhaps Mazzoni already felt the challenge of painting as the superior art that was to become so outspoken in the *Paragone* literature of the next century. Be that as it may, the Cinquecento not only took sculptural realism a step further but combined it with painted backdrops in such great tableaux as those by Gaudenzio Ferrari on the Sacro Monte of Varallo (fig. 10.10). Here we not only find once more the use of actual hair and clothing, as well as glass eyes, but painted extensions of the foreground scene. The transitions are often abrupt, but in Baroque ceilings such as that of the Gesu in Rome, sculpture and painting are so cunningly combined that some of the "realness" of the sculpture is transferred to the painted areas. Similar combinations may even be found in easel pictures, as in the partly three-dimensional *Dead Christ* by Samuel Percy.[14]

The almost forgotten sculptural tradition I have tried briefly to sketch here took the use of color and real-life materials, such as hair and cloth, for granted. It also made use of another technique: casts taken from living models, or at least parts of them, such as faces and hands. Here we encounter an aspect of sculptural realism that goes back at least as far as the time of Akhenaten, the fourteenth century B.C. A sculptor's workshop at Tell El Amarna has yielded a series of plaster heads that strongly suggest the use of life masks (fig. 10.11).[15] The area around the eyes has obviously been reshaped, but the rest seems to reproduce the life mask unchanged. These heads, needless to say, were not a final product but models from which the portrait itself would be carved. The method is comparable to the use of photographs by a painter; it establishes an objective standard of realism, which the artist must then reconcile with other demands. In Egypt, and in antiquity as a whole, one of these was permanence through the use of durable, hard-to-work materials that limited the degree to which real-life data contained in a cast could be retained.

How extensively the Greeks made use of life casts is hard to say, but they were at least familiar with the idea. According to Pliny, Lysistratus, Lysippus's brother, was the first to make such casts.[16] The story is often discounted as legend, an oblique commentary on Lysippus as a master of realism, yet I suspect it has a factual core of some sort.[17] While nobody can be sure whether or not the ancestor portraits of the Etruscans and Romans were based on life or death masks, the possibility cannot be dismissed. We do know that the Italian Early Renaissance produced such masks (Vasari credits Verrocchio with having introduced the practice), surely encouraged by references in ancient literature. They served as models for the heads of tomb effigies and portrait busts. The earliest surviving death mask, I believe, is that of Brunelleschi (1446). A decade later, Donatello used actual cloth for the mantle of his bronze *Judith* (fig. 10.12); in some places, the warp and woof show through the wax covering with which he had coated the cloth in preparing the model for the casting pit (fig. 10.13). Also, according to Bruni Bearzi, Donatello used life casts for the legs of Holofernes.[18] Perhaps this claim, difficult to verify, is no more than a tribute to Donatello's anatomical realism. I rather suspect, though, that Renaissance sculptors increasingly tended to do what an encyclopedia of the late eighteenth century reports as common practice: they kept casts of parts of the human body as well as of antique statuary in their workshops for study purposes.[19]

The use of life casts does not seem to have been denounced as "cheating" until Neoclassicism. Ironically, such an accusation was directed at Canova's early (and still rather Baroque) *Daedalus and Icarus* group.[20] In the nineteenth century it became a standard attack on any work of sculpture that was more realistic than the academic tradition was willing to tolerate, e.g., Mercié's *David*. The most famous—and, I think, the last—instance was Rodin's *Age of Brass;* the artist went to great lengths to prove the claim false.[21] The oddest case concerns Pauline Borghese, whom Canova portrayed, at her husband's insistence, as the victorious Venus, nude to the waist. She was famous for the beauty of her breasts, and Canova is said to have made a plaster cast of them. There is indeed such a cast—or at least a cast after a beautiful pair of breasts—in the Museo Napoleonico in Rome, but the identity of neither the caster nor the castee is well established.[22] That there was a realistic side to Canova's art as a portraitist, on the other hand, can be shown in such examples as his posthumous bust of the composer Cimarosa (fig. 10.14), which is timelessly nude but displays the fleshly chest of a fat elderly man.

That life casts were actually produced in sculptors' studios is evident from a number of nineteenth-century paintings, such as one by Edouard Dantan (fig. 10.15) that appeared in the Salon of 1887.[23] Needless to say, the subject lent itself to the display of pretty nude female models, but it also attests what must have been a widespread practice. The contents of sculptors' studios have rarely survived intact, even when the artist, following the precedent set by Canova's Gipsoteca at Possagno, bequeathed his original plasters to posterity. Rodin's studio at Meudon is essentially undisturbed and contains heaps of human limbs, yet none are life casts, even though Rodin used them as if they were. There exists, however, another intact sculptor's workshop, that of Vincenzo Vela at Ligornetto near Lugano, and there, for once, we actually find a number of life casts and can form an idea of why the artist made them and how he used them.

They fall into several distinct categories: life or death masks of faces; limbs, hands, feet; and one complete adult female back. Most of the limbs, hands, and feet, somewhat surprisingly, are of children. But let us start our trip through the basement of the Museo Vela with the most familiar group, the face masks. Such casts had been routinely used as a step in portraiture by Houdon, who took molds of George Washington's face and hands at Mount Vernon. Vela, in contrast, seems to have worked without such aids, except when the portrait was a posthumous one. My impression is that all the masks in his basement are death masks (figure 10.16 shows the most impressive male example). In at least one instance (fig. 10.17) he must have reworked the eyes and perhaps the mouth as well, to sharpen the expression. The subjects are unidentified, and I have been unable to correlate them with portraits actually executed. The fine cast of a woman's back likewise does not seem to have been put to use directly (fig. 10.18). The numerous casts of children's limbs and feet, however, had a special purpose: Vela was often called upon to model nude or seminude children, either for tomb figures or as portraits, and apparently he found that children do not make good sitters, so that he made casts of parts of them as a substitute for the living model. Limbs and feet (figs. 10.19, 10.20) were put to use in statues such as the *Praying Boy*, the *Boy with a Bird's Nest*, or *The Children of Marchesa Ala-Ponzone*.[24] In at least one instance, there is a direct correlation between the cast and its use: two female hands, cast separately, have been linked together with wire (fig. 10.21); they recur, modified but recognizable, as the hands of *Italy* in the group *Italy Thanking France* (fig. 10.22), which Vela made on commission in 1862 as a present for Napoleon III.

That Vela's method of using life casts was characteristic of the sculptors of his time is suggested by other examples, although not many have come to light so far. Perhaps the most remarkable is the cast of her own shoulders (fig. 10.23) by the gifted woman sculptor Marcello (her *nom de ciseau*, as it were; her true name was Adèle d'Affry, Duchess Castiglione-Colonna), used as an aid in modeling her most ambitious work, the *Pythian Sibyl* in the Paris Opéra. The cast has been thoroughly transformed in the work itself (fig. 10.24). Marcello also made casts of her own hands for the same statue, but these have not survived.[25]

In all these instances, the relation of the life cast to the artist's final product is quite straightforward. Neither Vela nor Marcello would have thought of the casts as works of art; they were no more than substitutes for the living model, valued because they helped to assure accuracy. For Vela in particular, "truth to life" was important: he was among the pioneers of what came to be known in later years as *verismo*, the Italian counterpart of realism in France but with a special flavor of its own, since it derives from *il vero*, which means both *truth* and *nature*. It was Vela who first put the classical mourners on Italian tombs into modern costume, as early as 1846,[26] and thereby set a precedent that was to be exploited in countless later monuments, especially in the Camposanto di Staglieno near Genoa. The mourning father by Rivalta on the Drago tomb (fig. 10.25) or Orengo's watchful mother are the marble ancestors of Duane Hanson's figures. The most famous (and deservedly so, I think) is Orengo's *Caterina Campodonico* of 1881, a poor pretzel vendor who paid for her monument with her life's savings. Nothing but complete fidelity to nature would have satisfied her. But let us note, too, that Orengo has endowed her with an impressive dignity of bearing.[27]

Vela was not only a realist, he was also something of a romantic. And it was romanticism that had elevated life casts of a certain kind to the rank of works of art. It instituted what might be called a cult of the death mask. Probably the earliest to become a cult object was that of Napoleon, taken by his doctor on St. Helena in 1821 (fig. 10.26). It reached Paris in 1833 and was immediately multiplied in bronze and cheaper materials.[28] There must have been countless such replicas, treated like secular icons by the emperor's admirers. Beethoven's mask was a close second,[29] and, later in the century, the *Inconnue de la Seine*, a death mask of a young woman whose body was said to have been found floating in the river. Life casts of hands and feet suddenly became popular, and these, unlike death masks, were viewed as works of art. Vela's share in this vogue consists of a bronze cast of his wife's left hand (fig. 10.27), obviously based on a mold of the hand itself but carefully finished and with the position of the fingers and the angle at the wrist controlled by the artist to maximize the hand's expressive potential. A second specimen (fig. 10.28), in marble, is again based on a cast but with a group of objects added to enhance its sentimental value—a pen, a pair of scissors, and a medallion portrait of Vela himself.[30] These are essentially private memorabilia. I can well imagine, however, that Vela produced such hands on commission as well. The most famous instance is probably the cast of the clasped hands of Robert and Elizabeth Browning by the American woman sculptor Harriet Hosmer, who sold bronze replicas of it by the dozens—if not hundreds—to Browning enthusiasts.[31] Clearly, the fact that they were cast from life did not deprive these hands of the status of a work of art; after all, Harriet Hosmer had the idea; she arranged the hands and made other formal decisions that went into the final product, such as the truncation at the wrists. A similar argument can be made for the marble portrait of Lady Cloncurry's left foot (fig. 10.29), commissioned by her husband during a visit to Rome in 1841 from the Irish sculptor John Hogan, who surely began by making a cast of the foot. Some husbands or lovers went a good deal further: when Clésinger, in 1847, exhibited his *Woman Bitten by a Snake*, there were rumors that the figure was based on a life cast of Madame Sabatier, made by Clésinger at the behest of the lady's current lover.[32] There is some evidence for the latter part of the story, but the cast has not survived, so that its relationship to the marble must remain conjectural. As for feet as *pars pro toto* images of feminine allure, the finest example—unfortunately, anonymous—is to be found at Compiègne (fig. 10.30). Said to be the cast of the right foot of the famous actress Rachel, it has been cunningly embellished with a turban, a string of pearls, and a bit of flowered lawn to evoke the presence of an odalisque.

As a final example of this kind of object—final also in view of its late date, 1917—we might consider a cast of Rodin's right hand, made three weeks before his death by one of his assistants and combined with a small female torso from the master's stock of such studies (fig. 10.31). It is all too easy to dismiss this as a pastiche. In the perspective of its long line of predecessors, however, it assumes a more dignified purpose as a memorial, an act of homage that is at the same time a commentary on Rodin's own *The Hand of God* (fig. 10.32), which is, of course, not derived from a life cast of the artist's hand but represents it by implication. No less than Michelangelo, Rodin was profoundly convinced of the sculptor's godlike power. He would surely have applauded the quotation from Varchi's *Due Lezzioni* cited near the beginning of this essay, although we have no reason to think that he knew it. But he just as surely disapproved of life casts, even if at the very end of his life he permitted his assistant to make a cast of his right hand in the act of holding *something* (not the torso, which was added separately and, one assumes, posthumously).

Rodin's entire thinking about sculpture centered on the concept of "animation": how to endow the forms with a sense of life and movement. Objectively, this is, of course, impossible, yet these qualities can be suggested, creating what might be termed an "illusion once removed from reality," much as the illusion of spatial depth in painting is not a real illusion but demands "a willing suspension of disbelief." From classic Greek times on, the highest praise that could be bestowed upon a statue has been that it seemed alive. Callistratus, in describing the figure of a Bacchante by Scopas, says that the marble, "though it had no power to move, knew how to leap in Bacchic dance and would respond to the god when he entered into its inner being. When we saw the face we stood speechless, so manifest upon it was the evidence of sense perception, though perception was not present."[33] To achieve this miracle, Callistratus adds, Scopas himself must have been possessed of that divine inspiration that brings forth the work of poets. Clearly, to Callistratus this illusion of the marble being alive was the highest kind of realism—a realism that has little if anything to do with the everyday appearance of things. Rodin strove for this kind of realism, and he must have understood that life casts were incompatible with his goal; that, in fact, they represented the opposite end of the scale. For life casts inevitably show life at a standstill, like Duane Hanson's *Couple with Shopping Bags* or their predecessors. Sculpture of the latter kind simply relinquishes every claim to animation for the sake of a three-dimensional *trompe-l'oeil.* From the fifteenth century on, these two opposed kinds of sculptural realism have existed side by side, clearly separated in their extreme forms but often interbreeding in a variety of interesting ways, as in Donatello's

Judith (see fig. 10.12), whose face certainly shows animation yet is framed by actual, and hence inert, cloth. Houdon's *Washington* does not look like a monochrome version of a figure from Madame Tussaud's museum, despite the fact that the artist began with a cast of the sitter's features. And Marcello knew how to integrate the anatomical forms of her own shoulders and hands with the intensely animated conception of her *Pythian Sibyl*. Still, even the most animated nineteenth-century sculpture before Rodin, such as Carpeaux's *Dance*, is constrained by an obligation to verisimilitude that could give rise to the ever-recurring suspicion that the artist had used life casts. Only with Rodin do we find the goal of animation so overpowering that he sacrificed not only anatomical verisimilitude but even the integrity of the human form to it. To leave things unfinished, in a state of becoming rather than being, was his most effective device for overcoming the dilemma of realism that had plagued his predecessors.

NOTES

1. The most striking formulation of the views summarized is to be found in Heinrich Wölfflin, *Grundbegriffe der Kunstwissenschaft*, based on a series of lectures the author had presented at the Berlin Akademie der Wissenschaften in 1912. Since the book was published during the First World War, in 1915, its influence, in Germany and abroad, had to await the 1920s. The English translation, under the title *Principles of Art History*, was widely used in undergraduate teaching during the 1930s and 1940s. Wölfflin freely acknowledges his indebtedness to such earlier scholars as Wickhoff, Riegl, Schmarsow, Dehio, and Frankl.

2. I owe my acquaintance with this passage to the kindness of Dr. Lea Mendelsohn. It is to be found in *Trattati d'Arte del Cinquecento*, ed. Paolo Barocchi (Bari, 1960), I, 48.

3. For a collection of the relevant passages, see Ernst Kris and Otto Kurz, *Die Legende vom Künstler* (Vienna, 1934), pp. 69 ff., now also available in translation (*Legend, Myth, and Magic in the Image of the Artist*, Yale University Press, 1979, pp. 61 ff.).

4. *Decameron*, VI, 5.

5. Cf. Myron L. Braunstein, *Depth Perception through Motion* (New York: Academic Press [Harcourt Brace Jovanovich], 1976).

6. The earliest known example of the "bulletin board" type of *trompe-l'oeil* seems to be a fragmentary Venetian panel of ca. 1500 attributed to Carpaccio in the J. Paul Getty Museum, Malibu; see Burton B. Frederickson, *Masterpieces of Painting. . . .*, 1980, no. 6. *Trompe-l'oeil* flies occur in several panels of the later fifteenth century in both Flanders and Italy, e.g., Petrus Christus, *Portrait of a Carthusian*, and Carlo Crivelli, *Virgin and Child*, both in the Metropolitan Museum of Art, New York.

7. This omission is remedied in the artist's more recent nudes.

8. See E. J. Pyke, *A Biographical Dictionary of Wax Modellers* (Oxford: Clarendon Press, 1973).

9. Published by Lise Lotte Moeller, in *Opuscula in Honorem C. Hernmarck* (Nationalmusei skriftserie, nr. 15), Nationalmuseum, Stockholm, 1966, pp. 178 ff.

10. See Aby Warburg, *Bildniskunst und Florentinisches Bürgertum* (Leipzig, 1902), p. 11 and Anhang I ("Votivstatuen aus Wachs"), pp. 29 ff. Reprinted in *Gesammelte Schriften,* ed. Gertrud Bing and Fritz Rougemont (Leipzig-Berlin, 1932; anastatic reprint, Nendeln, Liechtenstein, 1969) and *Ausgewählte Schriften . . .,* ed. Dieter Wuttke (Baden-Baden, 1979), pp. 65 ff. A broader treatment of the subject is Julius von Schlosser, "Geschichte der Portraitbildnerei in Wachs," *Jahrbuch der Kunstsammlungen des Allerhöchsten Kaiserhauses,* 29 (Vienna, 1910–11), pp. 171–258.

11. Prof. Kathleen Weil-Garris was kind enough to draw my attention to this monument.

12. See *Art de France* 3 (1963): 127, 132.

13. See H. W. Janson, *The Sculpture of Donatello* (Princeton, 1957), p. 158.

14. Victoria and Albert Museum, London; Pyke, *Biographical Dictionary,* fig. 215.

15. For a full discussion of this group of heads, see Günther Roeder, *Jahrbuch der Preussischen Kunstsammlungen,* 62, 1941, pp. 145 ff. I have been unable to verify the claim of P. Montet that death masks in plaster existed as early as the Old Kingdom, reported in *La sculpture, méthode et vocabulaire* (Paris, 1978), p. 103 (a handbook by numerous authors in the series Principes d'analyse scientifique, part of the Inventaire général des monuments et des richesses artistiques de la France).

16. *Natural History,* book 35, chapter 12, section 44.

17. See the skeptical remarks by Kris and Kurz, *Die Legende vom Künstler,* p. 27.

18. See Janson, *The Sculpture of Donatello,* p. 201.

19. Jacques Lacombe, *Arts et Métiers,* in *l'Encyclopédie méthodique* (Paris: Panckoucke, 1782–91), s.v. "Art du Moulage," cited in *La sculpture, méthode et vocabulaire,* p. 135.

20. I owe this information to the kindness of Hugh Honour.

21. See Ruth Butler, "Rodin and the Salon," in the catalog of the Rodin exhibition at The National Gallery of Art, 1981, which the author kindly permitted me to read in advance of its publication.

22. See Carlo Pietrangeli, *Il Museo Napoleonico* (Rome, 1950), p. 62.

23. Our illustration is taken from p. 249, *Salon de 1887, Catalogue illustré,* (Paris: Baschet).

24. This group, dating from the early 1860s, is illustrated in Nancy Scott, *Vincenzo Vela, 1820–1891,* Outstanding Dissertations in the Fine Arts (New York: Garland, 1979), fig. 133.

25. Henriette Bessis, *Marcello sculpteur* (Fribourg: Musée d'Art et d'Histoire, 1980), pp. 163 ff., cat. nos. 40c,d.

26. Tomb of Maddalena Adami-Bozzi, Pavia. See Scott, *Vincenzo Vela,* pp. 99 ff. and fig. 17.

27. The two works by Orengo are illustrated in Giovanni Grassi and Graziella Pellicci, *Staglieno* (Genoa: Sagep, 1974), figs. 24, 101.

28. See Robert Kashey and Martin L. H. Reymert, *Western European*

Bronzes of the Nineteenth Century, A Survey, exhibition catalog (New York: Shepherd Gallery, 1973), no. 12.

29. It was actually a life mask, the death mask being too grim to achieve popular appeal. Casts after both exist in the Hutton Collection at the Princeton University Library (nos. 4112 and 68, respectively). I am grateful to Mary Ann Jenson for access to this collection.

30. Its counterpart is a cast, translated into marble, of the artist's own hand holding sculptor's tools. Professor William Gerdts owns a related but slightly earlier example, the right hand of Pietro Tenerani holding sculptor's tools, carved in 1852 by Tenerani's pupil, E. Amadori.

31. A specimen is owned by the Art Institute of Chicago. Precedents for such "hand monuments" to famous writers probably go back to the 1830s, as suggested by the cast of Goethe's right hand, made in his old age, ca. 1825–30 (an example is in the Hutton Collection, Princeton University Library, no. 573).

32. See *The Romantics to Rodin, French Nineteenth-Century Sculpture from North American Collections,* ed. Peter Fusco and H. W. Janson, exhibition catalog, Los Angeles County Museum of Art (New York: Braziller, 1980), pp. 175 ff.

33. Callistratus, *Descriptions,* ed. and trans. A. Fairbanks (New York and London: Loeb Classical Library, 1931), pp. 380 ff.

The Contributors

Robert J. Bezucha is Professor of History at Amherst College, where he teaches the social and cultural history of modern Europe. He is the author of *The Lyon Uprising of 1834* (Harvard University Press, 1974) and the editor of *Modern European Social History* (D.C. Heath, 1972), as well as a contributor to several collected volumes.

Albert Boime is Professor of Art at the University of California at Los Angeles, where he teaches the social history of art of the nineteenth and twentieth centuries. He has published *The Academy and French Painting in the Nineteenth Century* (Phaidon, 1971) and recently *Thomas Couture and the Eclectic Vision* (Yale University Press, 1980).

Petra ten Doesschate Chu is Professor of Art History at Seton Hall University. She has published two books, *French Realism and the Dutch Masters* (Utrecht, 1974) and *Courbet in Perspective* (Prentice-Hall, 1977), as well as several articles, mostly in the field of nineteenth-century painting. She has organized various exhibitions at Seton Hall University and contributed to the catalogue of *The Realist Tradition* exhibition (1980).

Françoise Forster-Hahn is Professor of Art History at the University of California at Riverside, where she specializes in nineteenth- and twentieth-century European art and the history of photography. Among her publications are a monograph on Johann Heinrich Ramberg, *French and School of Paris Paintings in the Yale University Art Gallery*, and numerous articles in American and European journals on modern German art, art and technology, photography, and the social history of art. She is presently preparing a book on the German realist painter Adolph Menzel and a monograph on his major work, *The Iron Rolling Mill*.

Alison Hilton is Assistant Professor of Art History at Wayne State University, Detroit, Michigan, where she specializes in nineteenth- and twentieth-century European art and the evolution of Russian painting. She has published articles on Russian art and women artists of Russia and the United States, including a recent study on Constructivism in *Arts Magazine*. She is currently on an international exchange grant to the Soviet Union, where she is working on a book on Russian Folk Art.

H. W. Janson is Professor Emeritus in the Department of Fine Arts at New York University. His *History of Art* (Harry N. Abrams and Prentice-Hall, 1962) has become one of the standard introductory texts to the field of art history. He has published widely and his best-known works are *Apes and Ape Lore in the Middle Ages and the Renaissance* (The Warburg Institute, University of London, 1952), *The Sculpture of Donatello* (Princeton University Press, 1957), and *Sixteen Studies* (Harry N. Abrams, 1973). His contribution to the catalogue of *The Romantics to Rodin: French Nineteenth-Century Sculpture from North American Collections* (Los Angeles, 1979), is in preparation for his current project, a history of nineteenth-century sculpture.

Geneviève Lacambre is Chief Curator at the Musée d'Orsay, Paris. She has participated in numerous exhibitions and catalogues, including *French Symbolist Painters* (London/Liverpool, 1972), *Le Musée du Luxembourg en 1874* (Paris, 1974), *Le Symbolisme en Europe* (Rotterdam–Brussels–Baden-Baden–Paris, 1975–76), *The Second Empire, Art in France under Napoleon III* (Philadelphia, Detroit, Paris, 1978–79) and *Mucha* (Paris, Darmstadt, Prague, 1980). With her husband, Jean Lacambre, she published an annotated edition of Champfleury, *Le Réalisme* (Paris, 1973).

Hans A. Lüthy is Director of the Swiss Institute for Art Research in Zurich. His main research interests have focused on Swiss and French painting of the nineteenth century. He has published numerous articles and critical studies in art journals, many of them examining the French painter Théodore Géricault.

Kenneth McConkey teaches art history at Newcastle upon Tyne Polytechnic. He has made a special study of British reaction to French Naturalism in the 1880s and has developed a series of exhibitions and articles related to this theme. His best-known exhibitions have been *A Painter's Harvest, H.H. La Thangue*, 1978, *Sir George Clausen R.A.*, 1980 and *Peasantries*, 1981. In addition to preparing the entries on Bastien-Lepage for *The Realist Tradition* catalogue, he is currently preparing a book on Clausen and a larger survey of Rustic Naturalist painting in Europe and America.

Gabriel P. Weisberg was recently Andrew Mellon Professor in the Department of Fine Arts, University of Pittsburgh. As Curator of Art History and Education at The Cleveland Museum of Art, he organized *The Realist Tradition* exhibition and prepared the catalogue. Among his numerous publications are found a book on *François Bonvin* (Paris, 1980), *Japonisme: Japanese Influence on French Art, 1854–1910* (The Cleveland Museum of Art, 1975), and articles on aspects of realism,

Japonisme, Symbolism, and art nouveau. He is currently completing a monograph on S. *Bing and the Evolution of Art Nouveau* on a Guggenheim Foundation Fellowship.

Credits

CHAPTER 1 (**Bezucha**)

1.1 Jules Breton, *The Gleaners*, 1854, oil on canvas, Dublin, National Gallery of Ireland.

1.2 Jean François Millet, *The Gleaners*, 1857, oil on canvas, Paris, Musée du Louvre. Photo: Musées Nationaux.

CHAPTER 2 (**Weisberg**)

2.1 Isidore Pils, *The Death of a Sister of Charity*, 1850, oil on canvas, Toulouse, Musée des Augustins.

2.2 Gustave Brion, *The Potato Harvest during the Flooding of the Rhine in 1852, Alsace*, 1852, oil on canvas, Nantes, Musée des Beaux-Arts.

2.3 Gustave Courbet, *The Grain Sifters*, 1855, oil on canvas, Nantes, Musée des Beaux-Arts. Photo: Musées Nationaux.

2.4 Philippe Auguste Jeanron, *Peasants from the Limousin,* oil on canvas, Lille, Musée des Beaux-Arts.

2.5 Théodule Ribot, *The Cook Accountant*, 1862, oil on canvas, Marseille, Musée des Beaux-Arts.

2.6 Théodule Ribot, *The Returns*, 1865, oil on canvas, Marseille, Musée des Beaux-Arts.

2.7 Jules Breton, *The Grape Harvest at Chateau-Lagrange*, 1864, oil on canvas, Omaha, Joslyn Art Museum, Gift of the Friends of Art Collection, 1932.

2.8 Jules Breton, *Preliminary Drawing for "The Grape Harvest,"* Private Collection, France.

2.9 Jules Breton, *Preliminary Watercolor for "The Grape Harvest,"* Private Collection, France.

2.10 François Bonhommé, *Employee with Shears, Workman—Fourchambault,* 1839–40, pen drawing, sepia, Jarville, Musée de l'Histoire du Fer.

2.11 François Bonhommé, *Blanzy Mines: Open-Pit Mining at Lucy,* 1857, watercolor, Paris, Conservatoire National des Arts et Métiers, Musée National des Techniques.

2.12 François Bonhommé, *Workshop with Mechanical Sieves at the Factory of La Vieille Montagne,* watercolor, Paris, Conservatoire National des Arts et Métiers, Musée National des Techniques.

CHAPTER 3 (Boime)

3.1 Eugène-André Oudine, *Medal: The Accession of Napoleon III to the Empire*, 1852, Paris, Musée du Louvre. Photo: Musées Nationaux.

3.2 Edouard Detaille, *Napoleon III crowned with laurel and smoking a cigarette*, 1860s, pen and ink, Compiègne, Musée National du Château.

3.3 Isidore Pils, *The Battle of Alma*, Salon of 1861, oil on canvas, Versailles, Musée National du Château. Photo: Musées Nationaux.

3.4 Ernest Meissonier, *The Emperor Napoleon III at the Battle of Solferino*, Salon of 1864, oil on panel, Paris, Musée du Louvre. Photo: Musées Nationaux.

3.5 Ange-Tissier, *The Submission of Abd-el-Kader*, Salon of 1861, oil on canvas, Versailles, Musée National du Château.

3.6 Jean Léon Gérôme, *Reception of the Siamese Ambassadors by Napoleon III and the Empress Eugenie at Fontainebleau, 27 June 1861*, 1861–64, oil on canvas, Versailles, Musée National du Château. Photo: Musées Nationaux.

3.7 Gustave Courbet, *The Burial at Ornans*, 1850, oil on canvas, Paris, Musée du Louvre. Photo: Musées Nationaux.

3.8 Jean Léon Gérôme, *Age of Augustus*, Salon of 1855, wood engraving from *L'Illustration* (July 14, 1855).

3.9 Gustave Boulanger, *Rehearsal of "The Flute Player" in the Atrium of H.I.H. the Prince Napoleon*, 1861, oil on canvas, Versailles, Musée National du Château. Photo: Musées Nationaux.

3.10 Jean-Louis Hamon, *My Sister is Not at Home*, Salon of 1853, Location unknown.

3.11 Jean-Louis Hamon, *The Human Comedy*, 1852, oil on canvas, Compiègne, Musée National du Château.

3.12 Eugène Guérard, *Théâtre de Guignol* (Champs-Elysées), 1856, lithograph, Paris, Bibliothèque Nationale.

3.13 Jean-Louis Hamon, *Conjurer*, Salon of 1861, oil on canvas, Nantes, Musée des Beaux-Arts.

3.14 Auguste Toulmouche, *Forbidden Fruit*, Salon of 1865, Location unknown.

3.15 Jean François Millet, *Immaculate Conception*, 1858, Location unknown.

3.16 Jean Léon Gérôme, *Pope Pius Blessing Locomotives*, 1858, Rome, Musei di Roma. Photo: Gerald M. Ackerman.

3.17 William-Adolphe Bouguereau, *Entrance of the Emperor at Tarascon, 14 June 1856*, Salon of 1857, oil on canvas, Tarascon, Mairie de Tarascon. Photo: Albert Boime.

3.18 Louis Hersent, *Louis XVI Distributing Alms to the Poor during the Rigorous Winter of 1788*, 1817, oil on canvas, Versailles, Musée National du Château. Photo: Musées Nationaux.

3.19 Alexandre Antigna, *The Visit of the Emperor to the Slate Quarry Workers of Angers during the Floods of 1856*, Salon of 1857, oil on canvas, Angers, Musée des Beaux-Arts. Photo: Yvonne M. L. Weisberg.

3.20 Hippolyte Lazerges, *The Emperor Distributing Alms to the Flood Victims of Lyon*, Salon of 1857, oil on canvas, Lyon, Musée Historique.

3.21 Ange-Louis Janet-Lange, *Napoleon III Distributing Alms to the Flood Victims of Lyon in June 1856*, Salon of 1857, wood engraving from *L'Illustration* (1857).

3.22 Rosa Bonheur, *Ploughing in the Nivernais*, 1849, oil on canvas, Fontainebleau, Musée National du Château.

3.23 Jules Breton, *Misery and Despair*, Salon of 1849, lithograph (work destroyed).

3.24 Jules Breton, *Hunger*, 1850 (work destroyed).

3.25 Charles Gleyre, *Ruth and Boaz*, 1853/54, Location unknown.

3.26 Evariste Luminais, *Champ de Foire*, Salon of 1861, wood engraving from *L'Illustration*, August 31, 1861.

3.27 Isidore Pils, *Rouget de l'Isle Singing the Marseillaise for the First Time*, 1849, oil on canvas, Strasbourg, Musée Historique.

3.28 Isidore Pils, *Soldiers Distributing Bread to the Poor*, Salon of 1852, wood engraving from *L'Illustration*, 1852.

3.29 François Bonhommé, *Diploma for a Mutual Aid Society*, 1852, pen and ink, Jarville, Musée de l'Histoire du Fer.

CHAPTER 4 (Forster-Hahn)

4.1 Adolph Menzel, *Chodowiecki on the Jannowitz Bridge*, 1859, oil on canvas, Schweinfurt, Collection Georg Schäfer.

4.2 Adolph Menzel, *Commemorative Print for the Celebration of G. Schadow's Hundredth Birthday*, 1864, Berlin, Staatliche Museum.

4.3 Daniel Chodowiecki, *Cabinet d'un Peintre*, 1771, engraving, Berlin, Staatliche Museum.

4.4 Adolph Menzel, *Family by Lamplight*, 1843, engraving, Berlin, Staatliche Museum.

4.5 Daniel Chodowiecki, *The Death of Frederick II*, 1790, engraving, Berlin, Staatliche Museum.

4.6 Gottfried Schadow, *Frederick and His Whippets*, 1822, Potsdam, Sans Souci.

4.7 Adolph Menzel, *The Death of Frederick II*, from Franz Kugler's *History of Frederick the Great*, 1842, Berlin, Staatliche Museum.

4.8 Adolph Menzel, *Oil Sketch for "The Dinner Conversation,"* 1849, oil on paper, Berlin, Staatliche Museum, Nationalgalerie.

4.9 Adolph Menzel, *The Flute Recital*, 1852, oil on canvas, Berlin (West), Staatliche Museen Preussischer Kulturbesitz, Nationalgalerie.

4.10 Wilhelm von Kaulbach, *The Destruction of Jerusalem*, destroyed, formerly Berlin, Neues Museum.

4.11 Adolph Menzel, *Frederick the Great and His Men at Hochkirch, 1758*, 1856, oil on canvas, destroyed, formerly Berlin, Nationalgalerie.

4.12 Adolph Menzel, *The Meeting of Frederick II and Joseph II, 1769*, 1857, oil on canvas, Berlin, Staatliche Museen, Nationalgalerie.

4.13 Franz Krüger, *Parade in the Opera Square*, 1829, oil on canvas, Berlin, Staatliche Museen, Nationalgalerie.

4.14 Eduard Gaertner, *Klosterstrasse*, 1830, oil on panel, Berlin (West), Staatliche Museen Preussischer Kulturbesitz, Nationalgalerie.

4.15 Johann Erdmann Hummel, *The Granite Basin in the Berlin Lustgarten*, 1831, Berlin (West), Staatliche Museen Preussischer Kulturbesitz, Nationalgalerie.

4.16 Eduard Gaertner, *Unter den Linden*, 1853, oil on canvas, Berlin (West), Staatliche Museen Preussischer Kulturbesitz, Nationalgalerie.

4.17 Adolph Menzel, *Sunday in the Tuileries Garden*, 1867, oil on canvas, Dresden, Gemäldegalerie Neue Meister.

4.18 Adolph Menzel, *Weekday in Paris*, 1869, oil on canvas, Düsseldorf, Kunstmuseum der Stadt.

4.19 E. Guérard, *The Tuileries—allée des feuillants*, 1856, engraving. Photo: Bibliothèque Nationale, Paris.

4.20 Adolph Menzel, *King William's Departure on 31 July 1870*, 1871, oil on canvas, Berlin (West), Staatliche Museen Preussischer Kulturbesitz, Nationalgalerie.

4.21 Carl Blechen, *Iron Rolling Mill at Eberswalde*, 1835, oil on panel, Berlin (West), Staatliche Museen Preussischer Kulturbesitz, Nationalgalerie.

4.22 Carl Blechen, *Preparatory study for the "Iron Rolling Mill at Eberswalde,"* Berlin, Staatliche Museen, Kupferstichkabinett und Sammlung der Zeichnungen.

4.23 Adolph Menzel, *The Iron Rolling Mill*, 1875, oil on canvas, Berlin, Staatliche Museen, Nationalgalerie.

4.24 Adolph Menzel, *Memorial Sheet for Heckmann*, 1869, Berlin, Staatliche Museen.

4.25 Paul Meyerheim, *Forging the Locomotive Wheel*, 1873, oil on canvas, Berlin, Märkisches Museum.

4.26 Max Liebermann, *Women Plucking Geese*, 1871–72, oil on canvas, Berlin, Staatliche Museen, Nationalgalerie.

4.27 Max Liebermann, *Women Cleaning Vegetables*, 1872, oil on canvas, Winterthur, Switzerland, private collection.

CHAPTER 5 (Lüthy)

5.1 Friedrich Simon, *The Poacher*, 1852, oil on panel, Geneva, Collection Musée d'art et d'histoire.

5.2 Friedrich Simon, *The Locksmith*, 1852, oil on canvas. Photo: Swiss Institute for Art Research.

5.3 Albert Anker, *A Child's Burial*, 1863, oil on canvas, Aarau, Aargauer Kunsthaus. Photo: Zurich, Swiss Institute for Art Research.

5.4 Albert Anker, *The Little Friend on Her Deathbed*, 1862, oil on canvas, Bern, Kunstmuseum. Photo: Zurich, Swiss Institute for Art Research.

5.5 Karl Friedrich Schick, *The Dead Child*, ca. 1862, oil on canvas, Karlsruhe, Staatlich Kunsthalle.

5.6 Albert Anker, *Soup for the Poor*, 1893, oil on canvas, Bern, Kunstmuseum. Photo: Zurich, Swiss Institute for Art Research.

5.7 Ferdinand Hodler, *The Joiner*, 1875, oil on canvas, Zurich, Kunsthaus.

5.8 Ferdinand Hodler, *The Washerwoman*, ca. 1874, oil on canvas, Private Collection. Photo: Zurich, Swiss Institute for Art Research.

5.9 Ferdinand Hodler, *The Gymnastics Society Banquet*, 1877/78, oil on canvas, Zurich, Kunsthaus.

5.10 Ferdinand Hodler, *Temperance Café*, 1879, oil on canvas, Location unknown.

5.11 Ferdinand Hodler, *Devotion*, 1880, oil on canvas, Private Collection. Photo: Zurich, Swiss Institute for Art Research.

CHAPTER 6 (Hilton)

6.1 Vasilii Perov, *Drowned Woman*, 1867, oil on canvas, Moscow, Tretiakov Gallery.

6.2 Vasilii Perov, *Last Tavern at the Edge of Town*, 1868, oil on canvas, Moscow, Tretiakov Gallery.

6.3 Nikolai Ge, *The Last Supper*, 1863, oil on canvas, Leningrad, Russian Museum.

6.4 Aleksei Savrasov, *The Rooks Have Arrived*, 1871, oil on canvas, Moscow, Tretiakov Gallery.

6.5 Ivan Kramskoi, *Mina Moiseev*, 1882, oil on canvas, Moscow, Tretiakov Gallery.

6.6 Ilya Repin, *Tolstoi Plowing*, 1887, oil on canvas, Moscow, Tretiakov Gallery.

6.7 Iaroshenko, *Woman Student*, 1883, oil on canvas, Kiev, Museum of Russian Art.

6.8 Ilya Repin, *Barge Haulers on the Volga*, 1871–73, oil on canvas, Leningrad, Russian Museum.

6.9 Valerian Iakobi, *Halt of the Convoy of Prisoners*, 1861, oil on canvas, Moscow, Tretiakov Gallery.

6.10 Grigorii Miasoedov, *The Zemstvo Dines*, 1872, oil on canvas, Moscow, Tretiakov Gallery.

6.11 Konstantin Savitskii, *Repair Work on the Railroad*, 1873, oil on canvas, Moscow, Tretiakov Gallery.

6.12 Konstantin Savitskii, *To War*, 1880–87, oil on canvas, Leningrad, Russian Museum.

6.13 Vladimir Makovskii, *Evening Meeting*, 1875–97, oil on canvas, Moscow, Tretiakov Gallery.

6.14 Vladimir Makovskii, *On the Boulevard*, 1886–87, oil on canvas, Moscow, Tretiakov Gallery.

6.15 Ilya Repin, *Religious Procession in Kursk Province*, 1881–83, oil on canvas, Moscow, Tretiakov Gallery.

6.16 Ivan Kramskoi, *Christ in the Wilderness*, 1872, oil on canvas, Moscow, Tretiakov Gallery.

6.17 Ilya Repin, *Ivan the Terrible and his Son Ivan, November 16, 1581*, 1885, oil on canvas, Moscow, Tretiakov Gallery.

6.18 Ilya Repin, *Revolutionary Meeting*, 1883, oil on canvas, Moscow, Tretiakov Gallery.

6.19 Ilya Repin, *They Did Not Expect Him*, 1884–88, oil on canvas, Moscow, Tretiakov Gallery.

6.20 Ilya Repin, *The Unexpected Return*, 1883, oil on canvas, Moscow, Tretiakov Gallery.

CHAPTER 7 (**McConkey**)

7.1 Henry Herbert La Thangue, *The Last Furrow*, 1895, oil on canvas, Oldham Art Gallery.

7.2 Harry Furniss, *Drunk again! The very last furrow*, 1895 (after H. H. La Thangue, *The Last Furrow*).

7.3 Henry Herbert La Thangue, *The Man with the Scythe*, 1896, oil on canvas, London, The Tate Gallery.

7.4 Frederick Walker, *The Vagrants*, 1868, oil on canvas, London, The Tate Gallery.

7.5 Alphonse Legros, *The Tired Wanderer*, 1878, oil on canvas, Tyne and Wear Museums.

7.6 George Clausen, *High Mass at a Fishing Village on the Zuyder Zee*, 1876, oil on canvas, Nottingham Castle Museum.

7.7 Alexander Stanhope Forbes, *The Old Convent, Quimperlé*, 1882, oil on canvas, Location unknown.

7.8 Jules Bastien-Lepage, *Pas Mêche (Nothing Doing)*, 1882, oil on canvas, Edinburgh, National Gallery of Scotland.

7.9 Alexander Stanhope Forbes, *Preparations for the Market, Quimperlé*, 1883, oil on canvas, Dunedin Art Gallery Collection.

7.10 Frank Bramley, *Domino*, 1886, oil on canvas, Cork Municipal Art Gallery.

7.11 Sir John Lavery, *Under the Cherry Tree*, 1884, oil on canvas, Belfast, Ulster Museum.

7.12 Jules Bastien-Lepage, *Les Foins*, 1878, oil on canvas, Paris, Musée du Louvre. Photo: Musées Nationaux.

7.13 George Clausen, *Labourers after Dinner*, 1884, oil on canvas, Australia, Private Collection.

7.14 George Clausen, *The Stone Pickers*, 1887, oil on canvas, Tyne and Wear Museums.

7.15 Jules Bastien-Lepage, *Pauvre Fauvette*, 1881, oil on canvas, Glasgow, Glasgow Art Gallery and Museum.

7.16 Herbert Dalzeil, *The Cow Girl*, 1885, oil on canvas, Great Britain, Private Collection. Photo: Courtesy of the Fine Art Society.

7.17 Peter Henry Emerson, *Coming Home from the Marshes*, 1886, photograph.

7.18 Henry Herbert La Thangue, *The Return of the Reapers*, 1886, oil on canvas, Great Britain, Private Collection. Photo: Courtesy of the Fine Art Society.

7.19 Jean François Millet, *Going to Work*, 1850–51, oil on canvas, Glasgow, Glasgow Art Gallery and Museum.

7.20 Jules Bastien-Lepage, *Jeanne d'Arc écoutant Les Voix*, 1879, oil on canvas, New York, Metropolitan Museum of Art.

7.21 George Clausen, *The Girl at the Gate*, 1889, oil on canvas, London, The Tate Gallery.

CHAPTER 8 (Lacambre)

8.1 Eva Gonzalez, *Une Loge aux Italiens*, 1879, oil on canvas, Paris, Musée du Jeu de Paume. Photo: Musées Nationaux.

8.2 Jean Charles Cazin, *Hagar and Ishmael*, Salon of 1880, oil on canvas, Tours, Musée des Beaux-Arts (on loan from the Louvre). Photo: Musées Nationaux.

8.3 Emile Friant, *La Toussaint*, 1888, Salon of 1889, oil on canvas, Nancy, Musée des Beaux-Arts (on loan from the Louvre). Photo: Musées Nationaux.

8.4 Marie Bashkirtseff, *The Meeting*, 1884, Salon of 1884, oil on canvas, Paris, Musée d'Orsay. Photo: Musées Nationaux.

8.5 Alfred Roll, *Manda Lamétrie fermière*, 1887, Salon of 1888, oil on canvas, Paris, Musée d'Orsay. Photo: Musées Nationaux.

8.6 Fernand Cormon, *Cain*, 1880, Salon of 1880, oil on canvas, Paris, Musée d'Orsay. Photo: Bulloz.

8.7 Lionel Walden, *Docks at Cardiff*, 1896, Salon of 1896, oil on canvas, Paris, Musée d'Orsay. Photo: Musées Nationaux.

8.8 Léon Lhermitte, *La Paye des Moissonneurs*, 1882, Salon of 1882, oil on canvas, Château Thiérry, Hôtel de Ville.

8.9 Henri Gervex, *Rolla*, 1879, oil on canvas, Bordeaux, Musée des Beaux-Arts.

CHAPTER 9 (Chu)

9.1 Horace Lecoq de Boisbaudran, *Self-Portrait*, oil on canvas, Paris, Musée du Louvre. Photo: Musées Nationaux.

9.2 Reutemann, *Memory drawing after an engraving by Jean Lepautre*, Paris, Ecole Nationale Supérieure des Arts Décoratifs.

9.3 Emile Pierre Metzmacher, *Memory drawing after a cast of an architectural fragment*, Paris, Ecole Nationale Supérieure des Arts Décoratifs.

9.4 Alphonse Legros, *Memory drawing after cast of the "Discobolos,"* Location unknown.

9.5 Léon Lhermitte, *Memory drawing after detail of Poussin's "Time and Truth,"* Paris, Ecole Nationale Supérieure des Arts Décoratifs.

9.6 Nicholas Poussin, *Time and Truth*, oil on canvas, Paris, Musée du Louvre. Photo: Musées Nationaux.

9.7 Georges Bellenger, *Compositional drawing made from memory after observation of life model*, Location unknown.

9.8 Georges Bellenger, *Compositional drawing made from memory after observation of life model*, Paris, Ecole Nationale Supérieure des Arts Décoratifs.

9.9 Léon Lhermitte, *Memory drawing: Choir Rehearsal*, Location unknown.

9.10 Félix Régamey, *Memory drawing: Avenue de l'Observatoire*, London: Victoria and Albert Museum.

9.11 Jacques Valnay-Desrolles, *Memory drawing: Stone Quarry*, Paris, Ecole Nationale Supérieure des Arts Décoratifs.

9.12 Léon Lhermitte, *Memory drawing: Nine Peasant Women in Interior*, London, Victoria and Albert Museum.

9.13 Guillaume Régamey, *Memory drawing: Horse Stable*, Paris, Ecole Nationale Supérieure des Arts Décoratifs.

9.14 Jean Charles Cazin, *Memory drawing: Landscape*, Paris, Ecole Nationale Supérieure des Arts Décoratifs.

9.15 Léon Lhermitte, *Memory drawing: Landscape with Trees*, Paris, Ecole Nationale Supérieure des Arts Décoratifs.

9.16 Léon Lhermitte, *Compositional drawing made from memory after observation of life model*, Paris, Ecole Nationale Supérieure des Beaux-Arts.

9.17 Jean Charles Cazin, *Tobias*, 1880, oil on canvas, Lille, Musée des Beaux-Arts.

9.18 Henri Fantin-Latour, *Fairyland*, 1863, oil on canvas, Montreal, Museum of Fine Arts.

9.19 Léon Lhermitte, *The Quartet—Musical Evening at Amaury-Duval's*, 1881, charcoal drawing, Paris, Cabinet des dessins, Musée du Louvre. Photo: Musées Nationaux.

9.20 Auguste Rodin, *The Walking Man*, 1877–78, bronze, Washington, National Gallery of Art.

9.21 Edouard Manet, *Déjeuner sur l'herbe*, 1863, oil on canvas, Paris, Musée du Jeu de Paume. Photo: Musées Nationaux.

9.22 Paul Gauguin, *Ia Orana Maria*, 1891, oil on canvas, New York, The Metropolitan Museum of Art, Bequest of Samuel A. Lewisohn, 1951.

CHAPTER 10 (Janson)

10.1 *Trompe-l'oeil on back of fragmentary panel attributed to Carpaccio*. Malibu, J. Paul Getty Museum.

10.2 Duane Hanson, *Couple with Shopping Bags*, 1976, Kansas City, Missouri, Morgan Gallery. Photo: Courtesy O.K. Harris Gallery, New York.

10.3 John DeAndrea, *Reclining Woman*, 1970, Private Collection. Photo: Courtesy O.K. Harris Gallery, New York.

10.4 Jacques Talrich, *Jeremy Bentham* (detail), ca. 1830, London, University College. Photo: H. W. Janson.

10.5 Catherine Andras, *Horatio Nelson*, ca. 1805. London, Westminster Abbey. Photo: By courtesy of the Dean and Chapter of Westminster.

10.6 Mrs. Goldsmith, *William and Mary*, ca. 1690, London, Westminster Abbey. Photo: By courtesy of the Dean and Chapter of Westminster.

10.7 *Votive Equestrian Statue of Philip the Fair, formerly in Notre Dame Cathedral*, Paris, early fourteenth century; engraving, 1575.

10.8 *Equestrian Statue of Paolo Savelli*, soon after 1405, Venice, S. Maria dei Frari. Photo: Caprioli, Venice.

10.9   Guido Mazzoni, *Lamentation of Christ*, late fifteenth century, Modena, S. Giovanni. Photo: Alinari, Florence.

10.10 Gaudenzio Ferrarri, *Crucifixion*, ca. 1540, Sacro Monte, Varallo Sesia. Photo: Alinari, Florence.

10.11 Egyptian, *Male Portrait Head*, ca. 1360 B.C., East Berlin, Aegyptisches Museum. Photo: Courtesy of Bernhard Bothmer.

10.12 Donatello, *Judith and Holofernes*, ca. 1457, Florence, Palazzo Vecchio. Photo: Alinari-Brogi, Florence.

10.13 Detail of fig. 10.12.

10.14 Antonio Canova, *Domenico Cimarosa*, 1808, Rome, Protomoteca Capitolina.

10.15 Edouard Dantan, *Making a Life Cast*, 1887, Location unknown.

10.16 Vincenzo Vela, *Death Mask*, ca. 1870, Ligornetto (Ticino), Museo Vela. Photo: H. W. Janson.

10.17 Vincenzo Vela, *Death Mask*, ca. 1870, Ligornetto (Ticino), Museo Vela. Photo: H. W. Janson.

10.18 Vincenzo Vela, *Life Cast of a Woman's Back*, ca. 1870, Ligornetto (Ticino), Museo Vela. Photo: H. W. Janson.

10.19 Vincenzo Vela, *Life Cast of a Child's Leg*, ca. 1870, Ligornetto (Ticino), Museo Vela. Photo: H. W. Janson.

10.20 Vincenzo Vela, *Life Cast of a Child's Leg*, ca. 1870, Ligornetto (Ticino), Museo Vela. Photo: H. W. Janson.

10.21 Vincenzo Vela, *Life Cast of Two Female Hands*, 1862, Ligornetto (Ticino), Museo Vela. Photo: H. W. Janson.

10.22 Vincenzo Vela, *Italy Thanking France* (detail), 1862, Ligornetto (Ticino), Museo Vela. Photo: H. W. Janson.

10.23 Marcello (Adele d'Affry), *Life Cast of the Artist's Own Shoulders*, Fribourg, Fondation Marcello. Photo: H. W. Janson.

10.24 Marcello (Adele d'Affry), *Study for Pythia*, 1869–70, Fribourg, Fondation Marcello. Photo: H. W. Janson.

10.25 A. Rivalta, *Vincenzo Drago Monument*, ca. 1875, Genoa, Staglieno Cemetery. Photo: Alinari, Florence.

10.26 Dr. Francesco Antommarchi, *Death Mask of Napoleon*, 1821, Paris, Invalides, Musée de l'Armée. Photo: Giraudon, Paris.

10.27 Vincenzo Vela, *Left Hand of the Artist's Wife*, ca. 1860, Ligornetto (Ticino), Museo Vela. Photo: H. W. Janson.

10.28 Vincenzo Vela, *Left Hand of the Artist's Wife*, ca. 1860, Ligornetto (Ticino), Museo Vela. Photo: H. W. Janson.

10.29 John Hogan, *The Left Foot of Lady Cloncurry*, 1841, Dublin, Lyons House.

10.30 Anonymous Sculptor, *The Right Foot of Rachel*, ca. 1850, Compiègne, Musée du Château. Photo: H. W. Janson.

10.31 *Life Cast of Rodin's Right Hand*, 1917, Paris, Musée Rodin.

10.32 Auguste Rodin, *The Hand of God*, ca. 1895, New York, The Metropolitan Museum of Art.

Index